NO RULES
RULES

NO RULES RULES

Netflix and the
Culture of Reinvention

REED HASTINGS AND **ERIN MEYER**

RANDOM HOUSE
LARGE PRINT

Portrait illustrations by Henry Sene Yee

The Library of Congress has established a Cataloging-in-Publication record for this title.

ISBN: 978-0-593-15238-6

www.penguinrandomhouse.com/large-print-format-books

FIRST LARGE PRINT EDITION

Printed in the United States of America

10 9 8 7 6 5 4 3

This Large Print edition published in accord with the standards of the N.A.V.H.

CONTENTS

Introduction xi

▶ **SECTION ONE**

First Steps to a Culture of Freedom and Responsibility

1 FIRST BUILD UP TALENT DENSITY . . .
A Great Workplace Is Stunning Colleagues 3

2 THEN INCREASE CANDOR . . .
Say What You Really Think (with Positive Intent) 19

3 NOW BEGIN REMOVING CONTROLS . . .
a. Remove Vacation Policy 59
b. Remove Travel and Expense Approvals 83

▶ **SECTION TWO**

Next Steps to a Culture of Freedom and Responsibility

4 FORTIFY TALENT DENSITY . . .
Pay Top of Personal Market 113

5 PUMP UP CANDOR . . .
Open the Books 153

6 NOW RELEASE MORE CONTROLS . . .
No Decision-making Approvals Needed 193

▶ **SECTION THREE**

Techniques to Reinforce a Culture of Freedom and Responsibility

7 MAX UP TALENT DENSITY . . .
The Keeper Test 245

8 MAX UP CANDOR . . .
A Circle of Feedback 279

9 AND ELIMINATE MOST CONTROLS . . . !
Lead with Context, Not Control 305

▶ **SECTION FOUR**

Going Global

10 **Bring It All to the World!** 353

Conclusion 393

Acknowledgments 403

Selected Bibliography 407

Index 415

Reed Hastings is an entrepreneur who has revolutionized entertainment since cofounding Netflix in 1997, serving as its chairman and CEO since 1999. His first company, Pure Software, was launched in 1991 and was acquired just before Netflix launched. Hastings served on the California State Board of Education from 2000 to 2004 and is an active educational philanthropist. He has sat on the board of several educational organizations including DreamBox Learning, the KIPP Foundation, and the Pahara Institute. He received a BA from Bowdoin College in 1983 and an MSCS in artificial intelligence from Stanford University in 1988. Between Bowdoin and Stanford, Hastings served in the Peace Corps as a volunteer teacher in southern Africa.

Erin Meyer is the author of **The Culture Map: Breaking Through the Invisible Boundaries of Global Business** and a professor at INSEAD, one of the world's leading international business schools. Her work has appeared in **Harvard Business Review, The New York Times,** and Forbes.com. In 2019, Meyer was selected by the Thinkers50 as one of the fifty most in influential business thinkers in the world. She received an MBA from INSEAD in 2004, and she currently lives in Paris, France. In 1994 and 1995 Meyer also served in the Peace Corps as a volunteer teacher in southern Africa. Visit erinmeyer.com for more information.

INTRODUCTION

 Reed Hastings: "Blockbuster is a thousand times our size," I whispered to Marc Randolph as we stepped into a cavernous meeting room on the twenty-seventh floor of the Renaissance Tower in Dallas, Texas, early in 2000. These were the headquarters of Blockbuster, then a $6 billion giant that dominated the home entertainment business with almost nine thousand rental stores around the world.

The CEO of Blockbuster, John Antioco, who was reputed to be a skilled strategist aware that a ubiquitous, super-fast internet would upend the industry, welcomed us graciously. Sporting a salt-and-pepper goatee and an expensive suit, he seemed completely relaxed.

By contrast, I was a nervous wreck. Marc and I had cofounded and now ran a tiny two-year-old start-up, which let people order DVDs on a website and receive them through the US Postal Service. We had one hundred employees and a mere three hundred thousand subscribers and were off to a rocky start. That year alone, our losses would total $57 million. Eager to make a deal, we'd worked for months just to get Antioco to respond to our calls.

We all sat down around a massive glass table, and after a few minutes of small talk, Marc and I made our pitch. We suggested that Blockbuster purchase Netflix, and then we would develop and run Blockbuster.com as their online video rental arm. Antioco listened carefully, nodded his head frequently, and then asked, "How much would Blockbuster need to pay for Netflix?" When he heard our response— $50 million—he flatly declined. Marc and I left, crestfallen.

That night, when I got into bed and closed my eyes, I had this image of all sixty thousand Blockbuster employees erupting in laughter at the ridiculousness of our proposal. Of course, Antioco wasn't interested. Why would a powerhouse like Blockbuster, with millions of customers, massive revenues, a talented CEO, and a brand synonymous with home movies, be interested in a flailing wannabe like Netflix? What did we possibly have to offer that they couldn't do more effectively themselves?

But, little by little, the world changed and our business stayed on its feet and grew. In 2002, two years after that meeting, we took Netflix public. Despite our growth, Blockbuster was still a hundred times larger than we were ($5 billion versus $50 million). Moreover, Blockbuster was owned by Viacom, which at that time was the most valuable media company in the world. Yet, by 2010, Blockbuster had declared bankruptcy. By 2019, only a single Blockbuster video store remained, in Bend, Oregon. Blockbuster had been unable to adapt from DVD rental to streaming.

The year 2019 was also noteworthy for Netflix. Our film **Roma** was nominated for best picture and won three Oscars, a great achievement for the director Alfonso Cuarón, which underscored the transformation of Netflix into a full-fledged entertainment company. Long ago, we had pivoted from our DVD-by-mail business to become not just an internet streaming service, with over 167 million subscribers in 190 countries, but a major producer of our own TV shows and movies around the world. We had the privilege of working with some of the world's most talented creators, including Shonda Rhimes, Joel and Ethan Coen, and Martin Scorsese. We had introduced a new way for people to watch and enjoy great stories, which, in its best moments, broke down barriers and enriched lives.

I am often asked, "How did this happen? Why could Netflix repeatedly adapt but Blockbuster could not?" That day we went to Dallas, Blockbuster held all the aces. They had the brand, the power, the resources, and the vision. Blockbuster had us beat hands down.

It was not obvious at the time, even to me, but we had one thing that Blockbuster did not: a culture that valued people over process, emphasized innovation over efficiency, and had very few controls. Our culture, which focused on achieving top performance with talent density and leading employees with context not control, has allowed us to continually grow and change as the world, and our members' needs, have likewise morphed around us.

Netflix is different. We have a culture where No Rules Rules.

NETFLIX CULTURE IS WEIRD

 Erin Meyer: Corporate culture can be a mushy marshland of vague language and incomplete, ambiguous definitions. What's worse, company values—as articulated—rarely match the way people behave in reality. The slick slogans on posters or in annual reports often turn out to be empty words.

For many years, one of America's biggest corporations proudly exhibited the following list of values in the lobby of its headquarters: "Integrity. Communication. Respect. Excellence." The company? Enron. It boasted about having lofty values right up to the moment it came crashing down in one of history's biggest cases of corporate fraud and corruption.

Netflix culture, on the other hand, is famous—or infamous, depending on your point of view—for telling it like it is. Millions of businesspeople have studied the Netflix Culture Deck, a set of 127 slides originally intended for internal use but that Reed shared widely on the internet in 2009. Sheryl Sandberg, COO of Facebook, reportedly said that the Culture Deck "may well be the most important document ever to come out of Silicon Valley." I loved the Netflix Culture Deck for its honesty. And I loathed it for its content.

On the next page is a sample so you can see why.

Quite apart from the question of whether it is ethical to fire hardworking employees who don't manage to do extraordinary work, these slides struck me as pure bad management. They violate the principle that Harvard Business School professor Amy Edmondson calls "psychological safety." In her 2018 book, **The Fearless Organization**, she explains that if you want to encourage innovation, you should develop an environment where people feel safe to dream, speak up, and take risks. The safer the atmosphere, the more innovation you will have.

Apparently, no one at Netflix read that book. Seek to hire the very best and then inject fear into your talented employees by telling them they'll be thrown back out onto the "generous severance" scrap heap if they don't excel? This sounded like a surefire way to kill any hope of innovation.

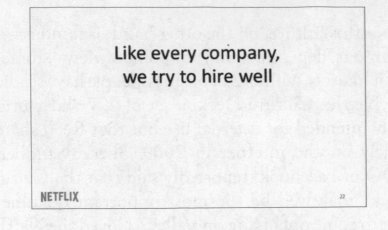

**Like every company,
we try to hire well**

NETFLIX   22

**Unlike many companies,
we practice:**

*adequate performance gets a
generous severance package*

NETFLIX   23

The other people should get a generous severance now,
so we can open a slot to try to find a star for that role

The Keeper Test Managers Use:

Which of my people,
if they told me they were leaving,
for a similar job at a peer company,
would I fight hard to keep at Netflix?

NETFLIX   26

Here's another slide from the deck:

Netflix Vacation Policy and Tracking

"there is no policy or tracking"

There is also no clothing policy at Netflix, but no one comes to work naked

Lesson: you don't need policies for everything

NETFLIX

71

Not allotting employees vacation days seemed downright irresponsible. It is a great way to create sweatshop conditions, where no one dares to take a day off work. And to wrap it up like a perk.

Employees who take holidays are happier, enjoy their jobs more, and are more productive. Yet many workers are hesitant to take the vacation allotted them. According to a survey conducted by Glassdoor in 2017, American workers took only about 54 percent of their entitled vacation days.

Employees are likely to take even less time off if you remove the vacation allotment altogether because of a well-documented human behavior, which psychologists refer to as "loss aversion." We humans hate to lose what we already have, even more than we like getting something new. Faced with losing something, we will do everything we can to avoid losing it. We take that vacation.

If you're not allotted vacation, you don't fear losing

it, and are less likely to take any at all. The "use it or lose it" rule built into many traditional policies sounds like a limitation, but it actually encourages people to take a break.

And here's a last slide:

Of course, no one would openly support a workplace based on secrets and lies. But sometimes it's better to be diplomatic than to offer opinions bluntly—for example, when a floundering team member needs a morale boost or a jolt of self-confidence. "Honesty sometimes" we can all get behind. But a blanket policy of "honesty always" sounds like a great way to break relationships, crush motivation, and create an unpleasant work environment.

Overall, the Netflix Culture Deck struck me as hypermasculine, excessively confrontational, and downright aggressive—perhaps a reflection of the kind of company you might expect to be constructed by an engineer with a somewhat mechanistic, rationalist view of human nature.

Yet despite all this, one fact cannot be denied . . .

NETFLIX HAS BEEN REMARKABLY SUCCESSFUL

By 2019, seventeen years after Netflix went public, its stock price had gone from $1 to $350. By comparison, $1 invested in the S&P 500 or NASDAQ index when Netflix went public would have grown to between $3 and $4 over the same period.

It's not just the stock market that loves Netflix. Consumers and critics love it too. Netflix original programming such as **Orange Is the New Black** and **The Crown** have become some of the most beloved shows of the decade, and **Stranger Things** became possibly the world's most-watched TV series. Non-English shows like **Elite** in Spain, **Dark** in Germany, **The Protector** in Turkey, and **Sacred Games** in India have all raised the bar for storytelling in their home countries and spawned a new generation of global stars. In the US, over the past few years Netflix has received more than three hundred Emmy nominations and taken home multiple Academy Awards. In addition, Netflix garnered seventeen nominations at the Golden Globes, more than any other network or streaming service, and in 2019 earned the No. 1 spot as the most highly regarded company in America on the Reputation Institute's annual national ranking.

Employees love Netflix also. In a 2018 survey conducted by Hired (a dot-com marketplace for tech talent), tech workers rated Netflix as the No. 1 company they'd most like to work for, beating companies like Google (No. 2), Elon Musk's Tesla (No. 3), and Apple (No. 6). In another 2018 "Happiest Employee" ranking, based on over five million anonymous reviews from workers at forty-five thousand large US companies compiled by the staff of Comparably, a compensation and careers site, Netflix was ranked as having the second-happiest employees of the many thousands ranked. (It trailed only HubSpot, a Cambridge-based software firm.)

Most interesting of all, unlike the vast majority of firms that fail when the industry shifts, Netflix had responded successfully to four massive transitions in the entertainment and business environment in just fifteen years:

- From DVD by mail to streaming old TV series and movies over the internet.
- From streaming old content to launching new original content (such as **House of Cards**) produced by external studios.
- From licensing content provided by external studios to building their own in-house studio that creates award-winning TV shows and movies (such as **Stranger Things, La Casa De Papel,** and **The Ballad of Buster Scruggs**).

- From a USA-only company to a global company entertaining people in 190 countries.

Netflix's success is beyond unusual. It's incredible. Clearly, something singular is happening, which wasn't happening at Blockbuster when they declared bankruptcy in 2010.

A DIFFERENT TYPE OF WORKPLACE

 Blockbuster's story is not an anomaly. The vast majority of firms fail when their industry shifts. Kodak failed to adapt from paper photos to digital. Nokia failed to adapt from flip phones to smartphones. AOL failed to adapt from dial-up internet to broadband. My own first business, Pure Software, could not adapt to changes in its industry either because our company culture wasn't optimized for innovation or flexibility.

I started Pure Software in 1991. At the beginning, we had a great culture. We were a dozen people, creating something new and having a blast. Like many small entrepreneurial ventures, we had very few rules or policies inhibiting our actions. When our marketing guy decided to work from his dining room because it "helped him think" to be able to pour himself a bowl of Lucky Charms cereal every time he felt the urge, he didn't have to get permission from management. When our facilities person wanted to buy fourteen leopard-print office chairs for our staff members because they were on bargain-basement sale at Office Depot, she didn't have to fill out a purchase order or get approval from the CFO.

Then Pure Software started to grow. As we hired new employees, a few did stupid stuff, leading to errors that cost the company money. Each time this happened, I put a process in place to prevent that mistake from occurring again. For example, one day our sales person at Pure, Matthew, traveled to Washington, DC, to meet with a prospective client. The client was staying at the five-star Willard InterContinental Hotel, so Matthew did too . . . at $700 a night. When I found out, I was frustrated. I had our HR person write a travel policy outlining how much employees could spend on airplanes, meals, and hotels, and requiring management approval beyond a specified spending limit.

Our finance person, Sheila, had a black poodle that she sometimes brought to the office. One day, I arrived at work to find the dog had chewed a big hole in the conference room rug. Replacing that rug cost a fortune. I created a new policy: no dogs at work without special permission from Human Resources.

Policies and control processes became so foundational to our work that those who were great at coloring within the lines were promoted, while many creative mavericks felt stifled and went to work elsewhere. I was sorry to see them go, but I believed that this was what happens when a company grows up.

Then two things occurred. The first is that we failed to innovate quickly. We had become increasingly efficient and decreasingly creative. In order to grow we had to purchase other companies that did have innovative products. That led to more business complexity, which in turn led to more rules and process.

The second is that the market shifted from C++ to Java. To survive, we needed to change. But we had selected and conditioned our employees to follow process, not to think freshly or shift fast. We were unable to adapt and, in 1997, ended up selling the company to our largest competitor.

With my next company, Netflix, I hoped to promote flexibility, employee freedom, and innovation, instead of error prevention and rule adherence. At the same time, I understood that as a company grows, if you don't manage it with policies or control processes, the organization is likely to descend into chaos.

Through a gradual evolution, over many years of trial and error, we found an approach for making this work. If you give employees more freedom instead of developing processes to prevent them from exercising their own judgment, they will make better decisions and it's easier to hold them accountable. This also makes for a happier, more motivated workforce as well as a more nimble company. But to develop a foundation that enables this level of freedom you need to first increase two other elements:

+ **Build up talent density.**

At most companies, policies and control processes
are put in place to deal with employees who exhibit
sloppy, unprofessional, or irresponsible behavior.
But if you avoid or move out these people, you don't
need the rules. If you build an organization made
up of high performers, you can eliminate most controls. The denser the talent, the greater the freedom
you can offer.

+ **Increase candor.**

Talented employees have an enormous amount
to learn from one another. But the normal polite
human protocols often prevent employees from
providing the feedback necessary to take performance to another level. When talented staff
members get into the feedback habit, they all get
better at what they do while becoming implicitly
accountable to one another, further reducing the
need for traditional controls.

With these two elements in place you can now . . .

- **Reduce controls.**

Start by ripping pages from the employee handbook. Travel policies, expense policies, vacation
policies—these can all go. Later, as talent becomes
increasingly denser and feedback more frequent

and candid, you can remove approval processes throughout the organization, teaching your managers principles like, "Lead with context, not control," and coaching your employees using such guidelines as, "Don't seek to please your boss."

FIRST

Build up talent density by creating a workforce of high performers

Introduce candor by encouraging loads of feedback

Remove controls such as vacation, travel, and expense policies

SECOND

Strengthen talent density by paying top of market

Increase candor by emphasizing organizational transparency

Release more controls such as decision-making approvals

THIRD

Max-up talent density by implementing the Keeper Test

Max-up candor by creating circles of feedback

Eliminate most controls by leading with context not control

Best of all, once you start developing this type of culture, a virtuous cycle kicks in. Removing controls creates a culture of "Freedom and Responsibility" (a term Netflix employees use so much that they now just say "F&R"), which attracts top talent and makes possible even fewer controls. All this takes you to a level of speed and innovation that most companies can't match. But you can't reach this level in one go.

The first nine chapters of this book cover this three-step implementation approach through three cycles, each cycle making a section. The tenth chapter looks at what happened when we began to take our corporate culture into a variety of **national** cultures—a transition that has led to interesting and important new challenges.

Of course, virtually every experimental project includes both successes and failures. Life at Netflix—like life in general—is a little more complicated than this tornado-shaped diagram suggests. That's why I asked someone from the outside to study our culture and write this book with me. I wanted an impartial expert to take a close look at how the culture actually plays out, day to day, within our walls.

I thought of Erin Meyer, whose book **The Culture Map** I had just finished reading. A professor at INSEAD business school outside of Paris, Erin had recently been selected by the Thinkers50 as one of the world's most influential business thinkers. She writes frequently about her research on cultural differences in the workplace for **Harvard Business Review,** and I learned in her book that she was also a Peace Corps volunteer teacher in Southern Africa ten years before I was. I sent her a message.

 In February 2015, I read an article in the **Huffington Post** titled, "One Reason for Netflix's Success—It Treats Employees Like Grownups." The article explained:

Netflix assumes that you have amazing judgment, ... And judgment is the solution for almost every ambiguous problem. Not process.

The flip side . . . is that people are expected to work at a super-high level or be quickly shown the door (with a generous severance package).

I became increasingly curious as to how an organization could operate successfully, in real life, following the stated methodology. A lack of process is bound to create pandemonium, and showing employees the door if they don't operate at a super-high level is bound to instigate terror in the workforce.

Then, a few months later, I woke up to find the following email in my inbox:

From: Reed Hastings
Date: May 31, 2015
Subject: Peace Corps and book

Erin,

I was Peace Corps Swaziland (1983–85). Now I'm the CEO of Netflix. I loved your book and we are having all of our leaders read it.

I'd love to have coffee sometime. I'm in Paris often.

Small world!

Reed

Reed and I got to know each other and eventually he suggested I interview Netflix employees to get a firsthand glimpse of what the Netflix culture is really like, and to gather data in order to write a book with him. This was a chance to find out how a company with a culture in direct opposition to everything we know about psychology, business, and human behavior can have such remarkable results.

I have conducted over two hundred interviews with current and past Netflix employees in Silicon Valley, Hollywood, São Paulo, Amsterdam, Singapore, and Tokyo, speaking with employees at every level, from executives to administrative assistants.

Netflix generally doesn't believe in anonymity, but I insisted that during my interviews all employees be given the option to conduct these interviews anonymously. Those who chose that option are referred to in this book by fictional first names only. However, true to the "honesty-always" culture at Netflix, many were happy to share all sorts of surprising and sometimes unflattering opinions and stories about themselves and their employer, while being identified openly.

YOU HAVE TO CONNECT THE DOTS DIFFERENTLY

In his famous commencement speech at Stanford University, Steve Jobs said: "You can't connect the dots looking forward; you can only connect them looking backwards. So you have to trust that the dots will somehow connect in your future. You have to trust in something—your gut, destiny, life, karma, whatever. This approach has never let me down, and it has made all the difference in my life."

Jobs is not alone. Sir Richard Branson's mantra is said to be "A-B-C-D," or "Always be connecting the dots." And David Brier and **Fast Company** released a fascinating video that claims the way we connect life's dots defines how we see reality, and thus how we make decisions and reach conclusions.

The point is to encourage people to question how the dots are connected. In most organizations, people join the dots the same way that everyone else does and always has done. This preserves the **status quo**. But one day someone comes along and connects the dots in a different way, which leads to an entirely different understanding of the world.

That's what happened at Netflix. Despite Reed's experience at Pure Software, he didn't exactly set out to build a company with a unique ecosystem. Instead, he sought organizational flexibility. Then a few things happened that led him to connect the dots of corporate culture differently. Gradually, as these elements came together, he was able—in hindsight only—to understand what it was about the culture that helped drive Netflix's success.

 In this book we'll be connecting the dots chapter by chapter, in the order that we discovered them at Netflix. We will also look at how they play out in the current Netflix work environment, what we've learned along the way, and how you might apply your own version of freedom and responsibility to your organization.

FIRST STEPS TO A CULTURE OF FREEDOM AND RESPONSIBILITY

First build up talent density...

1 ▶ A Great Workplace Is Stunning Colleagues

Then increase candor...

2 ▶ Say What You Really Think
(with Positive Intent)

Now begin removing controls...

3a ▶ Remove Vacation Policy

3b ▶ Remove Travel and Expense Approvals

This section demonstrates how a team or organization can begin to implement a culture of Freedom and Responsibility. These concepts build on one another. Although you may try implementing elements of each chapter in isolation, such an approach can be risky. Once you have built up talent density, you can safely address candor. Only then can you safely begin removing policies that control your staff.

FIRST BUILD UP TALENT DENSITY . . .

1

A GREAT WORKPLACE
IS STUNNING COLLEAGUES

 In the 1990s, I liked to rent VHS videos from the Blockbuster down the street from our house. I'd take two or three at a time and return them quickly to avoid late fees. Then one day I moved a pile of papers on the dining room table and saw a cassette that I'd watched weeks ago and forgotten to return. When I took the movie back to the store, the woman told me the fee: $40! I felt so stupid.

Later, that got me thinking. Blockbuster made most of its margin from late fees. If your business model depends on inducing feelings of stupidity in your customer base, you can hardly expect to build much loyalty. Was there another model to provide the pleasure of watching movies in your own living room without inflicting the pain of paying a lot when you forgot to return them?

In early 1997, when Pure Software was acquired,

Marc Randolph and I started thinking about opening a movies-by-mail business. Amazon was having good luck with books. Why not films? Customers would rent VHS cassettes from our website and be able to return them via the mail. Then we learned it would cost $4 to mail the VHS cassette each way. There wasn't going to be a big market. It was too expensive.

But a friend told me about a new invention called DVDs, which would be coming that fall. "They're like CDs but hold a movie," he explained. I raced to the post office and mailed myself several CDs (I couldn't find an actual DVD for my test). Each cost thirty-two cents to mail. Then I went back to my place in Santa Cruz and waited anxiously for them to arrive. Two days later they dropped through the mail slot, unharmed.

In May 1998, we launched Netflix, the world's first online DVD rental store. We had thirty employees and 925 movie titles, which was almost the entire catalog of DVDs available at the time. Marc was the CEO until 1999, when I took over and he became one of our executives.

By early 2001, we'd grown to 400,000 subscribers and 120 employees. I tried to avoid the leadership fumbles of my Pure Software days, and although we avoided implementing excessive rules and controls this time, I also couldn't characterize Netflix as a particularly great place to work. But we were growing, business was good, and work for our employees was OK.

LESSONS FROM A CRISIS

Then, in the spring of 2001, crisis struck. The first internet bubble burst, and scores of dot-coms failed and vanished. All venture capital funding stopped, and we were suddenly unable to raise the additional funds we needed to run the business, which was far from profitable. Morale in the office was low, and it was about to get lower. We had to lay off a third of our workforce.

I sat down with Marc and Patty McCord—Patty had come with me from Pure Software and was head of Human Resources—and we studied the contribution of each employee. We didn't have any obviously poor performers. So we divided the staff into two piles: the eighty highest performers who we would keep and forty less amazing ones we would let go. Those who were exceptionally creative, did great work, and collaborated well with others went immediately into the "keepers" pile. The difficulty was that there were many borderline cases. Some were great colleagues and friends but did adequate rather than great work. Others worked like crazy but showed uneven judgment and needed a lot of hand-holding. A few were exceptionally gifted and high performing but also complainers or pessimists. Most of them would have to go. It wasn't going to be easy.

In the days before the layoffs, my wife remarked how on edge I was, and she was right. I worried that motivation in the office would plummet. I was convinced that, after I'd let go of their friends and colleagues, those who stayed would think that the company wasn't loyal to employees. It was bound to make everyone angry. Even worse, the "keepers" would have to shoulder the work of those let go, which seemed certain to lead to bitterness. We were already short on cash. Could we bear a further collapse in morale?

The day of the layoffs arrived, and it was awful, as expected. Those who we laid off cried, slammed doors, and shouted in frustration. By noon it was finished, and I waited for the second half of the storm: the backlash from the remaining employees. . . . But, despite some tears and visible sorrow, all was calm. Then, within a few weeks, for a reason I couldn't initially understand, the atmosphere improved dramatically. We were in cost-cutting mode, and we'd just let go of a third of the workforce, yet the office was suddenly buzzing with passion, energy, and ideas.

A few months later the holidays arrived. DVD players were popular that Christmas, and by early 2002, our DVD-by-mail subscription business was growing rapidly again. Suddenly, we were doing far more work—with 30 percent fewer employees. To my amazement, those same eighty people were getting everything done with a passion that seemed higher than ever. They were working longer hours, but spirits were sky-high. It wasn't just our employees who were happier. I'd wake up in the morning and couldn't wait to get to the office. In those days, I drove Patty McCord to work every day and when I swung up to her house in Santa Cruz, she would practically leap into the car with this big grin: "Reed, what's going on here? Is this like being in love? Are these just some wacky chemicals and this thrill is going to wear off?"

Patty had put her finger on it. The entire office felt like it was filled with people who were madly in love with their work.

I'm not advocating for layoffs, and fortunately we haven't had to do anything like that at Netflix since. But in the days and months following those 2001 layoffs, I discovered something that completely changed the way that I understand both employee motivation and leadership responsibility. This was my road to Damascus experience, a turning point in my understanding of the role of talent density in organizations. The lessons we learned became the foundation of much that has led to Netflix's success.

But before we go on to describe those lessons, I should give Patty a proper introduction because she played a critical role in the development of Netflix for over a decade, and her protégé, Jessica Neal, runs HR for Netflix today. I first met Patty McCord while at Pure Software. In 1994 she called the office out of the blue and asked to speak to the CEO. My younger sister was answering the phones in those days, and she put Patty right through. Patty was raised in Texas, which I could hear faintly in the way she spoke. She said she was currently working for Sun Microsystems in the HR department, but she'd like to come to Pure Software and run HR for us. I invited her in for a cup of coffee.

During the first half of the meeting, I couldn't understand anything Patty was saying. I asked her to tell me her HR philosophy, and she said: "I believe that every individual should be able to draw a line between their contribution to the corporation and their individual aspirations. As the head of human capital management, I would work with you, the CEO, to increase the emotional intelligence quotient of our leadership and improve employee engagement." My head started to spin. I was young and unpolished and after she stopped, I said: "Is that how all HR people speak? I couldn't understand a word. If we are going to work together you are going to have to stop talking like that."

Patty was insulted, and she told me so straight to my face. When she got home that evening and her husband asked her how the interview had gone, she told him, "Bad. I got in a fight with the CEO." But

I loved the way she told me exactly what she thought of me. So I gave her the job, and since then we have had a frank, long-lasting friendship, which has persisted even after her departure from Netflix. It may be partly because we're so different: I'm a math wonk and a software engineer, she's an expert in human behavior and a storyteller. When I look at a team, I see numbers and algorithms that connect the people and discussions. When Patty looks at a team, she sees emotions and subtle interpersonal responses that are invisible to me. Patty worked for me at Pure Software until we sold it in 1997, and she joined us early at Netflix.

Patty and I spent dozens of car rides following the 2001 layoffs trying to figure out why the work environment had taken a sharp turn for the better and how we could maintain this positive energy. We came to understand that what Patty referred to as our dramatic increase in "talent density" was behind the improvements.

TALENT DENSITY: TALENTED PEOPLE MAKE ONE ANOTHER MORE EFFECTIVE

Every employee has some talent. When we'd been 120 people, we had some employees who were extremely talented and others who were mildly talented. Overall we had a fair amount of talent dispersed across the workforce. After the layoffs, with only the most talented eighty people, we had a smaller amount of talent overall, but the amount of talent per employee was greater. Our talent "density" had increased.

We learned that a company with really dense talent is a company everyone wants to work for. High performers especially thrive in environments where the overall talent density is high.

Our employees were learning more from one another and teams were accomplishing more—faster. This was increasing individual motivation and satisfaction and leading the entire company to get more done. We found that being surrounded by the best catapulted already good work to a whole new level.

Most important, working with really talented colleagues was exciting, inspiring, and a lot of fun—something that remains as true today with the company at seven thousand employees as it was back then at eighty.

In hindsight, I understood that a team with one or two merely adequate performers brings down the performance of everyone on the team. If you have a team of five stunning employees and two adequate ones, the adequate ones will

- sap managers' energy, so they have less time
  for the top performers,

- reduce the quality of group discussions, lowering the team's overall IQ,
- force others to develop ways to work around them, reducing efficiency,
- drive staff who seek excellence to quit, and
- show the team you accept mediocrity, thus multiplying the problem.

For top performers, a great workplace isn't about a lavish office, a beautiful gym, or a free sushi lunch. It's about the joy of being surrounded by people who are both talented and collaborative. People who can help you be better. When every member is excellent, performance spirals upward as employees learn from and motivate one another.

PERFORMANCE IS CONTAGIOUS

 From the 2001 layoffs, Reed learned that performance—both good and bad—is infectious. If you have adequate performers, it leads many who could be excellent to also perform adequately. And if you have a team consisting entirely of high performers, each pushes the others to achieve more.

Professor Will Felps, of the University of New South Wales in Australia, conducted a fascinating study demonstrating contagious behavior in the work environment. He created several teams of four college students and asked each team to complete a management task in forty-five minutes. The teams who did the best work would receive a financial reward of one hundred dollars.

Unbeknownst to the students, some teams included an actor, who played one of several roles: a "Slacker" who would disengage, put his feet up on the table, and send text messages; a "Jerk" who would speak sarcastically and say things like, "Are you kidding me?" and "Clearly, you've never taken a business class before"; or a "Depressive Pessimist" who would look like his cat had just died, complain the task was impossible, express doubt that the team could succeed, and sometimes put his head on the desk. The actor did so without tipping off the rest of the team that he was anything other than a regular student.

Felps first found that, even when other team members were exceptionally talented and intelligent, one individual's bad behavior brought down the effectiveness of the entire team. In dozens of trials, conducted over month-long periods, groups with one underperformer did worse than other teams by a whopping 30 to 40 percent.

These findings flew in the face of research going back decades, which suggested that individual team members conform to group values and norms. The behavior of the one individual quickly spread to the other group members, even though the groups were together for only forty-five minutes. As Felps explains, "Eerily surprising was how the others on the team would start to take on his characteristics." When the impostor was a slacker, the rest of the group lost interest in the project. Eventually someone else would announce that the task just wasn't important. If the actor was a jerk, others in the group also started being jerks: insulting one another, speaking abrasively. When the actor was a depressed pessimist, the results were the starkest. Says Felps: "I remember watching this video of one of the groups. You start out all the members are sitting up straight, energized, and excited to take on this potentially challenging task. By the end they have their heads actually on the desk, sprawled out."

 Felps demonstrated what Patty and I had already learned in 2001. If you have a group with a few merely adequate performers, that performance is likely to spread, bringing down the performance of the entire organization.

Most of us can remember moments in our own lives when we have seen this principle of infectious behavior play out firsthand, as I did when I was twelve years old.

I was born in 1960 in Massachusetts. I was a pretty average kid with no particular talent or standout ability. When I was in third grade, we moved to Washington, DC. Things would have been OK there, and I had a big group of friends, but on the sixth and seventh grade playground, there was one boy, Calvin, who began to organize fistfights. It wasn't that he picked on or bullied any of us. But this one kid, otherwise unremarkable, created a pattern of behavior that impacted the way the rest of us behaved and responded to one another. I didn't want to join in, but the shame of not fighting would have been worse than taking part. And it really mattered for the whole day who won or lost their fight. Without Calvin, our way of responding to one another and playing together would have been dramatically improved. When my father told us we were moving back to Massachusetts, I couldn't wait to leave.

After the 2001 layoffs, we realized that at Netflix we also had a handful of people who had created an undesirable work climate. Many weren't great at their jobs in myriad little ways, which suggested to others that mediocre performance was acceptable, and brought down the performance of everyone in the office.

In 2002, with a new understanding of what makes a great place to work, Patty and I made a commitment. Our number one goal, moving forward, would be to do everything we could to retain the post-layoff talent density and all the great things that came with it. We would hire the very best employees and pay at the top of the market. We would coach our managers to have the courage and discipline to get rid of any employees who were displaying undesirable behaviors or weren't performing at exemplary levels. I became laser-focused on making sure Netflix was staffed, from the receptionist to the top executive team, with the highest-performing, most collaborative employees on the market.

THE FIRST DOT

This is the most critical dot for the foundation of the whole Netflix story.

A fast and innovative workplace is made up of what we call "stunning colleagues"—highly talented people, of diverse backgrounds and perspectives, who are exceptionally creative, accomplish significant amounts of important work, and collaborate effectively. What's more, none of the other principles can work unless you have ensured this first dot is in place.

▶ TAKEAWAYS FROM CHAPTER 1

- Your number one goal as a leader is to develop a work environment consisting exclusively of stunning colleagues.

- Stunning colleagues accomplish significant amounts of important work and are exceptionally creative and passionate.

- Jerks, slackers, sweet people with nonstellar performance, or pessimists left on the team will bring down the performance of everyone.

Toward a Culture of Freedom and Responsibility

Once you have high talent density in place and have eliminated less-than-great performers, you are ready to introduce a culture of candor.

This brings us to chapter 2.

THEN INCREASE CANDOR . . .

2

SAY WHAT YOU REALLY THINK
(WITH POSITIVE INTENT)

 In my first few years as CEO at Pure Software, I managed the technology well. But I was still pretty miserable at the people part of leadership. I was conflict-avoidant. People would become upset if I addressed them directly with a problem, so I would try to work around issues when they arose.

I trace this personality trait back to my childhood. When I was a kid, my parents were supportive, but we didn't talk about emotions in our house. I didn't want to upset anyone, so I avoided any difficult topics. I didn't have many role models for constructive candor, and it took me a long time to get comfortable with it.

Without much thought, I carried this attitude over into my work. At Pure Software, for example, we had a very thoughtful senior leader called Aki, who was, I felt, taking too long developing a product. I got frustrated and upset. But instead of talking with Aki, I went outside the company and struck a deal with another set of engineers to get the project going. When Aki learned what I'd done, he was furious. He came to me and said, "You're upset with me, but you go around my back instead of just telling me how you feel?"

Aki was dead right—the way I'd handled the problem was terrible. But I didn't know how to talk openly about my fears.

The same problem affected my personal life. By the time Pure went public in 1995, my wife and I had been married for four years and we had one young daughter. It was the pinnacle of my professional life, but I didn't know how to be a good spouse. The next year when Pure acquired another company three thousand miles away, it got harder. I spent half of each week away, but when my wife expressed her frustration, I would defend myself, saying that everything I did was for the good of the family. When friends would ask her, "Aren't you excited about Reed's success?" she wanted to cry. She was distant from me, and I was resentful of her.

The problem turned around when we started going to a marriage counselor. He got each of us to talk about our resentments. I began to see our relationship through my wife's eyes. She didn't care about money. She'd met me, in 1986, at a party for returned Peace Corps volunteers and had fallen in love with the guy who'd just spent two years teaching in Swaziland. Now she found herself hitched to a guy obsessed with business success. What was there for her to be excited about?

Giving and receiving transparent feedback helped us so much. I saw I'd been lying to her. While I was saying things like, "Family is the most important thing to me," I'd been missing dinners at home and working all hours of the night. I see now that my words were worse than platitudes. They had been lies. We both learned what we could do to be better partners, and our marriage came back to life. (We've now been married twenty-nine years and have two grown kids!)

Afterward, I tried to take this same commitment to being honest back to the office. I began encouraging everyone to say exactly what they really thought, but with positive intent—not to attack or injure anyone, but to get feelings, opinions, and feedback out onto the table, where they could be dealt with.

As we began giving increasing amounts of candid feedback to one another, I saw that getting feedback had an added benefit. It pushed the performance in the office to new levels.

An early example involved our chief financial officer, Barry McCarthy. Barry was the first Netflix CFO, serving from 1999 to 2010. He was a great leader with vision, integrity, and an incredible ability to help everyone deeply understand our finances. But he was also a little moody. When the head of marketing, Leslie Kilgore, mentioned Barry's moodiness to me, I encouraged her to speak to him herself. "Tell him exactly what you've said to me," I suggested, inspired by my marriage counseling experiences.

Leslie was chief marketing officer from 2000 to 2012 and is currently on our board of directors. Her external persona is no-nonsense, but she has a dry, often surprising, sense of humor. Leslie spoke to Barry the next day and did a much better job than I ever could. She found a way to calculate how much money his moodiness was costing the business. She spoke to him in his own financial language, adding a shot of her infectious humor to the communication, and Barry was moved. He went back to his team, told them about the feedback he'd received, and asked them to call him out when his mood was influencing their actions.

The results were remarkable. In the subsequent weeks and months, many on the finance team spoke to me and Patty about the positive change in Barry's leadership. That wasn't the only benefit.

After Leslie gave constructive feedback to Barry, Barry gave constructive feedback to Patty and later to me. Seeing how well he had responded to Leslie's feedback, Barry's team dared to tell him, with a bit of humor, when his moodiness was slipping back in and started giving more feedback to one another. We hadn't hired any new talent or raised anyone's salaries, but day-by-day candor was increasing talent density in the office.

I saw that openly voicing opinions and feedback, instead of whispering behind one another's backs, reduced the backstabbing and politics and allowed us to be faster. The more people heard what they could do better, the better everyone got at their jobs, the better we performed as a company.

That's when we coined the expression "Only say about someone what you will say to their face." I modeled this behavior as best I could, and whenever someone came to me to complain about another employee, I would ask, "What did that person say when you spoke to him about this directly?" This is pretty radical. In most situations, both social and professional, people who consistently say what they really think are quickly isolated, even banished. But at Netflix, we embrace them. We work hard to get people to give each other constructive feedback—up, down, and across the organization—on a continual basis.

An employee on our legal team, Doug, gave this example of candor in action. He joined the company in 2016, and not long after he went on a business trip to India with a senior colleague named Jordan. As he explained, "Jordan is the kind of colleague who brings Rice Krispy treats for people on their birthdays. But he is also hard-driving and impatient." Although Jordan had emphasized the need to be relationship oriented and focus on building personal connections, when they arrived in India, his behavior didn't match his advice:

> We were having dinner with a Netflix supplier named Sapna at a restaurant on a hill with a view over Mumbai. Sapna has a big personality and a bigger laugh. We were having a great time but every time the topic veered off work, Jordan seemed irritated. Sapna and I were giggling about how her baby was already walking at ten months, while my seventeen-month-old nephew had developed a scooting technique, so it was unnecessary to use his legs to do anything. It was a great moment of camaraderie, the type of connection that was certain to improve business. But Jordan was radiating frustration. He pulled his chair back from the table and kept glancing nervously at his cell phone as if that would make the coffees come faster. I knew his behavior was hurting our efforts.

In any of his previous jobs, Doug would have said nothing, silenced by attitudes about protocol, hierarchy, and niceness. And he hadn't adapted to the Netflix culture fully enough to risk openly calling out his new colleague's behavior. Not until a week after they'd returned home did he manage to screw up his courage. "Let me be Netflix about it," Doug told himself. He added "Feedback from India trip" to the agenda for his next meeting with Jordan.

The morning of the meeting, Doug's stomach was churning when he stepped into the meeting room. Feedback was the first item on the agenda. Doug asked Jordan if he had any feedback for him, and Jordan provided some. That made it easier. Then Doug said, "Jordan, I don't like to give feedback. But I did see something while in India that I think could be helpful to you." Jordan remembers the rest like this:

Let me be clear. I think of myself as a relationship-building king. Every time I go to India, I lecture everyone on the team about building emotional bonds. That's why Doug's feedback hit me so hard. Because I was stressed, I acted like a robot, sabotaging my own objectives, without even noticing my behavior. I go to India every single month. Now I don't lecture others before going. Instead I start the trip by telling my colleagues, "Hey, this is my weakness! If I start glancing at my watch while Nitin is giving us a tour of the city, give me a big kick in the shin! I'll thank you for it later."

When giving and receiving feedback is common, people learn faster and are more effective at work.

The only unfortunate part was that Doug didn't pull Jordan aside and give him that feedback during that very dinner in India, so that he could have potentially saved the meal.

HIGH PERFORMANCE + SELFLESS CANDOR = EXTREMELY HIGH PERFORMANCE

 Imagine attending a nine o'clock Monday-morning meeting with a group of work colleagues. You're sipping a cup of coffee and listening to your boss ramble on about his plans for an upcoming retreat, when the voice in your head starts shouting furiously in disagreement with what he's saying. The agenda your boss is outlining sounds like one that's guaranteed to fail—and you're sure the program you thought up while watching **Grey's Anatomy** reruns last night would be more effective. You wonder, **Should I say something?** But you hesitate, and the moment soon passes.

Ten minutes later, one of your colleagues who is often long-winded and repetitive—but contagiously upbeat (and, as everyone knows, very sensitive)—begins updating the team on her latest project. The voice in your head sighs at the pointlessness of her presentation and the underlying inanity of the project itself. Again you wonder, **Should I speak up?** But again, your lips stay sealed.

You've probably experienced moments like these. You may not always remain silent. But often you do—and when you do, it's likely to be because of one of the following reasons:

- You think your viewpoint won't be supported.
- You don't want to be viewed as "difficult."
- You don't want to get into an unpleasant argument.
- You don't want to risk upsetting or angering your colleagues.
- You're wary of being called "not a team player."

But if you work for Netflix, you probably **do** speak up. During the morning meeting, you tell your boss his plan for the retreat won't work and that you have another idea you think will be better. After the meeting, you tell your colleague why you believe she should rethink the project she described. And for good measure, after stopping at the coffee machine, you visit with another colleague to mention that he came across as defensive when he was asked to explain a recent decision of his in the all-hands meeting last week.

At Netflix, it is tantamount to being disloyal to the company if you fail to speak up when you disagree with a colleague or have feedback that could be helpful. After all, you could help the business—but you are choosing not to.

When I first heard about the candor at Netflix, I was skeptical. Netflix promotes not just candid feedback but also **frequent** feedback, which, in my experience, just increases the chances that you will hear something hurtful. Most people have trouble un-hearing harsh remarks, which can lead to a negative spiral of thought. The idea of a policy that encourages people to voice their honest feedback frequently sounded not just unpleasant but very risky. But almost as soon as I began to collaborate with Netflix employees, I saw the benefits.

In 2016, Reed asked me to give a keynote address at the company's quarterly leadership conference in Cuba. This was the first time I'd done work for Netflix, but the participants had all read my book, **The Culture Map**, and I wanted to present something fresh. I worked extensively to prepare a customized presentation full of new material. Normally when I speak to large audiences, it's with tried-and-tested content. This time, when I walked out onstage I could hear my heart beating faster than normal. The first forty-five minutes went well. The audience of around four hundred Netflix managers from around the world was engaged, and each time I asked a question dozens of hands flew up.

I then invited the participants to form small groups for five minutes of discussion. As I came down from the stage and walked among the participants, hearing snippets of conversation, I noticed one woman speaking with particular animation in an American accent. When she saw me observing, she beckoned me over. "I was just saying to my colleagues," she explained, "that the way you are facilitating the discussion from the stage is undermining your message about cultural diversity. When you ask for comments and call on the first person who raises a hand, you're setting just the type of trap your book tells us to avoid—because only Americans raise their hands, so only Americans get the chance to speak."

I was taken aback. It was the first time anyone had given me negative feedback smack in the middle of a presentation and in front of a group of other participants. I started to feel queasy—especially when I realized that, of course, she was right. I had two minutes to make an on-the-fly adjustment. When I resumed my talk, I suggested that we hear a comment from each country represented in the audience—first the Netherlands, then France, then Brazil, the US, Singapore, and Japan. It worked beautifully, and there's no way I would have used this technique at that moment without that feedback.

This set the pattern for other interactions to follow. At moments when I was supposed to be interviewing Netflix employees, they would offer feedback to me about my own actions, sometimes before I'd even had a chance to ask a question.

For example, when I was interviewing Amsterdam-based Danielle Crook-Davies, she greeted me warmly, told me she loved my book and then before we even had a chance to sit down, said, "Can I offer you some feedback?" She continued to tell me that the reader on the audio version of my book was startlingly poor and was undermining my message with her tone of voice. "I hope you'll find a way to get it re-recorded. The book has so much great content, but the voice spoils it all." I was taken aback, but upon reflection, recognized she was right. I made the call that evening to get the book re-recorded.

Another time, while conducting interviews in São Paulo, a Brazilian manager began his interview with a friendly "I'd love to give you some feedback." We'd only just said hello, but I tried to act like I felt this was normal. He proceeded to tell me that the preparation email I'd sent out to interviewees was so structured it came off as bossy. "You told us yourself in your book how we Brazilians often prefer to leave things more implicit and flexible. But you didn't follow your own advice. Next time, you might send out an email with themes but not specific questions. You'll have a better reaction." I found myself gulping uncomfortably while this manager pulled out my email to show me where the problem sentences lay. Again, that feedback helped me. On following trips, before I sent a pre-interview preparation email out I ran it by my local contact, who often had useful ideas for how to get the local interviewees on board.

Given all the benefits of candid feedback, you might wonder why in most companies we give and receive so little of it. A quick look at human behavior explains why.

WE HATE CANDOR (BUT STILL WANT IT)

Few people enjoy receiving criticism. Receiving bad news about your work triggers feelings of self-doubt, frustration, and vulnerability. Your brain responds to negative feedback with the same fight-or-flight reactions of a physical threat, releasing hormones into the bloodstream, quickening reaction time, and heightening emotions.

If there is one thing we hate more than receiving criticism one-on-one, it is to receive that negative feedback in front of others. The woman who gave me feedback in the middle of my keynote address (and in front of her colleagues) helped me a lot. She had input that could benefit me and it couldn't wait. But receiving feedback in front of the group sends off danger alarms in the human brain. The brain is a survival machine, and one of our most successful survival techniques is the desire to find safety in numbers. Our brain is constantly on the watch for signals of group rejection, which back in more primitive times would have led to isolation and potentially death. If someone calls out a mistake you are making in front of your tribe, the amygdala, the most primitive part of the brain, which is on constant watch for danger, sets off a warning: "This group is about to reject you." Our natural animalistic impulse in the face of this is to flee.

At the same time, there's a wealth of research showing that receiving **positive** feedback stimulates your brain to release oxytocin, the same feel-good hormone that makes a mother happy when she nurses her baby. It's no wonder so many people prefer to dish out compliments rather than give honest, constructive feedback.

Yet research shows that most of us do instinctively understand the value of hearing the truth. In a 2014 study, the consulting firm Zenger Folkman collected data on feedback from almost one thousand people. They found that, despite the blissful benefits of praise, by a roughly three-to-one margin, people believe corrective feedback does more to improve their performance than positive feedback. The majority said they didn't find positive feedback to have a significant impact on their success at all.

Here are a few more telling statistics from the same survey:

- 57 percent of respondents claim they would prefer to receive corrective feedback to positive feedback.
- 72 percent felt their performance would improve if they received more corrective feedback.

- 92 percent agreed with the comment, "Negative feedback, if delivered appropriately, improves performance."

It's stressful and unpleasant to hear what we are doing poorly, but after the initial stress, that feedback really helps. Most people intuitively understand that a simple feedback loop can help them get better at their jobs.

THE FEEDBACK LOOP: CULTIVATING A CULTURE OF CANDOR

In 2003, the people of Garden Grove, California, a small community south of L.A., were struggling with a problem. Accidents involving cars and pedestrians were alarmingly frequent on streets with elementary schools. Authorities put up speed limit signs in order to get drivers to slow down, and police doled out tickets to violators.

Accident rates barely budged.

City engineers tried another approach, putting up dynamic speed displays. In other words, "driver feedback." Each included a speed limit sign, a radar sensor, and a readout announcing, "Your Speed." Passing drivers got real-time data on their speed and a reminder of how fast they should be going.

Experts were doubtful that this would help. Everyone has a speedometer on their dashboard. Furthermore, law enforcement doctrine has long held that people obey rules only when they face clear consequences for breaking them—why would the displays influence driving behavior?

But they did. Studies showed that drivers slowed down 14 percent—at three schools, the average speed fell **below** the posted speed limit. Fourteen percent is a big improvement from something as simple and low-cost as feedback.

A feedback loop is one of the most effective tools for improving performance. We learn faster and accomplish more when we make giving and receiving feedback a continuous part of how we collaborate. Feedback helps us to avoid misunderstandings, creates a climate of co-accountability, and reduces the need for hierarchy and rules.

Yet encouraging candid feedback in a company is a lot more difficult than putting up traffic signs. To foster an atmosphere of candor requires getting your employees to abandon years of conditioning and firmly held beliefs such as, "Only give feedback when someone asks you for it" and "Praise in public, criticize in private."

When considering whether to give feedback, people often feel torn between two competing issues: they don't want to hurt the recipient's feelings, yet they want to help that person succeed. The goal at Netflix is to help each other succeed, even if that means feelings occasionally get hurt. More important, we've found that in the right environment, with the right approach, we can give the feedback **without** hurting feelings.

If you would like to develop a culture of candor in your own organization or on your own team, you can take several steps. The first is not the most intuitive. You might think the first step for cultivating candor would be to begin with what's easiest: having the boss give copious feedback to her staff. I recommend instead focusing first on something much more difficult: getting employees to give candid feedback to the boss. This can be accompanied by boss-to-employee feedback. But it's when employees begin providing truthful feedback to their leaders that the big benefits of candor really take off.

TELL THE EMPEROR WHEN HE HAS NO CLOTHES

Like many people, growing up I heard the famous tale of "The Emperor's New Clothes," about a foolish man in power so convinced he was wearing the finest costume ever made that he paraded naked in front of his subjects. No one dared point out the obvious—except for a child with no understanding of hierarchy, power, or consequences.

The higher you get in an organization, the less

feedback you receive, and the more likely you are to "come to work naked" or make another error that's obvious to everyone but you. This is not just dysfunctional but dangerous. If an office assistant screws up a coffee order and no one tells him, it's no big deal. If the chief financial officer screws up a financial statement, and no one dares to challenge it, it sends the company into crisis.

The first technique our managers use to get their employees to give them honest feedback is regularly putting feedback on the agenda of their one-on-one meetings with their staff. Don't just ask for feedback but tell and show your employees it is expected. Put feedback as the first or last item on the agenda so that it's set apart from your operational discussions. When the moment arrives, solicit and encourage the employee to give feedback to you (the boss) and then—if you like—you can reciprocate by giving feedback to them.

Your behavior while you're getting the feedback is a critical factor. You must show the employee that it's safe to give feedback by responding to all criticism with gratitude and, above all, by providing "belonging cues." As Daniel Coyle, author of **The Culture Code**, describes them, such cues are gestures that indicate "your feedback makes you a more important member of this tribe" or "you were candid with me and that in no way puts your job or our relationship in danger; you belong here." I speak with my leadership team frequently about displaying "belonging cues" in situations when an employee is providing feedback to the boss, because an employee who is courageous enough to give feedback openly is likely to worry, "Will my boss hold it against me?" or "Will this harm my career?"

A belonging cue might be a small gesture, like using an appreciative tone of voice, moving phys- ically closer to the speaker, or looking positively into that person's eyes. Or it might be larger, like thanking that person for their courage and speaking about that courage in front of the larger team. Coyle explains that the function of a belonging cue "is to answer the ancient ever-present question glowing in our brains: Are we safe here? What's our future with these people? Are there dangers lurking?" The more you and others in your company respond to all candid moments with belonging cues, the more courageous people will be in their candor.

 Ted Sarandos, Netflix's chief content officer, is a leader on Reed's team who solicits feedback openly and displays belonging cues when he receives it.

Ted is responsible for every television show and movie available on Netflix. Ted has played a pivotal role in reshaping the entertainment industry and is frequently described as one of the most import- ant people in Hollywood. Ted is not a typical media mogul. He didn't finish college, and he acquired his film education working in Arizona video stores.

An article in the May 2019 **Evening Standard** described Ted like this:

> If Netflix were to make a mini-series about Ted Sarandos, its multi-millionaire chief content officer, it would surely start with him as a kid in the sixties, sitting cross-legged in front of the blue flicker of a TV screen in a poor neighborhood in Phoenix, Arizona, oblivious to the chaos of four siblings playing around him. He spent hours like this, the TV schedule his only routine.
>
> In his teens, he took a job in a video store and, during long, empty daytime hours, he began ploughing through the nine hundred films it stocked. He developed an encyclopedic knowledge of film and TV—plus a pretty good instinct for what people liked (someone once called him a "human algorithm"). So much for too much TV rotting your brain.

In July 2014, Ted tapped Brian Wright, a senior vice president at Nickelodeon, to lead young adult content deals. (Brian's first Netflix claim to fame is signing the deal for a show called **Stranger Things** just a few months into the job.) Brian tells this story about Ted receiving feedback publicly on Brian's first day at Netflix:

> In all my past jobs, it was all about who's in and who's out of favor. If you gave the boss feedback or disagreed with her in a meeting in front of others, that would be political death. You would find yourself in Siberia.
>
> Monday morning, it's my first day of this brand-new job, and I'm on hyperalert trying to find out what are the politics of the place. At eleven a.m. I attend my first meeting led by Ted (my boss's boss, who is from my perspective a superstar), with about fifteen people at various levels in the company. Ted was talking about the release of **The Blacklist** season 2. A guy four levels below him hierarchically stopped him in the middle of his point: "Ted, I think you've missed something. You're misunderstanding the licensing deal. That approach won't work." Ted stuck to his guns, but this guy didn't back down. "It won't work. You're mixing up two separate reports, Ted. You've got it wrong. We need to meet with Sony directly."
>
> I could not believe that this low-level guy would confront Ted Sarandos himself in front of a group of people. From my past experience, this was equivalent to committing career suicide. I was literally scandalized. My face was completely flushed. I wanted to hide under my chair.

When the meeting ended, Ted got up and put his hand on this guy's shoulder. "Great meeting. Thanks for your input today," he said with a smile. I practically had to hold my jaw shut, I was so surprised.

Later I ran into Ted in the men's washroom. He asked how my first day was going so I told him, "Wow Ted, I couldn't believe the way that guy was going at you in the meeting." Ted looked totally mystified. He said, "Brian, the day you find yourself sitting on your feedback because you're worried you'll be unpopular is the day you'll need to leave Netflix. We hire you for your opinions. Every person in that room is responsible for telling me frankly what they think."

Ted clearly demonstrated the two behavioral necessities to get employees to give the boss candid feedback. Don't just ask for feedback but tell and show your employees it is expected (such as his instructions to Brian). Then when you receive the feedback, respond with belonging cues; in this case, the hand Ted put on that guy's shoulder in the meeting.

Reed is another Netflix leader who frequently displays these two behaviors. And in return he receives more negative feedback than any other leader in the company. The proof is his 360-degree written assessment, which is open for everyone to contribute to, and where he consistently gets more feedback than any other employee does. Reed solicits feedback continually and religiously responds with belonging cues, sometimes even speaking publicly about how pleased he's been to receive a piece of criticism. Here is a paragraph from a memo he shared with all Netflix employees in spring 2019:

> 360 is always a very stimulating time of year. I find the best comments for my growth are unfortunately the most painful. So in the spirit of 360, thank you for bravely and honestly pointing out to me: "In meetings you can skip over topics or rush through them when you feel impatient or determine a particular topic on the agenda is no longer worth the time...On a similar note, watch out for letting your point-of-view overwhelm. You can short-change the debate by signalling alignment when it doesn't exist." So true, so sad, and so frustrating that I still do this. I will keep working on it. Hopefully, all of you got and gave very direct constructive feedback as well.

Rochelle King remembers clearly what it's like to give the CEO of the company constructive feedback. It was 2010, and she had been working as creative product director at Netflix for about a year. She reported to a vice president, who worked for the chief product officer, who in turn worked for Reed, so she was three levels below him. Her story of upward-facing candor at Netflix is a typical one:

> Reed was leading a meeting with about twenty-five directors, VPs, and some of the executive team. Patty McCord said something Reed didn't agree with. Reed got visibly irritated with Patty and sarcastically dismissed her comment. When he spoke, there was this sort of collective, public flinch and an under-the-breath gasp. Maybe Reed was too frustrated to notice the audience reaction, but I felt it was not a great leadership moment for him.

Rochelle took seriously the Netflix principle that to say nothing in circumstances like this would be tantamount to disloyalty. She spent that evening writing the following email to Reed and rereading it "a hundred times, because even if this is Netflix, it still felt a little risky." The email she finally sent said the following:

> Hi Reed,
>
> As part of the audience in the room yesterday, your comments to Patty came across to me as dismissive and disrespectful. I bring this up because at last year's retreat, you talked about the importance of creating an environment where people are encouraged to speak up and contribute to the conversation (whether in dissent or to augment).
>
> In the room yesterday, we had a mix of folks— directors and VPs—and some who don't know you well. The tone you used with Patty would prevent me, if I didn't know you as well, from voicing my opinion publicly in front of you in the future, for fear you might shut my ideas down. I hope you don't mind me letting you know.
>
> Rochelle

After hearing this story, I thought about my past jobs, from waitress at the Sri Lanka Curry House to training manager at a big multinational to director at a small Boston-based company and professor at a business school. I tried to remember whether, in any of these roles, I had ever heard someone politely yet candidly tell the head of the organization that his tone of voice in a meeting had been out of line. And my answer was one big, loud NO!

When I emailed Reed asking him if he remembered the incident with Rochelle five years earlier, he responded within minutes.

> Erin—I recall the room (King Kong) and where I was sitting and where Patty was. I recall feeling shitty afterwards about how I handled my frustration.
>
> —Reed

Minutes later he forwarded his own copy of the email Rochelle had sent him as well as the response he sent her.

> Rochelle—I appreciated a lot receiving that feedback and please continue to call me out if you see something that feels inappropriate to you.
>
> Reed

Rochelle's feedback was frank but thoughtful and genuinely intended to help Reed improve.

But the big risk in fostering a climate of candor is

all the ways people may both purposely and acciden-tally misuse it. That brings us to Reed's next step for developing a culture of candor in the workplace.

TEACH ALL EMPLOYEES TO GIVE AND RECEIVE FEEDBACK WELL

In Bradley Cooper and Lady Gaga's Oscar-winning film **A Star Is Born**, there is a scene in which candor done wrong is displayed in all its ugliness.

Lady Gaga is lying in a bath full of bubbles. She has recently been recognized as a musical star in her own right, receiving three Grammy nominations. Her mentor (and recently turned husband) comes into the bathroom having had too much to drink. And he tells her candidly how he feels about her new original song, which she just performed on **Saturday Night Live**.

```
You got nominated and that's great . . .
I'm just trying to figure it out. (Your
song) "Why You Come Around Me with an
Ass Like That." (eyes rolling . . . long
sigh) Maybe I failed you. You're embar-
rassing. I got to be honest with you."
```

Despite all the talk about feedback at Netflix, this type of candor would not fly. A climate of candor doesn't mean anything goes. The first few times Netflix employees gave me feedback I felt so startled I thought the rules of feedback were something like, "say what's on your mind, to hell with the cost." But Netflix managers invest significant time teaching their employees the right and wrong way to give feedback. They have documents explaining what effective feedback looks like. They have sections of training programs where people learn how and practice giving and receiving it.

You can do this too. After ploughing through all the Netflix materials on candor and hearing dozens of interviewees explain how it works, I've found the lessons can be summarized in the following 4A format.

4A FEEDBACK GUIDELINES

Giving Feedback

1. **AIM TO ASSIST:** Feedback must be given with positive intent. Giving feedback in order to get frustration off your chest, intentionally hurting the other person, or furthering your political agenda is not tolerated. Clearly explain how a specific behavior change will help the individual or the company, not how it will help you. "The way you pick your teeth in meetings with external partners is irritating" is wrong feedback. Right feedback would be,

"If you stop picking your teeth in external partner meetings, the partners are more likely to see you as professional, and we're more likely to build a strong relationship."

2. **ACTIONABLE:** Your feedback must focus on what the recipient can do differently. Wrong feedback to me in Cuba would have been to stop at the comment, "Your presentation is undermining its own messages." Right feedback was, "The way you ask the audience for input is resulting in only Americans participating." Even better would have been: "If you can find a way to solicit contributions from other nationalities in the room your presentation will be more powerful."

Receiving Feedback

3. **APPRECIATE:** Natural human inclination is to provide a defense or excuse when receiving criticism; we all reflexively seek to protect our egos and reputation. When you receive feedback, you need to fight this natural reaction and instead ask yourself, "How can I show appreciation for this feedback by listening carefully, considering the message with an open mind, and becoming neither defensive nor angry?"

4. **ACCEPT OR DISCARD:** You will receive lots of feedback from lots of people while at Netflix. You are re-

quired to listen and consider all feedback provided. You are not required to follow it. Say "thank you" with sincerity. But both you and the provider must understand that the decision to react to the feedback is entirely up to the recipient.

 In the example toward the beginning of this chapter, where Doug gave feedback to Jordan about how to adjust his behavior while working in India, we can see the 4As modeled beautifully. Doug saw how Jordan's transactional approach was sabotaging his own goals. His objective was to help Jordan to improve and to help the organization succeed (Aim to Assist). The feedback he provided was so practical that Jordan claims he now takes a different approach each time he works with India (Actionable). Jordan expressed thanks (Appreciation). He could have chosen to discard the feedback but this time he accepted it saying: "Now I don't lecture others before going. Instead I start the trip by telling my colleagues 'Hey, this is my weakness! If I start glancing at my watch while Nitin is giving us a tour of the city, give me a big kick in the shin!'" (Accept or Discard)

Most people, like Doug, find it especially difficult to give feedback in real time. Many have been deeply conditioned to wait for the right moment and the right conditions before telling the truth, so that the usefulness of the feedback often all but fades away. This brings us to the third priority for instilling a culture of candor on your team.

PREACH FEEDBACK ANYWHERE, ANYTIME

The only remaining question is when and where to give feedback—and the answer is anywhere and anytime. That might mean giving feedback in private, behind closed doors. Erin got her first Netflix feedback in front of a group of three or four people in the middle of a keynote. That is fine too. It can even be shouted out in front of a group of forty, if that's where it will help the most.

Rose, a VP on the Global Communications Team, provided an example:

> My forty colleagues had come together from around the world for a two-day meeting and I had sixty minutes on the agenda to present the marketing plan for the rollout of **13 Reasons Why** season 2.
>
> When we released season 1, the suicide on the show set off a firestorm of public controversy. For season 2, I wanted to take a different approach common in brand publicity, where my experience lies, but not common in traditional publicity, which had been the norm at Netflix.
>
> My plan included partnering with Northwestern University to conduct an independent study

looking at the impact of the series on teenage viewers. Netflix would not influence the study but hopefully the data would help better position the season 2 launch.

This sixty-minute presentation was Rose's one chance to get her marketing colleagues on board. Yet fifteen minutes in, the audience was pushing back: "Why would you invest that money when you don't even know what the results will be? Can a study be independent if we fund it?" Rose felt she was being attacked:

Each raised hand felt like another challenge. Everyone seemed to be shouting, "Do you know what you're doing?!" I heard myself talking faster with each challenge and the frustration in the room cycling up. The more the group questioned me, and the more worried I became that I wouldn't finish my content, the faster I talked.

Then Rose's close colleague Bianca waved her arm from the back of the room, offering a life vest . . . Netflix style: "Rose! This isn't working! You are losing the room! You sound defensive! You're talking too fast. You're not listening to the questions. You're repeating yourself without addressing the concerns. Take a deep breath. You NEED THE ROOM," she called out:

At that moment I saw myself as the audience was seeing me—breathless and talking more than listening. I took a deep breath. "Thank you, Bianca. You're right. I'm watching the time. I need everyone to understand the project. I'm here to listen and answer your questions. Let's go back. Who did I miss?" I consciously changed my energy, and this triggered a change in the room. Voice tones lowered. People started smiling. The aggressiveness in the meeting dissipated. I got the group on board. Bianca's candor saved me.

In most organizations, shouting criticism out in front of a group, while that person is in the middle of a presentation, would be considered inappropriate and unhelpful. But if you manage to inculcate an effective culture of candor, all involved would recognize that this feedback from Bianca was a gift. Bianca's intent was only to help Rose succeed (Aim to Assist). She outlined specific actions Rose could take to improve her performance (Actionable). Rose received the feedback with thanks (Appreciation). In this case, she followed the advice Bianca had provided, to the benefit of all (Accept or Discard). If you follow the 4A model, feedback can and should be given exactly when and where it will help the most.

In this case, Bianca meant well, but what if she hadn't? Someone with a bone to pick could pretend to follow the 4A guidelines but actually sabotage Rose's message or harm her reputation. If candor still feels risky to you, that's understandable. That brings us to the final point of advice for fostering a climate of candor.

CLARIFY AND REINFORCE THE DIFFERENCE BETWEEN BEING SELFLESSLY CANDID AND A BRILLIANT JERK

We've all worked with people who are obviously brilliant. You know the type: bursting with amazing insights, articulate, able to solve problems with a single blow. The denser the talent in your organization, the more brilliant people you're likely to have on the team.

But with a lot of brilliant people running around, you run a risk. Sometimes really talented people have heard for so long how great they are, they begin to feel they really are better than everybody else. They might smirk at ideas they find unintelligent, roll their eyes when people are inarticulate, and insult those they feel are less gifted than they are. In other words, these people are jerks.

If you are promoting a culture of candor on your team, you have to get rid of the jerks. Many may think, "This guy is so brilliant, we can't afford to lose him." But it doesn't matter how brilliant your jerk is, if you keep him on the team you can't benefit from candor. The cost of jerkiness to effective teamwork is too high. Jerks are likely to rip your organization apart from the inside. And their favorite way to do that is often by stabbing their colleagues in the front and then offering, "I was just being candid."

Even at Netflix, where we preach "No Brilliant Jerks," we often have an employee who has difficulty finessing the boundaries. When this happens, you need to jump in. Original Content Specialist Paula was one example. Paula was exceptionally creative and had an extensive network, which was an enormous asset. She put in long hours reading scripts and visualizing how to turn a potential TV series into a big hit. Paula tried to live the Netflix culture by being forthcoming and candid in all instances.

Often in meetings Paula spoke forcefully, repeating herself, sometimes pounding on the table to make her point. She frequently spoke over people if they weren't getting her gist. Paula was clearly very efficient too, working on her computer while others were speaking, especially if she didn't agree with their points. If people were long-winded or slow to get to the point, she would interrupt them and let them know, then and there. Paula did not feel she was being a jerk, just that she was living the Netflix culture with her honest feedback. Yet because of her difficult behavior, Paula no longer works at Netflix.

A culture of candor does not mean that you can speak your mind without concern for how it will impact others. On the contrary, it requires that everyone think carefully about the 4A guidelines. This requires reflection and sometimes preparation before you give feedback, as well as monitoring and coaching from those in charge. Justin Becker, an engineering manager for the Playback API team at Netflix, gave this example in a 2017 presentation titled: "Am I a Brilliant Jerk?"

> Early in my time at Netflix, an engineer in my group made a big mistake in my area of expertise and sent an email that dodged responsibility and showed no path to fix it. I was upset and called the engineer: my intent was to put him on the right path. I was blunt and criticized his actions. I didn't enjoy doing so, but I felt I was doing a good thing for the company.
>
> A week later, his manager stopped by my desk unexpectedly. He told me that he was aware of my exchange with the engineer and didn't think I was technically wrong, but did I know that the engineer had been demotivated and unproductive since I talked to him and was it my intent to make his staff unproductive? No, of course not.

The manager continued: Do you think you could have told my engineer what you needed to, in a way that left him feeling positive and motivated to fix it? Sure, I probably could do that. Good. Always do that in the future, please. I did.

The conversation lasted less than two minutes and was immediately effective. Notice that he did not accuse me of being a jerk. Rather, he asked: (1) "Are you intending to hurt the company?" and (2) "Are you able to act decently?" There's really only one right answer to those questions. If he had just said, "You are a jerk," I may have replied, "No, I'm not," but by asking questions instead, it put the onus on me to think about the answer and triggered a moment of self-reflection.

Justin had partly followed the 4A-feedback guidelines. He had intended to help the engineer get on the right path. He had emphasized that he had the company's interest in mind. Perhaps his message was even actionable. But he still came across as a jerk because he also broke part of the first candor rule, by giving feedback to get frustration off his chest. Following other general critical-feedback guidelines—such as "Never give criticism when you're still angry" and "Use a calm voice when giving corrective feedback"—could have helped too.

Of course, many of us have had moments of being

a jerk. In Justin's case, he had confused jerkiness with candor. Justin was able to adapt his behavior. He's still at Netflix today.

 In chapter 8, we will come back to this topic and explore a couple of other methods you can use to encourage candor on the team. In the meantime this is . . .

THE SECOND DOT

If you have a group of people who are highly talented, thoughtful, and well-meaning, you can ask them to do something that is not at all natural but nonetheless incredibly helpful to a company's speed and effectiveness. You can ask them to give each other loads of candid feedback and challenge authority.

▶ TAKEAWAYS FROM CHAPTER 2

- With candor, high performers become outstanding performers. Frequent candid feedback exponentially magnifies the speed and effectiveness of your team or workforce.

- Set the stage for candor by building feedback moments into your regular meetings.

- Coach your employees to give and receive feedback effectively, following the 4A guidelines.

- As the leader, solicit feedback frequently and respond with belonging cues when you receive it.

- Get rid of jerks as you instill a culture of candor.

With talent density and candor in place, you are ready to begin releasing controls and offering more workplace freedom.

Toward a Culture of Freedom and Responsibility

Most organizations have a wide variety of control processes to make sure employees are behaving in ways that benefit the company. Control mechanisms include policies, approval procedures, and management oversight.

First focus on developing a high-talent-density workplace. Second develop a culture of candor, assuring that everyone gives and receives a lot of feedback.

With a climate of candor, the boss is no longer the primary individual to correct an employee's undesirable behavior. When the entire community speaks openly about which individual behaviors advance the company, and which don't, the boss doesn't have to get so involved in overseeing an employee's work.

With these two elements in place, you are ready to begin removing controls. Chapters 3a and 3b will show you how.

NOW BEGIN REMOVING CONTROLS . . .

3a

REMOVE VACATION POLICY

Well before Netflix, I believed that the value of creative work should not be measured by time. This is a relic of an industrial age when employees did tasks that are now done by machines.

If a manager came to me and said, "Reed, I want to give Sherry a promotion because she works like crazy," I would be frustrated. What do I care? I want that manager to say, "Let's give Sherry a promotion because she's making a huge impact," not because she's chained to her desk. What if Sherry's accomplishing amazing things working a twenty-five-hour week from a hammock in Hawaii? Well, let's give her a big raise! She's extremely valuable.

Today, in the information age, what matters is what you achieve, not how many hours you clock, especially for the employees of creative companies like Netflix. I have never paid attention to how many hours people are working. When it comes to how we judge performance at Netflix, hard work is irrelevant.

Nevertheless, until 2003 we allocated vacation and tracked days off, just like every other company I knew. Netflix was following the pack. Each employee received a specific number of days off per year depending on seniority.

Then a suggestion from an employee led us to make a change. He pointed out the following:

> We are all working online some weekends, responding to emails at odd hours, taking off an afternoon for personal time. We don't track hours worked per day or week. Why are we tracking days of vacation per year?

There was no answer. An employee could be working from 9:00 a.m. to 5:00 p.m. (eight hours) or from 5:00 a.m. to 9:00 p.m. (sixteen hours). That's a 100 percent variation, yet no one monitored it. So why should I care if that employee works fifty weeks a year or forty-eight weeks a year? That's only a 4 percent variation. Patty McCord suggested we remove the policy altogether: "Let's just say our vacation policy is 'Take Some!'"

I liked the idea of telling people they were in charge

of their own lives and could decide for themselves when to work and when to take a break. Yet no other company I knew of was doing this. I worried how it would play out. During this time, I often woke in the night with one of two nightmares.

In the first, it's summer. I'm late for an important meeting. I rip into the office parking lot and sprint into the building. The preparation I have to do is gigantic. It will require the input of the entire office. I run through the front doors calling out names: David! Jackie! But the office is dead quiet. Why is the place empty? Finally, I find Patty in her office wearing this white feather boa. "Patty! Where is everybody?" I gasp, out of breath. Patty looks up from her desk with a smile. "Oh, hi, Reed! Everyone's on vacation!"

This was a serious concern. We were a small group of people with a lot to accomplish. If two of our team of five DVD buyers all took a monthlong vacation in the winter, that would cripple the office. Would ever-vacationing employees sink the company?

In the second nightmare, it's winter and there's a blizzard outside, like we used to have in Massachusetts when I was a child. The entire workforce is stuck in the office with heaps of snow blocking the door. Icicles the size of elephant tusks hang from the roof. The wind is whipping the windows. The office is stuffed with people. Some are lying on the kitchen floor asleep. Others are staring blankly at their computers. I'm furious. Why is no one working? Why is everyone so tired? I try to get the people asleep on the floor back to work. I tug them to a standing position, but when they head back to their desks they walk like zombies. In the back of my mind, I know why we are all stuck in this building exhausted. It's been years, and no one's taken any vacation.

I worried that people would stop taking vacation if it wasn't allotted to them. Would our "No Vacation Policy" become a "No Vacation" policy? Many of our biggest innovations happened when people took time off. One example was Neil Hunt, who was our chief product officer for almost twenty years. Neil is from the UK. Patty calls him "Brain-on-a-Stick" because he's six foot four, pencil thin, and especially smart. Neil oversaw many of the technical innovations that have made Netflix what it is today. He also has a passion for vacationing in the extreme outdoors.

When Neil left on vacation, often he went to an isolated place. Each time he came back he had a fantastic new idea for how to move the business forward. Once he and his wife took ice saws to the northern Sierra Nevada mountains and spent a week sleeping in igloos. When they returned, Neil had dreamed up a new mathematical algorithm to improve the way we select the movies to offer our customers. He was living proof of why companies benefit when their employees take vacations. Time off provides mental bandwidth that allows you to think creatively and see your work in a different light. If you are working all the time, you don't have the perspective to see your problem with fresh eyes.

Patty and I brought the executive team together to discuss the two contradictory anxieties that occupied my mind as we prepared to get rid of our vacation policy. We decided, despite some trepidation, to remove the vacation policy, but only as an experiment. The new system would allow all salaried staff to take off whenever they wanted for as long as they wanted. There would be no need to ask for prior approval and neither the employees themselves nor their managers would be asked or expected to track their days away from the office. It was left to the employee alone to decide if and when he or she felt like taking a few hours, a day, a week, or a month off.

The experiment worked well, and we still operate that way today, leading to plenty of benefits. Unlimited vacation helps attract and retain top talent, especially Gen Z-ers and millennials, who resist punching clocks. Removing the policy also reduces bureaucracy and the administrative costs of keeping track of who is out and when. Most important, the freedom signals to employees that we trust them to do the right thing, which in turn encourages them to behave responsibly.

That said, if you remove the vacation policy without taking a couple of other necessary steps, you may find either of my nightmares turning into your reality. The first is that . . .

LEADERS MUST MODEL BIG VACATION-TAKING

I recently came across an article by the CEO of a small company who tried the same vacation experiment as Netflix, but with considerably less success. He wrote:

> If I take two weeks off, will my coworkers think I'm a slacker? Is it okay to vacation more than my boss?. . . . I get it. For almost a decade, my company offered unlimited vacation time. As we grew to forty employees, questions like these began lingering beneath the surface. Last spring, my executive team decided it was time to put the policy up for a vote for all of our employees to decide. When my staff ultimately decided to strike down unlimited vacation in favor of a more finite policy based on tenure, I can't say I was surprised.

But I was surprised. Our unlimited vacation is so popular, I couldn't imagine this happening at Netflix. My first question was "Did the leader model taking big vacations?" Further in the article I found the answer:

> Even as CEO, under our unlimited plan, I realized I was only taking a yearly total of about two weeks off. Under the new (finite vacation) plan, I'm planning to use most if not all of my five weeks. To me, the fear of losing these days I've "earned" is what's motivating me to actually use them.

If the CEO is taking only two weeks' vacation, **of course** his employees feel the unlimited plan doesn't give them much freedom. They're bound to take more time off with three allotted weeks than with an indefinite number and a boss who models just two. In the absence of a policy, the amount of vacation people take largely reflects what they see their boss and colleagues taking. Which is why, if you want to remove your vacation policy, start by getting all leaders to take significant amounts of vacation and talk a lot about it.

Patty articulated this right from the beginning. During the 2003 leadership meeting, where we decided to launch the no-vacation-policy experiment, Patty insisted that in order for this to work we, the executive team, would have to take big vacations and talk about them a lot. Without a policy, the example the bosses set would become incredibly important. She told us that she wanted to see our postcards from Indonesia or Lake Tahoe posted all over the office, and that when Ted Sarandos got back from his July holiday to Southern Spain, she expected everyone to sit through his 7,000-photo slideshow.

With the absence of a policy, most people look around their department to understand the "soft limits" of what's acceptable. I have always been interested in travel and before we lifted our vacation policy I already tried to take a good amount. But after we lifted the policy I started talking a lot more about those vacations to anyone who was willing to listen.

 When I began collaborating with Reed I expected him to work like a maniac. Much to my surprise, he seemed to be frequently on vacation. He couldn't meet while I was in Los Gatos because he was hiking in the Alps, he complained about a stiff neck from lumpy pillows after a week in Italy with his wife, and an ex-employee told me that he and Reed had just returned from a week's scuba excursion in Fiji. By Reed's count, he takes six weeks of vacation a year, and from my limited experience, I would add "at least."

Reed's own modeling is fundamental to the success of the unlimited vacation policy throughout

Netflix. If the CEO doesn't model this, the method can't work. Even then, Reed's substantial vacation-taking has trickled down as intended in some areas of Netflix and not so well in others. When those leaders under Reed don't follow his example, their employees often sound a bit like the zombies from Reed's nightmares.

One example is marketing executive Kyle. He was a newspaper journalist before joining Netflix. Kyle loves the thrill and pressure that comes from working against tight deadlines: "It's the middle of the night, breaking news is just in. That paper is going to print in just a few hours. There's nothing more exciting than the weight of the ticking clock and the reward of finishing a project that should have taken days in a matter of hours." Kyle's kids are grown up. He's in his late fifties and until recently headed up one of the Netflix departments based in Hollywood. While at Netflix he continued to work like he was constantly under deadline—and everyone in his department did too. Kyle explained, "We all work like crazy, but that's because we are so passionate about our jobs." Kyle didn't take much vacation and didn't talk much about vacations, but those in Kyle's department heard his message loud and clear.

Marketing manager, Donna, for example, was one burnt-out example.

According to her Fitbit, Donna had slept four hours and thirty-two minutes the previous night.

Working late nights and getting up early in an effort to complete what she described as "valleys of uncompleted work" was status quo. Donna hadn't taken a nonworking vacation in four years, ever since the birth of her first of two children. "I took a few days off to visit my mother at Thanksgiving. I spent the entire time in the laundry room working."

Why didn't Donna use the freedom allotted to Netflix employees and take more time off? "My husband's an animation artist—he draws cartoons. I'm the one bringing home the bacon." Donna worked so much because that's what her boss and everyone on her team did, and she didn't want to look like she wasn't pulling her weight: "The Netflix culture has great ideals but sometimes the gap between the ideals and practice is big, and what should bridge that gap is leadership. When leaders don't set a good example . . . I guess I'm what happens."

As Netflix grows there are an increasing number of pockets where Reed's modeling and Patty's initial instructions don't seem to have trickled down. On these Netflix teams, the "no vacation policy" does feel a bit like a "no vacation" policy. But many leaders at Netflix are consciously following Reed's modeling, taking big vacations and making sure everyone is watching. And when they do, employees use the freedom Netflix provides in many surprising and beneficial ways.

Greg Peters, who replaced Neil Hunt as chief product officer in 2017, is one example. Greg gets to work at the normal hour of 8:00 a.m. and leaves the office by 6:00 p.m. to be home for dinner with his children. Greg makes a point of taking big vacations, including visiting his wife's family in Tokyo, and encourages his staff to do the same. "What we say as leaders is only half the equation," Greg explains. "Our employees are also looking at what we do. If I say, 'I want you to find a sustainable and healthy work-life balance,' but I'm in the office twelve hours a day, people will imitate my actions, not follow my words."

Greg's actions are speaking loud and clear and his people are hearing them.

John, an engineer on Greg's team, is one example. John drives a 1970s two-toned tan-brown Oldsmobile with vinyl front bench seats, wood-colored paneling, and a wayback. John loves the feeling of being transported back to the 1970s as he drives to his office at the Netflix Silicon Valley headquarters. The Oldsmobile gives him the space he needs for his mountain bike, his guitar, his Rhodesian ridgeback puppy, and his six-year-old twin girls. John feels a little guilty about his extraordinary work-life balance:

I've taken seven weeks of vacation already this year and it's only October. My bosses take a lot of vacation, but I don't think even they know how much I've had. No one's ever asked or blinked an eye. I bike, I'm a musician, and my kids need me. I often think, I'm making all this money . . . shouldn't I be working more? But I'm getting a ton done, so I tell myself that this incredible work-life balance I have . . . it's okay.

Others on Greg's team have found creative ways to organize their lives that would be impossible under a traditional vacation policy. Senior software engineer Sarah works seventy to eighty hours a week, but takes ten weeks of vacation a year (most recently for an anthropological trip to see the Yanomami tribe in the Brazilian Amazon). She considers it a rotation of several weeks of intense work followed by a week of doing something wildly different. "This is the great benefit to the Netflix vacation freedom," she explained. "Not that you can take more or less days off, but that you can organize your life in any crazy way you like—and as long as you do great work nobody bats an eyelid."

The behavior of the boss is so influential that it can even wipe out national cultural norms. Before becoming CPO, Greg served for a time as Netflix's general manager in Tokyo. In Japan, businesspeople are famous for long work hours and taking little time off. There are stories of people working so much there, they literally die from it. There's even a word for this phenomenon, **karoshi**. The average Japanese worker uses about seven vacation days a year, and 17 percent take none at all.

One evening over beer and sushi, Haruka, a manager in her early thirties, told me, "In my last job, I worked for a Japanese company. For seven years, I arrived at work at 8:00 a.m. and I took the last train home just after midnight. In seven years, I took one week of vacation, and only then because my sister in the US was getting married." Her experience is common in Japan.

Joining Netflix changed Haruka's life. "When Greg was here, he left the office every day before dinnertime, and so did the other employees. He'd take frequent vacations to Okinawa Island or to Niseko to take his kids skiing, and when he returned he'd show us all photos. He asked us about our vacations too, so we all started taking them. My biggest fear about leaving Netflix is that I'd have to go back to a life of suffocating long days and no breaks, because Netflix offers such incredible work-life balance."

Greg, an American, managed to get an entire office of Japanese people to work and vacation like Europeans. He didn't create rules or nag. He just modeled the behavior and communicated expectations.

 If you want to remove the vacation policy in your organization, lead by example. Even at Netflix where I model taking off six weeks a year and encourage my leadership team to do the same, Kyle and Donna's story demonstrates that getting big vacation-taking to trickle down requires ongoing reminders and attention. But if you and those on your leadership team set the example you want your team to follow, you won't have to worry about pulling vacationless zombies off your kitchen floor.

Leadership modeling is the first part of getting the unlimited vacation to work properly. The other concern many have about removing the vacation policy is that their teams will use the freedom to take off months on end at inconvenient moments, harming teamwork and sabotaging the business. That's what brings us to the second required step for a successful lifting of vacation policy. Do this well and it will also help you fix the problem of any leaders in your organization, like Kyle, who don't emulate the big vacation-taking their bosses are modeling and in doing so fail to achieve healthy work-life balance on their own teams.

SET AND REINFORCE CONTEXT
TO GUIDE EMPLOYEE BEHAVIOR

In 2007, Leslie Kilgore coined the expression "Lead with context, not control" (which we will explore further in chapter 9), but we didn't have this guiding principle when we removed the vacation policy in 2003. We had only the notion that the leaders must take a lot of vacation and talk about those vacations a lot. Beyond that, we hadn't thought much about the need to say anything specific or set context at all. We told people we would be neither allotting vacation days nor tracking days off. We left it at that. Within months, we started having problems.

We removed our vacation policy in 2003. In January 2004, a director in the accounting department came into my office and complained. "Thanks to your brilliant idea to remove the vacation policy, we're going to close the books late this year." A member of this director's team, tired of always having to work the first two weeks of January—the annual crunch period for accountants—had claimed her right to take those two weeks off, throwing the department into chaos.

Another day, I ran into a manager at the fruit bowl in the kitchen. Her eyes were puffy and her cheeks splotchy, like she'd been crying. "Reed, this vacation freedom is killing me!" Her team of four had a massive deadline looming. One employee was starting his paternal leave the following week. Now another had informed her that in two weeks' time she would be taking a monthlong Caribbean cruise. The manager didn't feel she could tell either of them no. "This is the price of the freedom we offer," she moaned.

This brings us to the second step critical for successfully removing your vacation policy. When you remove a policy, employees don't know how to operate with the absence. Some will be paralyzed until the boss tells them explicitly what actions are okay. If you don't tell them, "Take some time off," they won't. Others will imagine they have complete freedom to behave in wildly inappropriate ways like going on vacation at a time that causes pain to everyone else. This not only sabotages team effectiveness, but could ultimately lead the manager to throw up his hands and fire the employee, which is not good for anyone.

In the absence of written policy, every manager must spend time speaking to the team about what behaviors fall within the realm of the acceptable and appropriate. The accounting director should have sat down with the team and explained which months were okay to take vacation—and that January was off limits for all accountants. The puffy-eyed manager at the fruit bowl should have worked with the team to set vacation parameters, such as, "only one team member can be out at a time" and "make sure you're not causing the rest of the group undue grief before booking your vacation." The clearer the manager is when setting context, the better. That accounting director might say, "Please give at least three months' advance warning for a month out of the office, but a month's notice is usually fine for a five-day vacation."

As a company grows, the variety in how leaders set context and model behavior increases. Due to Netflix's rapid growth and change, it's easy to feel overwhelmed and under pressure. Any manager who isn't thoughtful and vigilant can quickly find a fleet of Donnas on the team. Kyle's mistake wasn't just that he didn't model big vacation-taking, but that he also didn't set context about the time off he expected his own team to take to maintain a healthy work-life balance. I've dealt with this type of scenario by trying to do a better job setting context myself as to demonstrate the context I expect our leaders to set with their own teams. One of the main occasions I use to set this example is our quarterly meeting, which brings together all directors and vice presidents in the company (top 10–15 percent of all employees) four times a year. Whenever I hear stories floating around about people not taking time off, it's time to put vacations on the agenda of a QBR meeting. This gives me an opportunity to talk about the type of environment we aspire to have and gives our leaders a chance to discuss, in small groups, techniques they use in order to achieve a healthy work-life balance for our workforce.

FREEDOM FROM VACATION POLICY ADDS VALUE—EVEN IF NO ONE USES IT

 After Netflix removed vacation tracking, other companies began doing the same, including Glassdoor, LinkedIn, Songkick,

HubSpot, and Eventbrite from the tech sector, as well as law firm Fisher Phillips, PR firm Golin, and marketing agency Visualsoft, to name just a few.

In 2014, the famous British entrepreneur Richard Branson adopted the nonpolicy for Virgin Management. He wrote an article about his decision, explaining it like this:

> I first learned of what Netflix was up to when my daughter Holly read the **Daily Telegraph** and immediately forwarded the piece to me with a clearly excited email saying, "Dad, check this out." It's something I have been talking about for a while and I believe it would be a very Virgin thing to do to not track people's holidays. She then went on to say, "I have a friend whose company has done the same thing and they've apparently experienced a marked upward spike in everything—morale, creativity, and productivity have all gone through the roof." Needless to say I was instantly intrigued and wanted to learn more.
>
> It is always interesting to note how often the adjectives "smart" and "simple" describe the cleverest of innovations—well, this is surely one of the simplest and smartest initiatives I have heard of in a long time and I'm delighted to say that we have introduced this same (non) policy at our parent company in both the UK and the US, where vacation policies can be particularly draconian.

Trenton Moss, the CEO of Webcredible, also got rid of his company's vacation policy, explaining how this attracts good candidates and increases employee satisfaction:

The Netflix ethos is that one superstar is better than two average people. We very much follow their lead. There is currently a huge demand for good user-experience practitioners, so holding on to staff is a big challenge (lifting vacation policy helps). Members of our team are always being tapped on LinkedIn, and many professionals in our business are millennials who are fleet of foot and like to keep moving. Unlimited holiday is easy to implement—you just have to create an environment of trust, and ours is built through three company rules: (1) always act in the best interests of the company, (2) never do anything that makes it harder for others to achieve their goals, (3) do whatever you can to achieve your own goals. Other than that, when it comes to setting holiday time, staff can do whatever they want.

Another company, Mammoth, learned something interesting when it decided to adopt the Netflix policy as a test and measure the response. CEO Nathan Christensen wrote the following:

We're a small business, and we liked the idea of a policy that conveys trust in our employees and reduces red tape. We agreed to try it for one year and then re-evaluate. During the year, the policy became one of our employees' most-valued benefits. In a survey we conducted just before we hit the one-year mark, our employees ranked unlimited vacation third-highest among the benefits we offer, just behind health insurance and our retirement plan. It beat out vision insurance, dental insurance, and even professional development, all of which still ranked highly.

Christensen's employees appreciated the benefit a lot, yet didn't take advantage of it: "They took roughly the same number of vacation days under our unlimited policy as they did the year before (about fourteen days, with most of our employees taking between twelve and nineteen days off)."

Netflix doesn't track vacation days, so there is no data on how much vacation employees are taking, on average, but one person did try to look into it. In 2007, a San Jose **Mercury News** journalist, Ryan Blitstein, conducted research on the subject. He arrived at the office one morning, excited to get the scoop. This was going to be a front-page Bay Area story: "Netflix's crazy time-off policy!" He asked Patty, "Do people take months off exploring exotic places? Do you still manage to get any work done?" Rather than answering, Patty sent an email to employees saying, "Feel free to chat with the journalist who'll be hanging around the office." He sat in the cafeteria asking Netflix staff a lot of questions.

At the end of the day, Blitstein was defeated. "There's no story here! No one is doing anything unusual. You know what your employees told me? They told me they love the vacation policy, but they vacation the way they've always vacationed. No more and no less. It's no scoop at all!"

GIVE FREEDOM TO GET RESPONSIBILITY

 I thought the sky might fall after we stopped tracking vacations, but nothing much changed except that folks seemed to be more satisfied and our more maverick employees, like the one who wanted to work eighty hours three weeks in a row and then go visit the Yanomami tribe in the Brazilian Amazon, were particularly appreciative of the freedom. We'd found a way to give our high performers a little more control over their lives, and that control made everybody feel a little freer. Because of our high-talent density, our employees were already conscientious and responsible. Because of our culture of candor, if anyone abused the system or took advantage of the freedom allotted, others would call them out directly and explain the undesirable impact of their actions.

About the same time, something else happened that provided a critical lesson. Patty and I both noticed people seemed to be taking more ownership around the office. Just little things, like someone started throwing out the milk in the refrigerator when it got sour.

Giving employees more freedom led them to take more ownership and behave more responsibly. That's when Patty and I coined the term "Freedom and Responsibility." It's not just that you need to have them both; it's that one leads to the other. It began to dawn on me. Freedom is not the opposite of accountability, as I'd previously considered. Instead, it is a path toward it.

With that in mind, I looked for other rules we could get rid of. The travel and expense policy was next.

CONTINUE REMOVING CONTROLS . . .

3b

REMOVE TRAVEL AND EXPENSE APPROVALS

In 1995, before Netflix, one of the sales directors at Pure Software, Grant, stormed into my office, ears flaming red, and slammed the door. Our employee handbook stated, **While visiting a client you can rent a car or take a taxi, but not both.** "I rented a car! The client's office is two hours away! A taxi would have cost a fortune. That was the right thing to do," Grant explained. "There was an evening event with a bunch of clients fifteen minutes from my hotel. I knew everyone would be drinking so I took a taxi. Now Finance won't reimburse my fifteen-dollar taxi because I had a rental car." Grant was angry on principle. "Would you have preferred I drink and drive?" Patty McCord and I spent an hour figuring out how to help and rewrite the handbook for future emergencies.

Months later Grant resigned. "When I saw how

senior management spends their time, I lost confidence in the company," he stated in his exit interview.

Grant was right. At Netflix, I didn't want **anyone** wasting time on this type of discussion. More so, I didn't want our talented employees to feel that dumb rules were preventing them from using their brains to do what was best. This was a clear way to kill the creative vibes that make for an innovative workplace.

In the early Netflix days, we were like any start-up. There weren't any written rules outlining who could spend what or which hotels to stay in when you traveled. The company was so small that each important purchase got noticed. Employees were free to buy what they needed, and if they went overboard someone would spot it and correct the behavior.

By 2004, however, we had been a public company for two years. That's about the time when most businesses begin to put a bunch of policies in place. Our CFO, Barry McCarthy, sent me a document outlining a proposal for a new expense and travel policy, which would reflect the types of rules most midsize to big companies were using. It had all sorts of details: which level of managers could fly business class, how much each employee could spend on office supplies without approval, the signatures needed if you wanted to buy something expensive like a new computer.

We'd recently removed the vacation policy, and, in the aftermath, I was dead set against putting any new control processes in place. We had proved that with the right employees, clear modeling from management, and enough context setting, we could get along perfectly fine without a bunch of rules. Barry agreed, but reminded me that we'd need to set crystal-clear context to help employees understand how to spend company money wisely.

I called a meeting in Half Moon Bay. On the agenda was how to articulate spending guidelines to employees in the absence of a policy. We looked at a series of cases. Some were clear-cut. If an employee sends a Christmas package to a family member by FedEx, that should not be billed to Netflix. But we soon found many situations were ambiguous. If Ted attends a party in Hollywood for work purposes and buys a box of chocolates for the host, can he charge that to Netflix? If Leslie works from home every Wednesday, is paper for her printer a valid business expense? What if her daughter uses this same paper for her school book report?

The only situation we could agree on was that if an employee steals from the company he should lose his job. But then a director named Chloe piped in: "I stole from the company on Monday. I had to work until eleven p.m. to finish a project. I didn't have anything to give my kids for breakfast the next morning, so I took four mini boxes of Cheerios from the kitchen." Well, that seemed reasonable. It only served to underline why setting rules and policies can never work well. Real life is so much more nuanced than any policy could ever address.

I suggested we just ask people to spend money frugally. Employees should think carefully before they buy anything, just like they would with their own money. We wrote our first expense guideline:

SPEND COMPANY MONEY AS IF IT WERE YOUR OWN

I felt great about that. I was frugal with my own money and frugal with company money and assumed others would be like me. But as it turned out, not everyone was as tightfisted, and the dramatically diverging styles of spending one's own money created problems. There was an example from David Wells, who joined our group as a VP of finance just as we were having those discussions in 2004. He later went on to be our CFO from 2010 to 2019.

> I was raised on a farm in Virginia. We lived a mile down a dirt road, way off of the beaten track. My dog Starr and I spent our days chasing bugs and swinging sticks over the two hundred acres of open woods that surrounded my house.
>
> I wasn't born with a silver spoon in my mouth and I don't require luxury. When Reed said to travel like I would with my own money, for me that meant flying economy and staying in modest hotels. I'm a finance guy and that just seemed fiscally responsible.
>
> A while into the new policy we had a leadership meeting in Mexico. I boarded the flight and was

walking back to my seat in economy. That's when I saw the entire Netflix content team sitting in first class, kicking back in cozy airline slippers. Those are expensive seats and the flight from L.A. to Mexico City is only a few hours. I went to say hello and a couple of them seemed embarrassed. But here's the clincher. They weren't embarrassed to be sitting in first class. They were embarrassed for me—that a key executive at the company would be sitting back in economy!

We saw quickly that **spend company money as if it were your own** was not actually how we wanted our employees to behave. One of the VPs, a guy named Lars who was making a substantial salary, used to joke that because of his love for luxury he lived paycheck to paycheck. The spending that accompanied this type of lifestyle is not what we were going for.

So we changed the spending and travel guideline to something even simpler. Today the entirety of the travel and expense policy still consists of these five simple words:

ACT IN NETFLIX'S BEST INTEREST

That works better. It is not in Netflix's best interest that the entire content team fly business from L.A. to Mexico. But if you have to take the red-eye from L.A. to New York and give a presentation the next morning it would likely be in Netflix's best interest that you fly business, so you don't have bags under your eyes and slurred speech when the big moment arises.

 What could be more intriguing than the possibility of spending money that is not your own to buy things that benefit you and your job, any way you see fit?

Think of the possibilities. You take a trip to Thailand to visit your colleagues and have a few meetings. The weather in Bangkok will do you good and the massages are amazing. You could replace that suitcase whose wheel broke on your last business trip—those Tumi suitcases are expensive! Of course, companies don't usually pay for luggage, but clearly it's because of business travel that the suitcase broke, so it can be justified.

On the other hand, if you're the owner of the company, the same five-word guideline may cause you to break out in an unexpected rash. Let your employees run around spending the company's money any way they choose, no approvals required? This is going to be expensive—it may even send the whole business into bankruptcy. Of course, some people are honest and frugal, but the vast majority are looking for a way to maximize personal gain.

This is not just a pessimistic hunch. Studies show that well over half the population will readily cheat the system to get more for themselves if they think they won't be caught.

Gerald Pruckner, a researcher at the University of Linz, and Rupert Sausgruber from the Vienna University of Economics, set up a study to find out how people would respond in just this type of scenario. They sold newspapers out of a box with no monitoring. The price was posted and passersby were supposed to put their payment into a slot if they took a copy. There was a message reminding people to be honest. About two thirds of people who took the paper didn't pay for it. That's a lot of dishonest people. It would be naive to believe only the honest third work for you.

Tantalizing and terrifying as this all sounds, the Netflix world of spending is very different from the newspaper experiment. It's neither as much fun nor as scary as you might think. That's because of the context set on the front end and the checks made at the back end. Employees have a lot of freedom to decide for themselves how to spend company money, but it's clearly not a free-for-all.

SET CONTEXT UP FRONT AND KEEP AN EYE ON SPENDING OUT BACK

 New recruits to Netflix are eager to understand what they should and shouldn't spend money on, and we provide them

with the context to make good choices. During the
ten years that David Wells was CFO he set the first
round of context for incoming recruits at our "New
Employee College." He explained it like this:

Before you spend any money imagine that you
will be asked to stand up in front of me and your
own boss and explain why you chose to purchase
that specific flight, hotel, or telephone. If you can
explain comfortably why that purchase is in the
company's best interest, then no need to ask, go
ahead and buy it. But if you'd feel a little uncomfortable explaining your choice, skip the purchase,
check in with your boss, or buy something cheaper.

This is what I mean by "context at the front end."
David's instruction to imagine explaining your
purchases to your bosses is not a simple exercise in
make-believe. If you aren't careful with your spending, you likely WILL have to explain your purchases.

At Netflix you don't have to complete a purchase
order and wait for approval to buy something. You
just buy it, take a photo of the receipt, and submit it
directly for reimbursement. But that doesn't mean no
one pays attention to what you spend. The finance
team offers two routes for eradicating unwise expen-
diture. Managers can choose which route to take or

can combine the two. The first method leans lightly toward an ethos of Freedom and Responsibility (or F&R, as we say at Netflix). The second choice jumps all in.

If the manager chooses to lean lightly toward F&R, it works like this: At the end of every month the finance team sends a link to each manager listing all receipts per employee for the previous weeks. The manager can click on those expenses and drill down to see what each person spent. Patty McCord, who chose this route while she worked for Netflix, diligently opened the email from finance on the thirtieth of each month and carefully reviewed the expenses of all employees in the HR department. Often, she found people **were** overspending. Patty recounts an incident from 2008 involving Jaime, a recruiter on her HR team:

> Late Friday afternoon I was getting ready to go home when a couple of the product folks came by to pick Jaime up to go to Dio Deka, the fancy Michelin-starred Greek restaurant in Silicon Valley. I said "You are going out for drinks?" But Jaime responded, "No, we're having a dinner meeting."
>
> The next month when I received my team's expenses, I saw a Dio Deka receipt from Jaime for four hundred dollars. That did not feel right. I said, "Hey Jaime, is this the bill from when you went out with the product team a few weeks ago?"

And it was! She explained that John had ordered a nice bottle of wine: "John and Greg like good wine." That just made me go ballistic!

I said: "If those two want to drink hundred-dollar bottles of wine they're welcome to! We pay them enough money to buy it themselves!"

That's when Patty set the context Jaime needed to hear:

"You can spend this kind of money taking a candidate out to dinner. And if the candidate orders a nice bottle of wine, okay, that's fine. That's part of your job. But here we paid for you all to go out drinking and dining on the company. That's crap! If you want to go have fun with your colleagues you pay yourself. If you need a place for a meeting, get a conference room. This was not in Netflix's best interest! Use good judgment."

Usually after just one or two conversations clarifying context your employees will get the hang of how to spend the company's money wisely and that will pretty much take care of it. When employees realize their managers are keeping an eye on expenses, they aren't likely to test the limits much. This is one way to curb spending, but many Netflix managers prefer a more radical version of Freedom and Responsibility.

For those managers who are ready to jump all in with F&R, there is another route, eliminating the administrative hassle of looking over receipts and leaving it to our internal auditing department to find abuse. But if they do find abuse, it's all over for the employee.

Leslie Kilgore explains it like this:

My marketing team was on the road nonstop. They selected their own flights and their own hotels. I went through a number of scenarios with them to help them make spending choices. If you're flying overnight and have to be operational the next morning, flying business makes sense. If you can fly overnight in economy to save money and arrive a day earlier, that's better and Netflix will pay for the extra hotel night. It's almost never in Netflix's best interest to fly business for short flights.

I told them I would never look at their expense reports, but that finance audits ten percent of all expenses annually. I trust them to behave frugally and carefully with the company's money and if finance finds any monkey business, that employee will be immediately fired. It's not one strike and a warning; it's "abuse the freedom and you're out"—plus you'll be used as an example to others for what not to do.

This is the nub of F&R. If your people choose to abuse the freedom you give them, you need to fire them and fire them loudly, so others understand the ramifications. Without this, freedom doesn't work.

SOME PEOPLE WILL CHEAT, BUT THE GAINS OUTWEIGH THE LOSSES

 When you offer freedom, even if you set context and clarify the ramifications of abuse, a small percentage of people will cheat the system. When this happens, don't overreact and create more rules. Just deal with the individual situation and move forward.

Netflix has had its cheaters. The most talked-about case concerned an employee in Taiwan who traveled a lot for business and was slipping in numerous luxurious vacations on the company's dime. His manager didn't check his receipts and finance didn't audit him for three full years. By the time he was caught he had spent over $100,000 on personal travel. Needless to say, he was fired.

In most instances, employees aren't so much defrauding the company as finding what they can get away with. The vice president of corporate operations, Brent Wickens, oversees all the company's office spaces around the world. One spring, a woman on his team, Michelle, made several business trips to Las Vegas. Brent did spot-check his own department's expenses, but it was only a few times a year.

One night I couldn't sleep so I clicked on the link in my email titled "Departmental expenses broken down by employee." I perused through a bunch of people in my group when something unusual popped out. Michelle had a travel expense listed as **Food and Drink** at the Wynn casino in Las Vegas for **twelve hundred dollars**. That was a lot of food and drink for a two-day trip! So, then I got curious and started looking at her expenses from past months. I saw several small items that didn't seem aboveboard. She'd gone to Boston for a Thursday conference and spent the weekend with her family. Friday night there was a restaurant expense for $180. Had she expensed her family's dinner?

I waited until Michelle and I were both in the office to ask her about these charges. But when I did, she froze. She had no explanation. No apology, no excuse, nothing to say. I let her go the next week. When she was packing her boxes, she kept saying that this was all a big mistake. I felt horrible and still don't understand clearly what happened. She's gone on to have a great career somewhere else. The freedom we offer wasn't a good match for her.

At the next Quarterly Business Review (QBR) leadership meeting, Netflix's chief talent officer at the time got up onstage and told Michelle's story to the 350 attendees, detailing the abuse but not identifying her by name or department. She asked participants to share the situation with their teams so everyone understood the gravity of cheating the system. Netflix brings these things out in the open for others to learn from. Brent felt bad for Michelle, but he understood the importance of telling everyone what had happened. Without this degree of transparency, freedom from expense approvals doesn't work.

The biggest expense resulting from the freedom is probably the number of people choosing to fly business class. Netflix has ongoing debates about whether to create a policy restricting business class travel, but senior managers still prefer the current approach. David Wells, while CFO, estimated travel expenses are about 10 percent higher than if Netflix had a formal approval system. But, according to Reed, that 10 percent is a small price to pay for the significant gains that come with it.

GREAT GAINS: FREE, FAST, AND (SURPRISINGLY) FRUGAL

 Remember Grant, the sales director from my days at Pure Software? When he came to complain about his taxi bill, he was angry. He felt like the company had pinned down his wings with all our red tape. He couldn't do what was right without feeling dragged down by a rule or policy.

When he said all that, I realized it was about our entire workforce. I had an image of our hundreds of employees, all as sparrows longing to fly, with big wads of red packaging tape fixing their wings to their desks. I hadn't intended to kill employee creativity and speed with bureaucracy. Spending policies had just seemed like a good way to minimize risk and save money.

But this is the most important message of this chapter: even if your employees spend a little more when you give them freedom, the cost is still less than having a workplace where they can't fly. If you limit their choices by making them check boxes and ask for permission, you won't just frustrate your people, you'll lose out on the speed and flexibility that comes from a low-rule environment. One of my favorite examples is from 2014, when a junior engineer saw a problem that needed to be solved.

Friday morning April 8, Nigel Baptiste, director of partner engagement, arrived at the Netflix Silicon Valley office at 8:15. a.m. It was a warm, sunny day, and Nigel whistled as he grabbed a cup of coffee in the open kitchen on the fourth floor and strolled back to the area where he and his team test Netflix streaming on TVs made by official partners like Samsung and Sony. But when Nigel arrived at his work space, he stopped whistling and froze. What he saw, or, rather, what he didn't see, sent him into a panic. He remembers it like this:

Netflix had invested a big chunk of money so that our customers could watch **House of Cards** on new 4K ultra high definition TVs. The problem was that until this moment basically no TVs supported 4K. We had this fresh super-crisp look, but few could see it. Now, our partner Samsung had come out with the only 4K television so far on the market. These TVs were expensive, and it wasn't clear if customers would buy them. My big goal that year was to work with Samsung to get lots of people watching **House of Cards** in 4K.

We had a minor media coup when journalist Geoffrey Fowler, who reviews high-tech products for the **Washington Post** and has about two million readers, agreed to test **House of Cards** on Samsung's new TV. His review would need to be great for 4K to take off. On Thursday Samsung engineers had come to Netflix with the 4K TV and checked it with my engineers to make sure Mr. Fowler would have a terrific viewing experience. Thursday evening, the TV tested, we all went home.

But Friday morning, when I arrived at the office, the TV was gone. After checking with facilities, I realized it had been disposed of with a bunch of old TVs we'd told them to get rid of.

This was serious. That TV was due in Fowler's living room in two hours. It was too late to call the Samsung people. We'd have to buy another TV before ten a.m. I started calling every electronic store in town. The first three calls resulted in: "I'm sorry sir, we don't have that TV." My heart was pounding in my throat. We were going to miss the deadline.

I was almost in tears when Nick, the most junior engineer on our team, sprinted into the office. "Don't worry, Nigel," Nick said. "I solved that. I came in last night, and I saw the TV had been disposed of. You didn't respond to my calls and texts. So I drove out to the Best Buy in Tracy, bought the same TV, and tested it this morning. It cost twenty-five hundred dollars, but I thought it was the right thing to do."

I was floored. Two and a half thousand dollars! Imagine, a junior engineer feeling so empowered that he spends that much without approval because he thinks it's the right decision. I felt a wave of relief. Due to all the sign-off policies this could never have happened at Microsoft, HP, or any other company I have worked for."

In the end, Fowler loved the high-definition streaming and wrote in his April 16 **Wall Street Journal** article: "Even the unflappable Francis

Underwood perspires in ultra-high definition. I spotted sweat on the upper lip of Kevin Spacey's fictitious vice president while streaming Netflix's 'House of Cards.'"

I don't want rules that prevent employees from making good decisions in a timely way. Fowler's review was worth hundreds of times more to both Netflix and Samsung than that TV. Nick had just five words to guide his actions: "Act in Netflix's best interest." That freedom enabled him to use good judgment to do what was right for the company. But freedom isn't the only benefit of removing your expense policy. The second benefit is that the lack of process speeds everything up.

 As companies grow from fast and flexible start-ups into mature businesses, they often create entire departments to monitor employee spending, which gives management a sense of control, but slows everything way down. Director of product innovation Jennifer Nieva provides an example from her time at Hewlett-Packard:

> I loved working at HP, but that week in 2005 I was so frustrated my ears were practically smoking.
>
> I'd been asked to run a big project, and it was understood from the outset that I would need to find several highly specialized outside consultants

who would work with me for six months. I looked at eight consulting firms and chose one. They quoted me $200k for the six months of work and I was eager to get started. The consultants were available now, but if I waited too long, they'd be reassigned to another client.

I followed the process and entered a request for spending approval into the HP procurement system. Then I looked over everything. There were TWENTY names that needed to sign off before I could get started. My boss, my boss's boss, my boss's boss's boss, but also over a dozen names I'd never heard of, people I soon learned were sitting in our procurement department in Guadalajara, Mexico.

Was I going to lose these consultants I'd taken so long to find? My boss signed, her boss signed, his boss signed. Then I started calling the procurement department, first daily and later hourly. Most of the time no one answered. Finally, I called a woman named Anna who picked up. I used every ounce of charm I could to get her to help me. The approval took six weeks and I called Anna so many times that, when she made the next step in her career, she asked me to write a LinkedIn recommendation for her.

Think of the impact on organizational speed of having hundreds—maybe thousands—of Jennifers dealing with the same barricades on a monthly basis. Processes provide management with a sense of control, but they slow everything way down. Jennifer's story has a second half, which is more satisfying:

> In 2009, I joined Netflix as a marketing manager. After three months I prepared a three-million-piece direct-mail campaign. We were using snail mail to send out brochures with photos of our most popular movies. The project had a sticker price of almost a million dollars. I printed the Statement of Work and found my boss. "Steve, how do I get the approval process started for this million-dollar expense?" I asked, braced for the worst. "You just sign it and fax it back to the vendor," he told me. I kid you not. I nearly hit the floor.

From Nigel's and Jennifer's examples, we see how a simple expense guideline like "act in the company's best interest" gives your employees both freedom of choice and the ability to move fast. But freedom and speed aren't the only benefits. A third, and more surprising benefit, is that some employees actually spend less when the expense policy is lifted. Claudio, a Hollywood-based director in the consumer insight department, supplied an example that illustrates why:

My job requires customer entertaining. At Viacom, my last employer, there was a clear policy explaining what kind of restaurants we could take clients to, who should pay for what, and how much alcohol the company was willing to reimburse. I liked that. It made me feel safe that I was coloring within the lines. The rule was that, while dining with a client, I could pay for the first bottle of wine only. So I would say at the beginning of the meal, "Viacom will pay for dinner and for the first bottle of wine. After that we each pay for our own drinks." Knowing the rule, sometimes we might spend to the limit, by ordering lobster and a particularly expensive bottle of wine. But the rule was clear from the start, so we could work with it.

After a few weeks at Netflix, I was preparing for my first customer dinner. I asked my boss, Tanya, "What's the policy for expensing meals with customers?" Her response was infuriating: "There's no policy. Use your best judgment. Act in Netflix's best interest." I felt she was testing to see if I had good judgment.

At that meal I was determined to show Tanya how frugal I was. I ordered one of the cheaper meals on the menu and decided to have just one beer (less expensive than wine). At the end of the meal, when I saw the clients were getting ready for a round of drinking I made an excuse, paid the bill, and said good night. No way was I going to pay for their party.

Throughout my time at Netflix, I've come to see that Tanya was not trying to test me. She doesn't analyze my dinner receipts at all. Still, without a rule you never know when your judgment will come into question. I feel safest sticking to the same practice of careful ordering I used that first night. No lobster and no expensive wine.

Claudio's story demonstrates the curious impact of rules. When you set them, some people will look eagerly for a way to take advantage of them. If Viacom told employees, "Order one starter, one main course, and one bottle of wine for two people," they might order caviar, lobster, and a bottle of champagne. That's within the rules but very expensive. When you tell people to behave in the company's best interest, they order Caesar salads, chicken breasts, and a couple of beers. The organization with the policy is not necessarily the one saving money.

THE THIRD DOT

 Once you have a workforce made up nearly exclusively of high performers, you can count on people to behave responsibly. Once you have developed a culture of candor, employees will watch out for one another and ensure their teammates' actions are in line with the good of the company. Then you can begin to remove controls and give your staff more freedom. Great places to start are the lifting of your vacation, travel, and expense policies. These elements give people more control over their own lives and convey a loud message that you trust your employees to do what's right. The trust you offer will in turn instill feelings of responsibility in your workforce, leading everyone in the company to have a greater sense of ownership.

▶ TAKEAWAYS FROM CHAPTER 3A (VACATION)

- When removing your vacation policy, explain that there is no need to ask for prior approval and that neither the employees themselves nor their managers are expected to keep track of their days away from the office.

- It is left to the employee alone to decide if and when he or she feels like taking a few hours, a day, a week, or a month off work.

- When you remove the vacation policy, it will leave a hole. What fills the hole is the context the boss provides for the team. Copious discussions must take place, setting the scene for how employees should approach vacation decisions.

- The practices modeled by the boss will be critical to guide employees as to the appropriate behavior. An office with no vacation policy but a boss who never vacations will result in an office that never vacations.

▶ TAKEAWAYS FROM CHAPTER 3B (TRAVEL AND EXPENSE)

- When removing travel and expense policies, encourage managers to set context about how to spend money up front and to check employee receipts at the back end. If people overspend, set more context.

- With no expense controls, you'll need your finance department to audit a portion of receipts annually.

- When you find people abusing the system, fire them and speak about the abuse openly—even when they are star performers in other ways. This is necessary so that others understand the ramifications of behaving irresponsibly.

- Some expenses may increase with freedom. But the costs from overspending are not nearly as high as the gains that freedom provides.

- With expense freedom, employees will be able to make quick decisions to spend money in ways that help the business.

- Without the time and administrative costs associated with purchase orders and procurement processes, you will waste fewer resources.

- Many employees will respond to their new freedom by spending less than they would in a system with rules. When you tell people you trust them, they will show you how trustworthy they are.

Toward a Culture of Freedom and Responsibility

The summer after we successfully lifted the vacation policy, I was preparing to run a race with Patty McCord's eleven-year-old son, Tristan. As we trained by running along the Santa Cruz coast, I found myself reflecting on my experience a decade earlier at Pure Software.

The first couple of years at Pure Software we had been a small group working with no rules or policies. But by 1996 we'd grown, largely through acquisition, to seven hundred employees. As we brought in new people, some of them acted irresponsibly, costing us money. We responded as most companies do: we put policies in place to control people's behavior. Every time we acquired a company, Patty would take our handbook and their handbook and merge the two together.

All these rules meant that going to work was less fun—and our most maverick employees, who were also the most innovative, left the company for more entrepreneurial environments. Those who chose to stay preferred familiarity and consistency. They learned policy adherence as the ultimate value. I realized during those long runs with Tristan that at Pure Software we had, without much thought, dummy-proofed the work environment. The result was that only dummies wanted to work there (well, not really dummies—but you get what I mean).

That summer, I realized that Netflix had reached a point where it was likely to go down the same route as Pure Software if we didn't actively work against it. The company was getting big, and it was increasingly difficult for our leaders to keep track of what everyone was up to. This would normally be the time to introduce more policies and control processes in order to deal with the complexity that comes with growth. But after the success of our vacation and expenses policy experiments, I began to wonder whether we could do the opposite. Were there other rules we could do without? Instead of increasing employee control as we grew, could we increase employee freedom?

We decided that rather than putting more rules and procedures in place, we would continue to do two other things:

1. We would find new ways to increase talent density. In order to attract and retain the best people, we would have to make sure that we offered the most attractive methods of compensation.

2. We would find new ways to increase candor. If we were going to remove controls, we would need to make sure that our employees had all the information they needed to make good decisions without management oversight. This would require increasing organizational transparency and eliminating company secrets. If we wanted employees to make good decisions for themselves, they would have to understand as

much about what was going on in the business as those at the top.

These two points are the topics of the next two chapters.

FYI: Tristan crushed me in the race.

SECTION TWO

NEXT STEPS TO A CULTURE OF FREEDOM AND RESPONSIBILITY

Fortify talent density . . .

4 ▶ Pay Top of Personal Market

Pump up candor . . .

5 ▶ Open the Books

Now remove more controls . . .

6 ▶ No Decision-making Approvals Needed

In the coming section, we'll take the process of implementing a culture of Freedom and Responsibility to a deeper level. In our talent-density chapter, we'll discuss compensation processes for attracting and retaining top performers. In our candor chapter, we'll move from talking about providing honest individual feedback, as explored in chapter 2, to organizational transparency.

FORTIFY TALENT DENSITY . . .

4

PAY TOP OF PERSONAL
MARKET

 One Friday afternoon in 2015, manager of original content Matt Thunell felt his heart pounding as he paged through a brand-new script. Squeezed into a corner table at a noisy Hollywood hot spot, agent Andrew Wang ate his lunch quietly as Matt read. From selecting screenplays to producing pilots, Matt's known as one of the most talented creative executives in the business. One of his skills: fostering bonds with the right agents. Wang hadn't shared the **Stranger Things** draft with anyone yet, but because of their great relationship, he slipped Matt the script right there at the lunch table.

Matt raced back to the office and passed the document to Brian Wright (the ex-Nickelodeon VP we met in chapter 2). Brian is known throughout the TV world for his uncanny ability to sense what audiences will watch. "That script was beautiful," Brian gushes. "Great characters and moving at a breakneck speed." The arguments others would make were obvious: "The **tween** protagonists are too old for kids and too young for adults, so, uninteresting to most viewers," or "It's an eighties period piece that'll only interest a niche audience." Brian saw differently: "Everyone was going to watch this show. **Stranger Things** was going to be big and Netflix was going to make it."

By spring 2015, the script was purchased, and the deadline was looming. But Netflix didn't have a studio yet. Hits like **House of Cards** and **Orange Is the New Black** had been made by other studios and then licensed exclusively to Netflix. Netflix hadn't produced content itself. Now Netflix was entering a new phase. "Ted had made it clear, future original shows we would produce ourselves."

At this stage, Netflix had only a handful of people on the production team, far less than the many dozens of people a studio usually requires. Matt remembers it like this:

> We managed to pull off **Stranger Things** because each member of the team was wildly competent. Rob is a super-brilliant negotiator. So when one of the show's stars didn't want to sign a multi-year contract, he knew exactly what to say. Laurence was the finance guy. He's supposed to be watching

the money. But he did his entire finance job while spending all other waking moments doubling as a production executive—things like renting spaces for the writers to work in. Laurence and Rob did the work of about twenty people.

Stranger Things season 1 took just over a year to finish. It aired on July 15, 2016. A few months later, it was nominated for best drama series at the Golden Globes.

The success of Netflix is founded on these types of unlikely stories: small teams consisting exclusively of significantly above-average performers—what Reed refers to as **dream teams**—working on big hairy problems. Here's Matt again:

At most places, there are some great employees and some just okay ones. The okay ones are managed while the stars are relied upon to give everything they can. At Netflix, it's different. We live in a walled garden of excellence, where everyone is a high performer. You go into these meetings and it's like the talent and brain power in the room could generate the office electricity. People are challenging one another, building up arguments, and each of them is practically smarter than Stephen Hawking. That's why we get so much done at such incredible speed here. It's because of the crazy high talent density.

The high talent density at Netflix is the engine that drives Netflix success. Reed learned this simple but critical strategy after the layoffs in 2001. More complicated was figuring out what steps to take in order to attract and retain that top talent.

OFFER ROCK-STAR PAY

 In the first few years of Netflix, we were growing fast and needed to hire more software engineers. With my new understanding that high talent density would be the engine of our success, we focused on finding the top performers in the market. In Silicon Valley, many of them worked for Google, Apple, and Facebook, and they were being paid a lot. We didn't have the cash to lure them away in any numbers.

But, as an engineer, I was familiar with a concept that has been understood in software since 1968, referred to as the "rock-star principle." The rock-star principle is rooted in a famous study that took place in a basement in Santa Monica. At 6:30 a.m. nine trainee programmers were led into a room with dozens of computers. Each of them was handed a manila envelope explaining a series of coding and debugging tasks they would need to complete to their best ability in the next 120 minutes. Millions of keystrokes have since been devoted to discussing the results on the internet.

The researchers expected to find that the best of the nine programmers would outperform his average counterpart by a factor of two or three. But of the group of nine, all of whom were at least adequate programmers, the best far outperformed the worst. The best guy was twenty times faster at coding, twenty-five times faster at debugging, and ten times faster at program execution than the programmer with the lowest marks.

The fact that one of these programmers would so dramatically outperform another has caused ripples across the software industry ever since, as managers grapple with how some programmers can be worth so much more than their perfectly adequate colleagues. With a fixed amount of money for salaries and a project I needed to complete, I had a choice. I could hire ten to twenty-five average engineers or I could hire one "rock-star" and pay significantly more than what I'd pay the others, if necessary.

Since then I have come to see that the best programmer doesn't add ten times the value. She adds more like a hundred times. Bill Gates, whom I worked with while on the Microsoft board, purportedly went further. He is often quoted as saying:

"A great lathe operator commands several times the wages of an average lathe operator, but a great writer of software code is worth ten thousand times the price of an average software writer." In the software industry, this is a known principle (although still much debated).

I started thinking about where this model applied outside the software industry. The reason the rock-star engineer is so much more valuable than his counterparts isn't unique to programming. The great software engineer is incredibly creative and can see conceptual patterns that others can't. She has an adjustable perspective, so when she gets stuck in a specific way of thinking, she has ways to push, pull, or prod herself to look beyond. These are the same skills needed in any creative job. Patty McCord and I started to look at where exactly the rock-star principle might apply within Netflix. We divided jobs into operational and creative roles.

If you're hiring someone for an operational position, say window washer, ice-cream scooper, or driver, the best employee might deliver double the value of the average. A really good scooper can probably fill two or three times the number of cones an average one could. A really good driver might have half the average number of accidents. But there's a cap on how much value one ice-cream scooper or one driver can deliver. For operational roles, you can pay an average salary and your company will do very well.

At Netflix, we don't have a lot of jobs like that. Most of our posts rely on the employee's ability to innovate and execute creatively. In all creative roles, the best is easily ten times better than average. The best publicity expert can dream up a stunt that attracts millions more customers than the average one. Going back to the **Stranger Things** scenario, Matt Thunell's relationship with Andrew Wang and many similar agents makes him hundreds of times more successful than a creative executive who doesn't have those relationships. Brian Wright's ability to see that **Stranger Things** will be a success, when other studios believe the tween-aged protagonists won't be popular, makes him thousands of times more valuable than a content vice president who doesn't have that script sixth sense. These are all creative jobs and they all follow the rock-star principle.

In 2003 we didn't have much money but we had a lot to accomplish. We had to think carefully about how we'd spend the little we had. We determined that for any type of operational role, where there was a clear cap on how good the work could be, we would pay middle of market rate. But for all creative jobs we would pay one incredible employee at the top of her personal market, instead of using that same money to hire a dozen or more adequate performers. This would result in a lean workforce. We'd be relying on one tremendous person to do the work of many. But we'd pay tremendously.

This is the way we have hired the majority of employees at Netflix ever since. The approach has been remarkably successful. We have exponentially increased our speed of innovation and our output.

I've also found having a lean workforce has side advantages. Managing people well is hard and takes a lot of effort. Managing mediocre-performing employees is harder and more time consuming. By keeping our organization small and our teams lean, each manager has fewer people to manage and can therefore do a better job at it. When those lean teams are exclusively made up of exceptional-performing employees, the managers do better, the employees do better, and the entire team works better—and faster.

IT'S NOT JUST WHAT YOU PAY, IT'S ALSO HOW YOU PAY IT

 Reed's strategy sounds great. But if you run a start-up no one's ever heard of, you may well wonder whether top performers will come work for you, even if you are ready to pay.

The research suggests that they will. A 2018 survey by OfficeTeam asked twenty-eight hundred workers what reasons would motivate them to pack up their desk and quit their jobs. Some 44 percent of respondents, well over any other category, stated they would leave their current job for one that pays more.

The main reason workers would quit their current job:

- For more money — **44%**
- For a company with a higher purpose/stronger mission — **12%**
- Don't feel appreciated — **12%**
- Bored/unchallenged by work — **12%**
- Bad commute/want something closer to home — **7%**
- Corporate culture is not a fit — **7%**
- Unhappy with boss — **6%**

I QUIT

If you work for a small, unknown company, and hope to apply Reed's theory, you'll probably find the person you need.

But it's not just how much you pay people that matters. The form of payment is also important. At the vast majority of companies, highly paid white-collar employees receive a salary plus a bonus, which is paid if they meet a set of predetermined goals. A large part of the top talent's pay is contingent on performance.

This is not as great as it sounds. When Reed and Patty were figuring out how to attract rock-stars to Netflix, they needed to differentiate the company from those they were poaching from. They came up with a plan, which is still in place today.

Let's imagine you've spent all your savings developing an ultramodern scooter that will take people to work by flying above the traffic. You find one crazily talented marketer and want to choose a compensation method that will motivate him to work hard, do his very best, and stay with the company for years to come. You're considering two options:

1. Pay him an annual salary of $250,000.

2. Pay him a $200,000 salary plus a 25 percent bonus based on how much he achieves.

If you're like many managers, you'd choose option 2. Why put all that money into salary when you could use it to give the new recruit an incentive to do his best work?

Pay-per-performance bonuses seem to make a lot of sense. Part of an employee's pay is guaranteed and part of it (usually 2 to 15 percent but up to 60 or even 80 percent for senior executives) is linked to performance. If you bring a lot of value to the company, you get your bonus. If you miss your goals, you don't get paid. What could be more logical? Performance-related bonuses are almost universally deployed in the US, and frequently elsewhere.

But Netflix doesn't use them.

BONUSES ARE BAD FOR FLEXIBILITY

 In 2003, we learned that bonuses are bad for business at about the same time that I came across the rock-star principle. Patty

McCord and I were preparing for a weekly management team meeting. On the agenda was a new bonus structure for the executive team. We were excited to be a grown-up company and we wanted to offer our senior managers at Netflix the kind of packages they'd get elsewhere.

We spent hours coming up with the right performance objectives and trying to link them to pay. Patty suggested we link the bonus of our chief marketing officer, Leslie Kilgore, to the number of new customers we signed on. Before Netflix, Leslie had worked for Booz Allen Hamilton, Amazon, and Procter & Gamble. Her compensation at all these places was metric oriented, with compensation tied to achieving predefined objectives. So she seemed a good person to start with. We wrote down Key Performance Indicators (KPIs) to calculate how much extra Leslie should make if she achieved her goals.

At the meeting I congratulated Leslie on the thousands of new customers we'd recently signed on. I was about to announce how this would bring her a huge bonus if she continued like that, when she interrupted me. "Yes, Reed, it's remarkable. My team has done an incredible job. But the number of customers we sign on is no longer what we should be measuring. In fact, it's irrelevant." She went on to show us numerically that, while new customers had been the most important goal last quarter, it was now the customer retention rate that really mattered. As I listened, I felt a wave of relief. Thankfully, I hadn't already tied Leslie's bonus to the wrong measure of success.

I learned from that exchange with Leslie that the entire bonus system is based on the premise that you can reliably predict the future, and that you can set an objective at any given moment that will continue to be important down the road. But at Netflix, where we have to be able to adapt direction quickly in response to rapid changes, the last thing we want is our employees rewarded in December for attaining some goal fixed the previous January. The risk is that employees will focus on a target instead of spot what's best for the company in the present moment.

Many of our Hollywood-based employees come from studios like WarnerMedia or NBC, where a big part of executive compensation is based on specific financial performance metrics. If this year the target is to increase operating profit by 5 percent, the way to get your bonus—often a quarter of annual pay—is to focus doggedly on increasing operational profit. But what if, in order to be competitive five years down the line, a division needs to change course? Changing course involves investment and risk that may reduce this year's profit margin. The stock price might go down with it. What executive would do that? That's why a company like WarnerMedia or NBC may not be able to change dramatically with the times, the way we've often done at Netflix.

Beyond that, I don't buy the idea that if you dangle cash in front of your high-performing employees, they try harder. High performers naturally want to succeed and will devote all resources toward doing so whether they have a bonus hanging in front of their nose or not. I love this quote from former chief executive of Deutsche Bank John Cryan: "I have no idea why I was offered a contract with a bonus in it because I promise you I will not work any harder or any less hard in any year, in any day because someone is going to pay me more or less." Any executive worth her paycheck would say the same.

 Research confirms Reed's hunch. Contingent pay works for routine tasks but actually decreases performance for creative work. Duke University professor Dan Ariely describes what he found in a fascinating study that he wrote in 2008:

We presented eighty-seven participants with an array of tasks that demanded attention, memory, concentration, and creativity. We asked them, for instance, to fit pieces of metal puzzle into a plastic frame, and to throw tennis balls at a target. We promised them payment if they performed the tasks exceptionally well. About a third of the subjects were told they'd be given a small bonus, another third a medium-level bonus, and the last third could earn a high bonus based on how well they performed.

We did this first study in India, where the cost of living is low, so we could pay people amounts substantial to them but within our budget. The lowest bonus was 50 cents—equivalent to what participants could receive for a day's work. The highest bonus was $50, five months' pay.

The results were unexpected. The people offered medium bonuses performed no better, or worse, than those offered low bonuses. But what was most interesting was that the group offered the biggest bonus did worse than the other two groups across all the tasks.

We replicated these results in a study at the Massachusetts Institute of Technology, where undergraduate students were offered the chance to earn a high bonus ($600) or a lower one ($60) by performing one task that called for some cognitive skill (adding numbers) and another one that required only a mechanical skill (tapping a key as fast as possible). We found that as long as the task involved only mechanical skill, bonuses worked as would be expected: the higher the pay, the better the performance. But when we included a task that required even rudimentary cognitive skill, the outcome was the same as in the India study: the offer of a higher bonus led to poorer performance.

This finding makes perfect sense. Creative work requires that your mind feel a level of freedom. If part of what you focus on is whether or not your performance will get you that big check, you are not in that open cognitive space where the best ideas and most innovative possibilities reside. You do worse.

 I've certainly found this to be true at Netflix. People are most creative when they have a big enough salary to remove some of the stress from home. But people are less creative when they don't know whether or not they'll get paid extra. Big salaries, not merit bonuses, are good for innovation.

The big surprise when we decided not to pay bonuses on top of salary was how much more top talent we were able to attract. Many imagine you lose your competitive edge if you don't offer a bonus. We have found the contrary: we gain a competitive edge in attracting the best because we just put all that money into salary.

Imagine you were looking for work and received two job offers. One place offered you $200,000 plus a 15 percent bonus and another offered you $230,000. Which would you choose? Of course, you'll choose the bird in the hand over the bird in the bush: $230,000. You know your compensation up front—no games.

By avoiding pay-per-performance bonuses you can offer higher base salaries and retain your highly motivated employees. All this increases talent density. But nothing increases talent density more than paying people high salaries and increasing them over time to assure they remain top of market.

PAY HIGHER SALARIES THAN ANYONE ELSE WOULD

Shortly after committing to pay whatever was necessary to hire and retain the best employees, Han, a director of engineering, came to me and said that he'd found an amazing candidate for an open position. This candidate, Devin, had a rare skill set that would be an enormous asset to the team. But the salary he was requesting was nearly double what the other programmers on the team were getting. It was even more than Han was making. "I know he'd be great for Netflix, but is it right to pay that much?" Han wondered.

I asked Han three questions:

1. Were any of the programmers on his current team good enough to take the job at Apple that Devin had just left? No.
2. Would three of Han's current employees collectively be able to make the same contribution that Devin could make? No.
3. If a fairy godmother suggested he could silently and without duress swap a few of his current programmers for Devin, would that be good for the company? Yes.

I suggested that Han could easily afford to hire Devin. We would hire a fewer number of programmers in the future and use that money to pay Devin what he was asking for. Han looked thoughtful. "Devin's skills are in really hot demand right now. If we are going to change our hiring strategy to pay Devin, I want to make sure we pay him enough not just to convince him to take the job, but to assure he isn't soon lured away by another higher-paying competitor."

We decided to scour the market to find out how much our competitors would be willing to pay for Devin's talents. Then we would pay him just over the very top of that range.

Devin's team went on to create many of the foundational features that make up the Netflix platform today. I wanted all of our employees to be as influential as Devin had been, so we decided to apply the same method to determine the salaries of all future new hires.

PAY TOP-OF-PERSONAL-MARKET SALARIES

At most companies, negotiating a salary is like buying a used car. You want the job, but you don't know the maximum the company is willing to compensate, so you try to guess what to ask for and what to accept.

The company uses your ignorance to hire you at the lowest salary possible. This is a great way to get an employee for less than she's worth, only to have her spirited away to another company at a higher price point a few months later.

Following this logic, the book **Negotiating Your Salary: How to Make $1000 a Minute** by Jack Chapman recommends the best way to get a good deal with a new employer:

> **HIRING MANAGER:** We've squeezed our budget and found we can offer you a salary of $95,000 a year! We're excited and hope you are too!

> **YOU:** (Stay silent. Sing a song in your head. Count the spots on the rug. Roll your tongue over your braces.)

> **HIRING MANAGER:** (now nervous) We may be able to go up to $110,000 however. That will be a big stretch but we hope you will accept.

> **YOU:** (continue to sing silently to yourself)

Netflix, on the other hand, **wants** to pay what will attract and keep talent, so their conversation with employees is focused on making it clear that (a) they estimate well what their prospective employee could make at any other company and (b) they'll be paying just above that.

Take the experience of Mike Hastings (no relation to Reed). If you go to the Netflix website, you might wonder why the film **Okja** is recommended for you. It's because every show and movie on Netflix has been tagged into a group of categories. **Okja** is categorized as Fight the System, Cerebral, Visually Striking, and Offbeat. If you watch other Cerebral, Fight the System movies, **Okja** will pop up for you. Mike's one of the people who makes this possible.

Mike was working in Ann Arbor, Michigan, for Allmovie.com when he got an interview to join the Netflix team that does the tagging. He was keen to move to Silicon Valley, "but the cost of living is so high in California, I didn't know how much money to ask for." So he read some books on salary negotiations and talked to a few friends. All of them recommended he keep any precise information close to the chest. "You'll probably undervalue yourself, and Netflix will try to take advantage of that," one friend said. With a regional salary converter, Mike determined that, if he got cornered, he'd ask for double what he was currently making, "which seemed like a lot."

He rehearsed how he would politely dodge all salary questions, "but during the interview I told the recruiter what I was making and what I was hoping to make and then kicked myself all the way back to Michigan for being so stupid." Mike was lying on his bed in Ann Arbor, staring at his favorite Hitchcock poster, when the Netflix recruiter called. "They offered thirty percent more than the hundred percent salary increase I'd asked for! I must have gasped because my boss-to-be clarified, 'That's top of market for your job and skill set here.'"

STAYING ON TOP

At first, a new hire will feel motivated by his top-of-the-range salary. But soon his skills will grow and competitors will start calling to offer higher salaries. If he is worth his salt, his market value is going to rise, and the risk that he'll move will grow. So it's paradoxical that when it comes to adjusting salaries, just about every company on earth follows a system that's likely to decrease talent density by encouraging people to find a job elsewhere. Here's an email from PR Director João describing the problem he had at his previous employer:

> Before Netflix I worked for an American advertising agency in São Paulo and I loved it. This was my first job out of college and I gave every ounce of myself. Sometimes I slept on

the floor of the copy room in the office to not lose work minutes in commute. I was incredibly lucky signing four huge clients and within twelve months I was bringing in more business than those who had been at the company for many years before me. I was so excited to build my career at this company I loved. I knew my senior colleagues had great salaries—double, even triple mine and I trusted at annual salary review time I'd get a big raise bumping me up closer to my contribution level.

End of year, I had my first performance review and received overwhelmingly positive feedback (98/100) and the company was boasting their most profitable year to date. I wasn't expecting my salary would double, but my boss promised he'd take care of me. In the back of my mind I expected a ten percent to fifteen percent raise.

The day of the raise meeting I was so excited I sang with the radio all the way to work. Imagine my disappointment when my boss offered me a five percent raise. To tell the truth I nearly started crying. The worst part was the way my manager conveyed it, with an enthusiastic "congratulations!" and saying this is the best raise he was giving this year. I

> responded shouting inside my head "Do you think I'm stupid?"
>
> After that, my relationship with my boss plummeted. I kept lobbying for a bigger raise. My boss wailed that he didn't want to lose me and raised the five percent increase to seven percent. Beyond that he said my expectations were "unreasonable" and "naive" and that no company gives annual raises bigger than that. That's when I started looking for another job.

João was extremely valuable to his company. His boss hired him at a salary that motivated him. But in just one year João's own growing accomplishments made him infinitely more valuable to his employer and attractive to competitors. Why would his employer offer him a raise that so clearly failed to match his market worth?

The answer to this question is that when it comes to review time, instead of looking at what that employee is worth on the market, most companies use "raise pools" and "salary bands" to determine raises. Imagine that Santa has eight elves each currently paid $50,000, and every year on December 26 he increases their salaries. He and Mrs. Claus put aside a big pot of money for raises, let's say 3 percent of total salary costs (between 2 percent and 5 percent is standard for American companies). Three percent of $400,000 = $12,000.

The Clauses must now decide how to divide it up. Sugarplum Mary is their top performer, so they want to give her a 6 percent raise—leaving $9,000 to distribute among her colleagues. But she insists she'll leave if she doesn't get a 15 percent raise, which reduces the pool to just $4,500 for seven other elves, all with large families of elf mouths to feed. Santa has to punish all his other little helpers to pay Sugarplum her market worth. This is likely what happened to João. Assuming his boss had a 3 percent raise pool, that 5 percent he offered was already extremely generous. Going up to 7 percent meant the rest of the team really had to suffer. Paying João the 15 percent higher salary he could get on the open market? Impossible!

Salary bands create a similar problem. Let's say at Santa's workshop the salary band for an elf is $50,000 to $60,000. Sugarplum is hired at $50,000, and the first three years Santa raises her salary 5 to 6 percent, to $53,000, then $56,000, then $58,800. But by year four, although Sugarplum is now more experienced and high performing than ever, she can only get a 2 percent raise. She's at the top of her band! Time to look for a new workshop, Sugarplum.

Research confirms what João and Sugarplum already suspected. You'll get more money if you change companies than if you stay put. In 2018, the average annual pay raise per employee in the US was about 3 percent (5 percent for top performers). For an employee quitting her job and joining a new company, the average raise was between 10 percent and 20 percent. Staying in the same job is bad for your pocketbook.

Here's what happened to João:

Netflix hired me at nearly triple my salary and I moved to Hollywood. Nine months later salary adjustments were the last thing on my mind. I went for my weekly walking meeting with my boss Matias around the big block of the Netflix Hollywood building. Partway around the block there is a big dim sum dumpling with blue eyes and a red tongue painted on the wall of a restaurant. At that spot, Matias mentioned that he was going to give me a twenty-three percent raise in order to keep my salary at top-of-market rate. I was so shocked I had to sit down next to the dim sum.

I continued to have lots of success and felt I was very well paid. A year later, at annual salary review time, I wondered if I'd get another enormous raise. Matias surprised me again. This time he said, "Your performance has been excellent, and I'm delighted to have you on this team. The market for your position hasn't changed much, so I'm not planning on giving you a raise this year." That seemed fair to me. Matias said if I didn't think so, I should come to him with some data showing the current market for my position.

I still like to think about what my first boss told me—that I was naive. Knowing how the corporate world works I see he was right. I was naive in understanding the processes of business. But on the other hand, isn't it naive for so many corporations to use a raise process that pushes all your best talent out the door?

João makes a strong case. So why do companies still follow the normal raise methods? Reed's theory is that the raise pools and salary bands used at most companies worked well when employment was often for life and an individual's market value wasn't likely to skyrocket in a matter of months. But clearly those conditions don't apply anymore, given how fast people switch jobs today and the changing nature of our modern economy.

But the pay-top-of-market model at Netflix is so unusual that it is hard to understand.

How is any manager supposed to know, on an ongoing basis, what top of market IS for each of her employees? You'd have to invest dozens of hours throughout the year making uncomfortable phone calls to people you barely know to find out how much money they and their staff are making. Netflix legal director Russell found this to be just as frustrating as you might imagine:

The most valuable player on my team in 2017 was a lawyer named Rani. Rani moved from India to

California when she was a teenager. Her mother was a mathematics professor at Stanford and her father a well-known chef of innovative Indian cuisine. Rani, as a lawyer, was somehow the intersection of a brilliant mathematician and a brilliant cook. She was able to manipulate precise and intricate ideas in a way I'd never seen before. She possessed this third sense that I can best refer to as "finesse," which made her a superior lawyer.

I hired Rani at a high salary—which I felt was a generous top-of-market offer—and she had a great first year on the job. When it got to be raise time I had a problem. Unlike the other lawyers on my team Rani has a unique job, so it was difficult to find any market data for the role. Some of the others were getting big raises that year—up to twenty-five percent—due to clear market changes.

I spent dozens of hours trying to find data for Rani. After a lot of research, I called fourteen contacts at different companies, but none of them would share salary figures with me. So, I started calling headhunters. Finally, I received three figures from recruiters. They were all over the place, but the top one was only five percent over what Rani was already making. From that data, a five percent raise put Rani at top of market. So that's what I raised her.

Oh boy, was that a bad day! When I told Rani her raise she started grinding her teeth and she wouldn't meet my eyes. As I explained how I'd come up with the figure her eyes shifted to the window. It was like she was already calculating which company to move to next. When I stopped speaking, she sat silently for a very long time and then said, with a slight quiver in her throat: "I'm disappointed." I suggested if she felt the raise didn't reflect her market worth, she should bring me data. She did not.

For the next comp review cycle, I implored Human Resources to help. The numbers HR dug up were nearly thirty percent higher than the figures I had found in my own search the previous year. This time Rani also stepped up and called her own contacts. She gave me the names of four people at other companies doing similar jobs with salary figures comparable to what HR had shown me. I had underpaid her the year before because the data I had was not a good reflection of the actual range.

Getting salary comparisons for yourself or for your staff isn't just time-consuming and cumbersome. It often requires calling people in your network and asking the embarrassing question, "How much money do you make?"

But this isn't the only concern. What about how incredibly expensive this all must be? Mathias gave

João a 23 percent raise that he didn't ask for and wasn't even thinking about. Russell gave Rani a 30 percent raise in year two. How many companies can afford to give their employees these types of pay increases? Wouldn't your profit margin have to be sky-high? Otherwise annual raises would put you out of business.

The answer to both of these questions is yes. Yet overall the investment pays off.

In a high-performance environment, paying top of market is most cost-effective in the long run. It is best to have salaries a little higher than necessary, to give a raise before an employee asks for it, to bump up a salary before that employee starts looking for another job, in order to attract and retain the best talent on the market year after year. It costs a lot more to lose people and to recruit replacements than to overpay a little in the first place.

Some employees will see their salaries grow dramatically in a short time. If the market value for an employee shifts up because her skill set increases or there's a shortage of talent in her field, we shift her salary up with it. The salaries of other employees may be flat year to year, despite their doing great work.

The one thing we try to avoid doing when possible is adjusting salaries down if the market rate falls (although we might do this if someone moves from one location to another). That would be a sure way to reduce talent density. If we couldn't afford our payroll expenses for some reason, we would need to increase talent density by letting go of some employees, thereby lowering our costs without lowering any individual salaries.

Figuring out top of market can take a lot of time, but not as much time as finding and training a replacement when your best people leave for more money at another company. Even though it can be tough, it is Russell's job (with help from HR) to understand what other organizations would pay Rani. It's a responsibility that Rani should share. No one should know your market range better than (first) you and (second) your boss.

But there is one person at every moment who likely **does** know your market worth better than either you or your boss does. And that is someone worth talking to.

WHEN RECRUITERS CALL, ASK "HOW MUCH?"

 Let's return for a moment to Sugarplum Mary. Who is the one person in the world who knows Sugarplum's value better than she, Mrs. Claus, and even Santa himself? It's the recruiter at the elf workshop down the way. By definition, what she is offering is exactly market value at that moment. If you really want to know what you're worth, talk to recruiters.

Recruiters call Netflix employees (and probably your talented employees) frequently, trying to get them to interview for other jobs. You can bet the hiring company's got money and they're willing to pay. What would you like your employees to do when they get these calls? Take the phone into the bathroom and turn on the faucet while they whisper into the phone? If you haven't given them clear instructions, that's probably exactly what they do—and they did the same thing at Netflix, until 2003 when the company started having pay-top-of-personal-market discussions.

 Not long after that, Chief Product Officer Neil Hunt came to Patty and me to report that one of his most valuable engineers, George, had received an offer for a higher-paying job at Google. We were both against offering George more money to stay and we felt he'd been disloyal interviewing for another job behind our back. On the drive back to Santa Cruz that afternoon Patty huffed, "No one employee should be irreplaceable!" But overnight both Patty and I started thinking about how much value the company would lose if George left.

When Patty jumped into my car the next morning, she said, "Reed, my head cracked in the night. We're

being stupid! George is not replaceable. Not really."
She was right. There were only four people in the
world who had the same algorithm programming
knowledge, and three of them worked at Netflix.
If we let George go, other companies might try to
target the remaining two.

We brought together the top executive team—
including Neil, Ted Sarandos, and Leslie Kilgore—
to discuss what to do about George in particular
and all the recruiters coming after our talent in
general.

Ted had a strong opinion, based on his own experience at a previous employer. This was his story:

> When I lived in Phoenix I worked for a Houston-
> based home video distributor. My company
> offered me a job as branch manager of the Denver
> distribution center. It was a big promotion for me
> then—and I took it. They gave me a nice raise
> and agreed to pay for my Denver housing for six
> months while I sold my Phoenix house.
>
> But after six months in Denver, I couldn't sell
> my house. I was financially under water. I started
> renting a lousy apartment in Denver with my wife,
> while still paying for this great house in Phoenix
> that I couldn't live in. Then a recruiter called from
> Paramount. I took the call because I was so miser-
> able with my housing. They offered me a position
> with a lot more money that allowed me to move

back to Phoenix. I was happy in my job, but this offer solved all my problems.

I went to my boss and told him I was leaving. He said, "Why didn't you tell us that you couldn't sell your house? We value you. We can change your deal in order to keep you!" They gave me more money to match the Paramount deal and bought my Phoenix house. I thought, "For the last six years I never took a recruiter's call and now I see my market value was climbing all the while. I've been underpaid for years because I viewed it as an act of disloyalty to have the conversation about making sure I was paid what I was worth."

I was really upset with my boss. I felt like asking, "If you knew what I was worth, why didn't you offer it to me?" Then as I grew up, I realized: Why would he? It's my own responsibility to know what I'm worth and ask for it!

After Ted told this story he said: "George was right to go interview at a competitor to find out what his worth is—and we would be stupid not to pay him his top-of-market value, now that we know also. In addition, if there are other people on Neil's team who Google would offer that same job to, we should up their salaries to the same level. That's their current market value."

Leslie came forward and told us she was already doing as Ted was suggesting:

Whenever I hire a new employee, I tell them to read **Rites of Passage at $100,000 to $1 Million+**, which back in the eighties and nineties was **the** handbook for executive recruiters. It tells you how to know your market value and how to talk to recruiters to get that data.

I say to all my people, "Understand your market, understand the book, go and meet these recruiters—and I give them a list of names of the recruiters specializing in their jobs. I want all my employees to make an active choice to stay. I don't want them to stay because they lack options. If you're good enough to work at Netflix, you're good enough that other options will be out there. If you feel like you have a choice, you can make a good decision. Working at Netflix should be a choice, not a trap.

After listening to Ted and Leslie, I was persuaded. Their comments were completely in line with everything else we were implementing around pay-top-of-personal-market salaries. We decided not only to give George a raise but also that Neil should also determine who else on his team Google would offer that job to—then bump up their salaries. That's what pay-top-of-personal market is all about. Then we told **all** our employees they should start taking those calls from recruiters and tell us what they learned. Patty developed a database where everyone could input the salary data points they received from calls and interviews.

After that, we told all managers that they shouldn't wait for their people to come to them with a competitor's offer before raising salaries. If we didn't want to lose an employee and we saw her market value rising, we should increase her pay accordingly.

At just about every company on earth, interviewing for another job would anger, disappoint, or alienate your current boss. The more valuable you are to your manager, the more annoyed he will be, and it's not difficult to see why. When an excellent new employee decides to go and just check out a job at the company down the road, you risk losing your entire investment. If during the interview, she finds the new position is so much more exciting than what she's doing now, you'll lose her—or at the very least her enthusiasm. That's why managers at most companies make their employees feel like traitors for speaking to recruiters at other companies.

Netflix doesn't see it this way. VP of content Larry Tanz remembers how he learned this lesson. It was 2017 and Netflix had just reached the hundred-million-member mark. Larry was getting ready for a bash at the Hollywood Shrine Auditorium, where Adam Sandler would perform. He was grabbing his coat to head for the door when the phone rang: "It was a Facebook recruiter asking me to come in for an interview. I felt it was wrong to be even speaking to her, so I murmured that I wasn't interested."

Four weeks later, Ted Sarandos, Larry's boss, was giving a monthly update to his staff: "The market's heating up and you are going to be getting calls from recruiters. You'll likely get calls from Amazon, Apple, and Facebook. And if you're not sure that you're being paid top of market, you should take those calls and find out what those jobs are paying. If you find out they are paying more than we pay you, you need to let us know." Larry was surprised: "Netflix is probably the only company where they encourage you to speak to and even interview with the competition."

On a trip to Rio a few weeks after that, Larry received a second call from Facebook: "We were meeting with the famous Brazilian singer Anitta in her living room to discuss her upcoming Netflix documentary **Vai Anitta**. For the two hundred million people in Brazil, Anitta is like Madonna and Beyoncé combined, so when my cell buzzed, I didn't answer it." But when Larry heard Facebook's message, he called back. "They asked me to come in but wouldn't tell me what the job paid. I said I wasn't looking for a job, but I'd come and talk with them."

Larry told his boss he was going to the interview. "That already felt odd. At most companies, going to interview with a competitor is considered a lack of loyalty." Larry did get a job offer from Facebook and it paid more than he was making. Ted, as promised, raised his salary to the current market rate.

Now Larry encourages his own staff to take those calls from the recruiters: "But I also don't wait for them to come to me. If I see someone could make more money somewhere else, I give them the raise right away." To retain your top employees, it's always better to give them the raise **before** they get the offers.

Of course, this worked out for Larry, who got a higher salary, and for Ted, who kept the talented Larry. But Ted's instructions sound extremely risky. How many others have taken those calls, fallen in love with the job they interviewed for, and left his team? Ted explains his reasoning like this:

> When the market heats up and recruiters are calling, employees get curious. No matter what I say, some of them are going to have those talks and go to those interviews. If I don't give them permission, they'll sneak around and then leave without giving me a chance to retain them. A month before I made that statement, we lost an amazing executive whose talents we will not be able to replace. When she came to me, she'd already accepted the other job. There was nothing I could do. When she told me that she'd loved working at Netflix but she'd received a forty percent pay raise, my heart sank. I could have matched that if I'd known her market

value had changed! That's why I want my employees to know they can talk to other companies as much as they want, as long as they do it openly, and tell us what they learn.

The question Ted receives from new employees today is, "Are you sure you want me to take that call, Ted? Isn't that disloyal?" His response is the same it's been since George came to Neil with that Google offer: "It's disloyal to sneak around and hide who you are speaking to, but openly interviewing and giving Netflix the salary data benefits all of us."

The rule at Netflix when recruiters call is: "Before you say, 'No thanks!' ask, 'How much?'"

THE FOURTH DOT

In order to fortify the talent density in your workforce, for all creative roles hire one exceptional employee instead of ten or more average ones. Hire this amazing person at the top of whatever range they are worth on the market. Adjust their salary at least annually in order to continue to offer them more than competitors would. If you can't afford to pay your best employees top of market, then let go of some of the less fabulous people in order to do so. That way, the talent will become even denser.

▶ **TAKEAWAYS FROM CHAPTER 4**

- The methods used by most companies to compensate employees are not ideal for a creative, high-talent-density workforce.

- Divide your workforce into creative and operational employees. Pay the creative workers top of market. This may mean hiring one exceptional individual instead of ten or more adequate people.

- Don't pay performance-based bonuses. Put these resources into salary instead.

- Teach employees to develop their networks and to invest time in getting to know their own—and their teams'—market value on an ongoing basis. This might mean taking calls from recruiters or even going to interviews at other companies. Adjust salaries accordingly.

Toward a Culture of Freedom and Responsibility

Now that your talent density is increasing you are almost ready to take dramatic measures to increase employee freedom. But first you'll need to take candor up a notch.

At most companies, the majority of employees—even if they are highly talented—can't be given significant levels of decision-making freedom, because they don't know all the company secrets that allow top management to make informed decisions.

Once you have a company full of those rare responsible people who are self-motivated, self-aware, and self-disciplined, you can begin to share with them unprecedented amounts of company information—the type of knowledge most companies keep under lock and key.

This is the subject of chapter 5.

PUMP UP CANDOR . . .

5

OPEN THE BOOKS

In 1989, after the Peace Corps but before Pure Software, I was a twenty-nine-year-old software engineer at a struggling start-up called Coherent Thought. One Friday morning, I arrived at my cubicle and, through the glass wall of the conference room in front of my desk, I saw the senior management standing huddled next to the window with the door closed. What startled me was how still they were. On a recent trip, I had watched a gecko that was about to be devoured by a large white egret. He froze in terror with one leg midair. That was how these managers looked. Their lips were moving frantically but their bodies were completely still. Why didn't they sit down? That image made me uncomfortable and I started to worry.

The next morning, I arrived at work early and the managers were already back in the conference room.

That day they sat in chairs but every time someone opened the door to get coffee, I could hear the fear escaping from the room. Was the company in trouble? What were they talking about?

To this day, I still don't know. Maybe I would have freaked out if I had been told. But back then, I resented bitterly that they didn't trust me enough to tell me what was going on, despite the fact that I was working hard and committed to the company's success. They had some big secret that they were keeping from the entire workforce.

Of course, we all have secrets. Most of us believe inherently that secrets keep us safe. As a young man, my instinct was to keep secret any risky or uncomfortable information. In 1979, at nineteen, I went to Bowdoin College in Maine, a small, comfortable undergraduate school. By pure luck, my freshman roommate was a Californian named Peter. Early in the year, we were in our dorm room folding our laundry and he mentioned casually that he was a virgin. He said it like it was the most normal thing to share, as simple as getting a cup of coffee. And here I was, a virgin too, and totally mortified that someone would learn my truth.

When he told me, I couldn't tell him my secret back. I was too embarrassed, even in the face of his honesty. My silence, I learned later, made it difficult for Peter to trust me in those early days. How can you trust someone when you feel they are hiding things from you? Peter, on the other hand, would talk frankly about his emotions, fears, and mistakes, and I was blown away by his comfort with bringing everything out in the open. I felt trust for him in a way I had never so quickly experienced. That friendship was transformative for me, because I saw that letting go of secrets and speaking transparently brought incredible advantages.

I'm not suggesting that it's advisable or even appropriate to talk about your sex life with your colleagues. Peter, of course, was not a work friend. But secret-keeping at work is even more prevalent and more harmful than in a student dormitory.

 According to a study by Michael Slepian, a professor of management at Columbia Business School, the average person keeps thirteen secrets, five of which he or she has never shared with anyone else. A typical manager, I would suggest, has even more.

According to Slepian, if you are anything like an average person, there's a 47 percent chance that one of your secrets involves a violation of trust, a 60-plus percent chance that it involves a lie or a financial impropriety, and a roughly 33 percent chance that it involves a theft, some sort of hidden relationship, or unhappiness at work. That's a lot of confidential content to be keeping in your closet, and it takes a psychological toll: stress, anxiety, depression, lone-liness, low self-esteem. Secrets also take up a lot of space in our brains. One study showed people spend twice as much time thinking about their secrets as they do actively concealing them.

On the other hand, when you share a secret, it floods the receiver with feelings of confidence and loyalty. If I tell you some huge mistake I made or share information that could sabotage my success, you think, **Well, if she'd tell me that, she'd tell me anything**. Your trust in me skyrockets. There is no better way to build trust quickly than to shine a light directly on a would-be secret.

Before continuing this discussion, we need a bet-ter term than would-be secret. The problem with the word **secret** is that once you tell someone, it's not a secret anymore.

STUFF OF SECRETS = SOS

SOS will be our term (not a Netflix term) for infor-mation you might commonly choose to keep quiet because it would be dangerous to divulge. Sharing the information might lead to a negative judgment, risk upsetting people, cause mayhem, or break up a relationship. Otherwise we wouldn't feel an urge to keep it to ourselves.

SOS information at work might be things like the following:

- You are considering a reorganization and people might lose their jobs.
- You've fired an employee but explaining why would hurt his reputation.
- You have "secret sauce": information you don't want to leak out to your competitors.
- You made a mistake that could hurt your reputation, maybe ruin your career.
- Two leaders are in conflict, and if their teams knew, it would lead to unrest.
- Employees could go to jail if they share certain financial data with a friend.

Organizations are full of SOS. Every day, managers grapple with the questions: "Should I tell my people? And if so, at what risk?" But keeping quiet brings risks too, as Reed's fear and falling productivity at Coherent Software demonstrated all those years ago.

 Just about all managers like the **idea** of transparency. But if you're serious about creating a high sharing environment, the first thing to do is to look at the symbols around your office that may accidentally be suggesting to everyone that secrets are being kept. I once went to visit a fellow CEO at another Silicon Valley company. This guy talks a lot about the importance of organizational transparency, and there have been articles in the news about the bold steps he's taking to increase openness in the workplace.

When I arrived, I took the elevator to the top floor of the corporate headquarters. The receptionist led me down a long quiet corridor. The CEO's office was in the corner. His door was open (as he talks about having an "open door policy"), but sitting outside was a secretary, who looked like she was guarding him. I'm sure this guy had a good reason for having a quiet corner office with a door that he locks at night and a guard who makes sure no one slips in unnoticed. But that office screams: "We are keeping secrets in here!"

That's why I don't have my own office or even a cubicle with drawers that close. During the day, I might grab a conference room for some discussions, but my assistant knows to book most of my meetings in other people's work spaces. I always try to go to the work spot of the person I'm seeing, instead of making them come to me. One of my preferences is to hold walking meetings, where I often come across other employees meeting out in the open.

It's not just about offices. Any locked area is symbolic of hidden things, and signifies we don't trust one another. On an early trip to our Singapore offices, I saw that our employees had been given lockers in which they could lock their things when they left every evening. I insisted we get rid of the locks.

But these kinds of signals are not enough on their own. It's up to the leader to live the message of transparency by sharing as much as possible with everybody. Big things, small things, whether good or bad—if your first instinct is to put most information out there, others will do the same. At Netflix, we call this "sunshining," and we make an effort to do a lot of it.

 The first time I met with Reed to begin interviews for this book, I assumed we'd be in a conference room with a door or in a quiet corner where he'd be able to answer sensitive questions. Instead he led me to an open balcony area where we sat at a table within earshot of everyone. Reed told animated stories about one of his first jobs selling vacuum cleaners door-to-door, getting into fistfights in junior high, a serious car accident when he and an old girlfriend were hitchhiking across Africa, and early challenges in his marriage. Others walked past the table frequently. His voice never dropped a decibel.

A few months later, I sent the first draft of the first chapter of this book to Reed for his feedback. The next week, I was interviewing a manager in the Netflix Amsterdam office when the interviewee referenced a specific passage from the draft I'd sent Reed. My face must have revealed my confusion because he explained, "Reed sent that chapter out to everyone."

"**All** Netflix employees?" I asked.

"Well not **everyone**, just the top seven hundred managers. He was showing us what the two of you are up to."

As soon as the interview was over, I reached for the phone. The conversation I would have with Reed played in my head: "What are you thinking? You can't send out unfinished chapters to hundreds of people! I haven't fact-checked it." But as I dialed his number, I imagined Reed's response. "You don't want me to send out unfinished chapters? Why not?" To which, I realized, I had no convincing response.

KNOWING WHEN TO SHARE

Transparency sounds great. You never hear leaders saying they promote organizational secrecy. But transparency isn't without its risks. With his instinct to share, Reed sent an unfinished chapter out to seven hundred people. Dozens of those seven hundred managers could have come complaining to me about the inaccuracy of what I'd written. That didn't happen, but it might have.

There are reasons for keeping secrets, and often it is not at all obvious when to be transparent and when to keep quiet. To try and figure out how Reed made his judgment calls, I gave him a test, which I'll now share with you.

I described four scenarios that might call for keeping a secret and asked Reed to choose between alternative responses, give his reasoning, and present similar real-life dilemmas from Netflix.

You can take the quiz too. Before you read Reed's response, ask yourself what you would do and why. Then see if you agree with him.

A QUIZ FOR REED (AND YOU)

QUIZ SCENARIO 1:
INFORMATION THAT WOULD BE
ILLEGAL TO LEAK

You are the founder of a start-up with one hundred employees. You've always believed in organizational transparency, teaching your staff to understand the P&L statements and making all financial and strategic information available to them. But next week your company is going public and things will change. After that, if you share the quarterly numbers with your workforce before you announce them to Wall Street and one employee tells a friend, the company stock could crash, and the leaker could go to prison for insider trading. What will you do?

a. Continue to share all the numbers quarterly, but only AFTER you've shared them with Wall Street.

b. Continue to keep giving the staff all numbers before anyone else knows but stress that, if they leak this information, they could be sent to jail.

Answer from Reed: remove the umbrella

 My response to Quiz Scenario 1 is (b): continue sharing quarterly financial data with employees before announcing it publicly—while also warning them about the dire potential consequences of leaks.

I first learned about open-book management in 1998. Netflix was one year old, and I attended a leadership development course at Aspen Institute. There were executives from many companies and we discussed several provocative readings. One of them was a case study about a manager called Jack Stack.

Jack, a manager in Springfield, Missouri, successfully revives a remanufacturing plant once owned by International Harvester. The plant is about to be closed but he raises money and stages a leveraged buyout. Then, in an effort to motivate his workforce, he sets himself two goals:

1. Create a work culture of financial transparency, making every aspect of the business visible to every employee.
2. Invest a substantial amount of time and effort training every staff member how to read and understand, in detail, the weekly operating and financial reports.

Jack teaches his workforce, from the top engineer to the lowest worker on the shop floor, to read the company's financial reports. He instructs these people without a high school education on the ins and outs of reading a profit and loss statement—something a lot of highly educated vice presidents can't do well at many companies. Then he provides weekly operating and financial data to every worker in the company, so they can see how the organization is progressing and how their work contributes to the success. This ignites feelings of passion, responsibility, and ownership in the workforce beyond what he could have hoped for. That company has done incredibly well over the past forty years.

When we discussed that case at Aspen, one of the other leaders didn't agree with Jack's approach: "I see my job as holding an umbrella over my workers to protect them from getting distracted by stuff that doesn't have anything to do with their work. I hire them each to do something they excel at and love doing. I don't want them to have to waste hours hearing about business details that they don't care about, and that isn't their strength."

I disagreed: "This guy Jack managed to instigate feelings of ownership by guiding people to understand the reasons behind the work they are doing. I don't want my employees to feel like they're **working for** Netflix; I want them to feel like they are **part of** Netflix." That's when I decided, if you're going to work at Netflix, no one is going to hold an umbrella over your head. You're going to get wet.

Back at work we started holding "all-hands" meetings every Friday. Patty McCord would stand on a chair like a town crier to get everyone's attention and we would head out into the parking lot, which was the only place we had enough space for everyone in the company. I would pass out copies of the P&L and we would go through the weekly metrics. How many shipments had we done? What was the average revenue? How well were we able to fill client requests for their first and second choice of movies? We also created a strategy document that was filled with information we wouldn't want our competitors to know, and posted it on the bulletin board next to the coffee machine.

We opened this information up to build feelings of trust and ownership in our employees, in the hope of getting the same reaction from the workforce as Jack Stack did. And it worked. I closed that umbrella, and no one complained. Since then all financial results, as well as just about any information that Netflix competitors would love to get their hands on, has been available to all of our employees. Most notable is the four-page "Strategy Bets" document on the home page of the company's intranet.

My goal was to make employees feel like owners and, in turn, to increase the amount of responsibility they took for the company's success. However, opening company secrets to employees had another outcome: it made our workforce smarter. When you give low-level employees access to information that is generally reserved for high-level executives, they get more done on their own. They work faster without stopping to ask for information and approval. They make better decisions without needing input from the top.

In most businesses, without even realizing it, senior managers stunt the abilities and intelligence of their own workforce by keeping financial and strategic information hidden. Although just about all companies talk about empowering staff, in the vast majority of organizations, real empowerment is a pipe dream because employees aren't given enough information to take ownership of anything. Jack Stack explained this well:

The most crippling problem in business is sheer ignorance about how business works. What we see is a whole mess of people going to a baseball game and nobody telling them what the rules are. That game is business. People try to steal from first base to second base, but they don't even know how that fits into the big picture.

If a manager doesn't know how many customers the company has signed on in the past weeks and months, and what strategy discussions are in the works, how does he know how many people he can afford to hire? He has to ask his boss. If his boss doesn't know the details of the company's growth, she can't make a good decision either, so she has to go to her own boss. The more employees at all levels understand the strategy, financial situation, and the day-to-day context of what's going on, the better they become at making educated decisions without involving those above them in the hierarchy.

Jack Stack, of course, is not the only leader of a private company who shares all financial data with the workforce. It's when a company goes public that top managers start to say, "Now we have to grow up and be more careful with information. Now we have to avoid risk and ensure no secrets get into the wrong hands."

This brings us back to Quiz Scenario 1, where my advice is don't open the umbrella just because you go public. After the Netflix IPO in 2002, I faced the same dilemma as the fictional manager in Erin's quiz. One Friday, I picked Patty up for our drive to work and she wailed, "At EVERY other public company only a few top-level insiders see the quarterly financials until it's released to Wall Street. If that information leaks, the employee goes to JAIL! What are we going to do?"

But I was committed. "If we suddenly begin keeping financial data from employees, what would it symbolize? That our employees were outsiders in their own company!" I responded. "We will not become more secretive as we get bigger. You know what, we're going to do the opposite. Every year we are going to work to be bolder, and share even more information than before."

We are perhaps the only public company that shares financial results internally in the weeks before the quarter is closed. We announce these numbers at a quarterly business review meeting with our top seven hundred or so managers. The financial world sees this as reckless. But the information has never been leaked. When it does one day leak (I imagine it will), we won't overreact. We'll just deal with that one case and continue with transparency.

For our employees, transparency has become the biggest symbol of how much we trust them to act responsibly. The trust we demonstrate in them in turn generates feelings of ownership, commitment, and responsibility.

Almost daily a new employee expresses to me how astounded he is by the transparency at Netflix. This gives me great joy. For example, vice president of investor relations and corporate development Spencer Wang, who previously worked as an analyst on Wall Street, shared this story about his first week on the job:

> Netflix is, of course, a subscription-based business, so in order to derive our revenue, you multiply the average price of a subscription (which everyone knows) by our number of subscribers. This number is top secret until we report it publicly once a quarter. Any investor who gets it early can illegally use it to trade Netflix stock and make a lot of money. If someone from Netflix leaks it, he or she could go to jail.
>
> It was 8:00 a.m. on a Monday morning in March. I was brand new and feeling a little skittish, getting a feel for the place. I grabbed a coffee, settled down at my desk, and opened my computer. There, in my mail, was a message titled Daily Membership Update March 19, 2015. It detailed with graphs and data how many new subscribers we'd signed on yesterday by country.
>
> My heart jumped. Should data this sensitive be going through regular email? I hugged the computer close to my chest and moved against the wall, so no one would sneak a peek over my shoulder.

> Later our CFO—my boss—stopped by my desk. I showed him the email. "This is super useful but dangerous too if it leaks out. How many people receive it?" I asked. I thought he'd say: Reed, me, you. Full stop. But his response was crazy. "Any employee can sign up for it. It's open to everyone in the company who's interested."

Of course, transparency, like all of our cultural principles at Netflix, does sometimes go wrong. In March 2014, a director of content acquisitions downloaded reams of confidential data and took it with him when he left to work for a competitor. This led to headaches and lawsuits and took a lot of our time. But when one employee abuses your trust, deal with the individual case and double your commitment to continue transparency with the others. Do not punish the majority for the poor behavior of a few.

QUIZ SCENARIO 2:
POSSIBLE ORGANIZATIONAL RESTRUCTURING

 You have been in discussions with your boss at headquarters about a possible organizational restructuring that would lead to several project managers on your team losing their jobs. You are only in

discussions at this point and there is a 50 percent chance it won't happen. Will you tell your project managers now or wait until you are certain?

a. Let time take its course. No need to cause stress now. Plus, if you tell your project managers today, they'll likely start looking for new jobs and you risk losing excellent employees.

b. Compromise. You're worried your employees might be blindsided if you let them go without any warning. Yet you don't want to freak them out unnecessarily either. You hint that changes are in the air without spelling out what's actually happening. When you hear about another company hiring project managers you discreetly leave the job announcement on their desks so that they can start considering other options.

c. Tell them the truth. You sit them down and explain there is a 50 percent chance that some of their jobs will be eliminated in six months. You stress that you appreciate them a lot and hope they will stay—but you wanted to be transparent, so they had all the information they needed to consider their futures.

Answer from Reed: upset the apple cart

My response to Quiz Scenario 2 is (c): tell them the truth.

No one wants to hear there's a possibility they'll lose their job. The idea of change is always unsettling and often distressing, even on a small scale, like being moved to another department or being asked to work out of another office. If you tell people before you're certain, you'll incite anxiety, leading to distraction and inefficiency, and maybe stir up employees to look for work elsewhere. Why upset the applecart before you're sure?

But if you want to build a culture of transparency and you don't tell your people about the potential change until it's finalized, you'll show your staff you're a hypocrite who can't be trusted. You preach transparency and then whisper about their jobs behind their backs. My advice is to lean hard into transparency. Go ahead and shake that applecart. Some apples might get bruised and others might fall off the cart but that's okay. Once things have settled down, your workforce will trust you all the more.

Of course, every case is a little different, and at Netflix each employee has a different opinion about such emotionally sensitive situations. Sometimes we share information and employees love it; sometimes they wish we'd kept that information to ourselves. We asked Netflix employees to volunteer their answers to Quiz Scenario 2, and here are two responses.

The first, from VP of digital products Rob Caruso, was similar to my reaction, largely because he'd felt the ramifications of being at a company that didn't share sensitive information openly:

Before Netflix I worked at HBO as the VP of digital products. At HBO, no matter what level you get to, you feel like there are five more closed doors that you're never going to crack. All strategic discussions are shared only on a need-to-know basis. And in the vast majority of situations, top management believes you don't need to know. I'm not picking on HBO—I think this is a pretty standard corporate approach.

One day in December we had a big deadline and I arrived at work so early the place was dead quiet. I remember the weather was bad, and I'd worn an old pair of sneakers instead of my normal dress shoes because of the slush in the streets. When I entered the office there was a note on my desk asking me to stop by the president of the division's office when I came in. That made me nervous because he'd never asked for an impromptu meeting before. I thought immediately that I shouldn't have worn those old sneakers.

The president was sitting in his office with another really friendly looking guy who he introduced as my new boss. I felt this pain of fear when he said it—what did this mean for me and the team? After ten minutes I saw this was all great news. No one had been fired. The new boss was terrific. The company message was: "We are going to invest in your department and we've hired a new leader who can really elevate your initiatives."

But leaving that office, instead of feeling elated as I should have, I felt a bitter sense of mistrust. I hadn't even known this was in discussions. How many people knew this job search had gone on without telling me? This was just one more top management secret that made me feel like a stranger in my own company.

Secretiveness was so omnipresent that when I left HBO to join Netflix I had a big shock.

I'll never forget our first Netflix Quarterly Business Review meeting (QBR). I'd only been at the company a week or so. I walked into the auditorium alone. I barely knew anybody yet and I was expecting the same type of dog-and-pony sales job we had at leadership meetings at past employers. There were four hundred managers in this big auditorium and after Reed gave a short hello they turned the lights off onstage and put up a white slide that read in black block letters:

YOU GO TO JAIL IF YOU TRADE ON THIS . . .
OR IF YOUR FRIEND DOES.
CONFIDENTIAL. DO NOT SHARE.

Finance VP Mark Yurechko hopped up onstage with a big grin. He talked us through the quarter's finances, stock price trends, and how he expected today's numbers would impact the stock price. In my decades of working for other companies, never had I seen anything close to this. A few of the very top executive team were privy to this information, no one else.

Over the next twenty-four hours, the ins and outs of current strategic dilemmas—including reorgs and other big changes that Reed and his top team were grappling with—were put on the table, and we debated them in small groups. I was like, "Oh my goodness, this is so open!"

Netflix treats employees like adults who can handle difficult information and I love that. This creates enormous feelings of commitment and buy-in from employees. For the Quiz Scenario 2, I choose response (c): share. Just tell those employees the truth. They might freak out, but at least they know you're honest with them. And that counts for a lot.

Rob's thinking is in line with mine and I beamed with pride when I heard it. But the second response, from project manager of original content Isabella, is actually more interesting, because it illustrates that transparency decisions are usually difficult and no answer is perfect. Here's what she said:

I had almost exactly the same situation as described in Quiz Scenario 2. What I learned is that although transparency sounds great in reality, often it's so much better not to know.

To set the scene, my husband and I had been looking for a new house near the Netflix office in L.A. for fourteen months to reduce my daily commute. Finally, after visits to about a hundred houses that weren't right, I'd found my dream home—the kind with an open floor plan, where you can talk to someone in the upstairs bedroom right from the downstairs kitchen with no walls blocking your communication. Here I could sing to my daughter while clearing the table and she was in bed.

I loved my job and I was good at it. I was working on the Chelsea Handler talk show. Usually we post an entire season of a Netflix show at once. But **Chelsea** ran three times a week and we had twenty-four hours after each filming to get it translated in a bunch of languages and have it posted online. My job was to manage all of that. Then one day, my boss Aaron put a meeting on my calendar, which he titled, "The Future."

We were sitting in the Out of Africa conference room. That room is all yellow—yellow walls, rug, carpet, and chairs. Aaron pulled up a chair right in front of me and said: "Nothing's been decided. But it's fifty-fifty the program management role you play will be eliminated. We are discussing a reorg and your job might go away, but I won't know for six to twelve months." My head started to spin. The yellow rug turned into the yellow ceiling and I had difficulty focusing on his face.

After that I lapsed into a crisis. We let the house go to another buyer. How could I buy a house when I might lose my job? Then I got angry. Why did Aaron have to cause me stress for something totally unknown? I would watch TV in the evenings with my two boys. When that Netflix logo popped up, instead of feeling pride as I had previously, I was flooded with anxiety and resentment. The stupid thing was that my job DIDN'T go away. It sort of morphed into another job. I'd given up the house and had all those months of stress for absolutely nothing at all.

That's why I vote for (a)—why ruin your employees' lives for no reason?

Isabella's right that it's stress-inducing to learn you might lose your job and frustrating to find out later that you had all those sleepless nights for nothing. But despite her vote for answer (a), I believe her story only boosts the argument for answer (c): **share.**

Imagine the situation had unfolded differently. Suppose Aaron had decided not to tell her until he was sure, and she'd gone ahead and purchased that house. Then imagine she finished the move and arrived at work one day only to hear Aaron say, "I'm so sorry! Your job has been axed and you're out of work." Then she would have been really mad that he'd been in discussions that would impact her life decisions without letting her know.

It's not our job at Netflix to get involved in your housing situation or any other major aspect of your life. But it is our job to treat you like an adult and give you all the information we have, so that you can make informed decisions.

All this said, transparency is our guideline, but we are not purists. I do have a Google Doc that is open only to my six direct reports. Here we can write anything—including stuff like "concerns over Ira's performance"—and it's not open to the rest of the company. But these instances are few. In general, whenever in doubt, we try to open up the process as early as possible, to create buy-in, and to help people see that, although things will always be changing, at least they will be kept informed.

QUIZ SCENARIO 3:
POST-FIRING COMMUNICATION

 You have decided to let go a senior member of the marketing team, a man named Kurt. He is hardworking, kind, and generally effective. But at odd moments he becomes verbally clumsy, putting his foot in his mouth and getting the company in trouble both when addressing employees and speaking externally. The liability has become too great.

When you tell him he's lost his job, he's devastated. He tells you how attached he is to the company, his employees, and the department. He asks you to tell everyone that he decided to leave on his own accord. How will you communicate about the firing to your staff?

a. Tell the whole truth to those who benefit from knowing it. You send an email to Kurt's colleagues at Netflix explaining that Kurt, although hardworking, kind, and effective, sometimes becomes verbally clumsy, putting his foot in his mouth and getting the company in trouble. The liability has become so great that you've decided to let him go.

b. Tell some of the truth. You inform the team Kurt's left, but you're not at liberty to discuss details. He's gone. What do the reasons matter? Give the guy a break and save his reputation.

c. Announce that Kurt decided to leave on his own accord because he wanted to spend more time with his family. Kurt worked hard for you. You already fired him. You don't need to humiliate him to boot.

Answer from Reed: leave the spin in the gym

 My response to Quiz Scenario 3 is (a): tell the whole truth.

Manipulating your message to make the organization, yourself, or another employee appear better than reality is so common across the business world that many leaders don't even realize they're doing it. We "spin" by selectively sharing the facts, overemphasizing the positive, minimizing the negative, all in an attempt to shape the perception of others.

Here are a couple more examples of spin you might recognize:

- "After working as a key player in Ramon's department, Carol is looking for an opportunity to leverage her administrative talents in another area."
  - Translation: "Ramon doesn't want Carol on his team any more. Will someone else take her so we don't have to fire her?"
- "In order to increase synergies across the company, Douglas will transition into a role supporting Kathleen. The gifted teams working for these two individuals will

come together as one to tackle the exciting initiative of boosting organizational sales."
- Translation: "Douglas is being demoted to work for Kathleen. All of Douglas's direct reports are now being folded into Kathleen's department."

Spinning the truth is one of the most common ways leaders erode trust. I can't say this clearly enough: don't do this. Your people are not stupid. When you try to spin them, they see it, and it makes you look like a fraud. Speak plainly, without trying to make bad situations seem good, and your employees will learn you tell the truth.

I understand that it can be difficult. Any leader who tries to be more transparent quickly recognizes that the good of bringing things out in the open sometimes competes with the good of respecting an individual's right to privacy. Both are important. But when someone is let go, everyone wants to understand why. What happened will eventually come out. But if you explain plainly and honestly why you've fired someone, gossip ceases and trust increases.

Several years ago, we had a messy example when we let go of one of our executives for lacking transparency in his own communication. Jake was being considered for a promotion when a few people on his team came forward to say he had been overly political with the team, and that they didn't feel he took feedback well. They provided examples of times they gave him frank feedback and he retaliated in backhanded or hurtful ways. One example stood out as particularly inappropriate. When his boss and HR tried to speak with him, he spun his story further, breaking trust with those he worked most closely with.

When his boss fired Jake, he had a typical moment of doubt. Should he send out an email transparently stating what had happened, or should he let Jake leave quietly, perhaps stating that we had all mutually agreed it was time for a change?

But transparency is the only answer that matches our principles. So his boss sent out the following email to those who worked with Jake (this is an abridged version).

> Dear all,
>
> With mixed emotions, I've decided to exit Jake.
>
> Jake was an internal candidate for a promotion to a senior level executive position. While conducting due diligence for this promotion, some more information has been shared with me that Jake has not consistently displayed the qualities of a leader in all cases that we demand or expect.
> Specifically, it is now clear that Jake was not forthright with us around a major employee issue that impacted the business even when directly asked.

> Jake made a meaningful impact over his many
> years at Netflix and for some, this will come
> as a shock. He did a lot of great work. But
> I'm confident that the feedback I've collected
> is clear and led to us needing to make this
> change.

Of course it is possible to be too candid when revealing why someone has been let go. It's important to respect the dignity of the person leaving as well as to take into consideration cultural differences in different world markets when figuring out how much to disclose. I recommend our managers seek to be as transparent as possible while also ensuring they can respond yes to the question, "Would I feel comfortable showing the person I let go of the email I sent?"

In this case, Jake's actions happened in the office. When it comes to speaking openly about an employee's personal struggles, things get even more complicated. And in these cases I recommend a different approach.

The fall of 2017, one of our leaders, who unbeknownst to us, struggled with alcohol addiction and fell off the wagon on a business trip. He immediately entered rehab. What should we tell his staff? His boss believed that we should follow the Netflix culture and tell everyone the truth. Human Resources insisted that he should have the right to choose what he shared about his personal challenges. In this case, I agreed with HR. When it comes to personal struggles, an individual's right to privacy trumps an organization's desire for transparency. Here we didn't take the most transparent route. But we didn't spin either. We told everyone that the guy had taken two weeks off for personal reasons. It was up to him to share more details if he chose.

Generally, I believed that if the dilemma is linked to an incident at work, everyone should be informed. But if the dilemma is linked to an employee's personal situation, it's up to that person to share details if he chooses.

QUIZ SCENARIO 4:
WHEN YOU SCREW UP

You are still the founder of a start-up with one hundred employees. This is a tough job, and despite your best efforts, you make a series of serious mistakes. Most notably you hire and fire five sales directors within five years. You keep thinking you've found a good candidate. But each time, as you begin to work together, you realize the new recruit doesn't have what it takes to do the job. You realize that these mis-hirings are entirely due to your poor judgment. Do you admit this to your workforce?

a. No! You don't want the group to lose confidence in your ability to lead. Some of your best people might even leave in search of a better boss. On the other hand, everyone can see that a fifth sales manager has just been let go. You have to say *something*—but only a few words about how difficult it is to find good sales directors. Focus your efforts on finding a great one next time.

b. Yes! You want to encourage your staff to take risks and to see mistakes as an inevitable part of that process. Besides, when you speak openly about your errors it makes others trust you more. At the next company meeting, you tell the group how embarrassed you are to have flubbed the hiring and managing of the sales director for the fifth time in a row.

Answer from Reed: whisper wins and shout mistakes

 My response to Quiz Scenario 4 is (b): Yes! Admit that you screwed up.

Earlier in my career, in the early days of Pure Software, I was too insecure to talk openly about mistakes with my staff, and I learned an important lesson. I was making a lot of leadership mistakes and it weighed on me heavily. Beyond my general incompetence at people management, I had indeed hired and fired five sales directors in five years. The first two times, I could blame the person

I'd hired, but by the fourth and fifth failures, it was clear the problem was me.

One thing I have always done is put the company before myself. Certain my own incompetence was bad for the organization, I went to the board and, as if in the confessional, detailed my inadequacies and offered my resignation.

But the Pure board didn't accept it. Financially, the company was doing well. They agreed that I'd made mistakes with people management but claimed that, if they hired someone new, that person would make mistakes also. Two fascinating things happened during that meeting. One was that, as expected, I felt immense relief because I had told the truth and come clean about my errors. The other was more interesting: the board seemed to believe in my leadership more after I had opened up and made myself vulnerable to them.

I went back to the office and, at our next all-employee meeting, did the same thing I'd done in the boardroom. I outlined my mistakes in detail and expressed my regret for having hurt the company. This time, not only did I feel more relief and build trust with my staff, but also people began telling me about all sorts of mistakes they made, mistakes they'd been previously sweeping under the rug. That offered them relief, improved our relationships, and gave me more information so I could do a better job managing the business.

In 2007, almost a decade later, I joined the Microsoft board. Steve Ballmer, the Microsoft CEO at the time, is this big, boisterous, friendly guy. He would talk very transparently about his mistakes, saying stuff like: "Look here, see how I really screwed this thing up." This led me to feel connected to him. What an honest thoughtful guy! And I realized: oh, it's just normal human behavior to feel more trusting of someone who is open about mistakes.

Since then, every time I feel I've made a mistake, I talk about it fully, publicly, and frequently. I quickly came to see the biggest advantage of sunshining a leader's errors is to encourage everyone to think of making mistakes as normal. This in turn encourages employees to take risks when success is uncertain . . . which leads to greater innovation across the company. Self-disclosure builds trust, seeking help boosts learning, admitting mistakes fosters forgiveness, and broadcasting failures encourages your people to act courageously.

That's why, when it comes to Quiz Scenario 4, I have absolutely no reservations. Humility is important in a leader and role model. When you succeed, speak about it softly or let others mention it for you. But when you make a mistake say it clearly and loudly, so that everyone can learn and profit from your errors. In other words, "Whisper wins and shout mistakes."

Reed speaks so frequently and openly about his mistakes as CEO of Pure Software that the experience sounds like one giant catastrophe, in spite of the fact that annual revenues doubled four years in a row before Morgan Stanley took it public in 1995, and it was sold two years later for $750 million, some of which went to Reed and became the seed money for Netflix.

Research backs up Reed's claims about the positive ramifications of the leader speaking openly about mistakes. In her book, **Daring Greatly: How the Courage to Be Vulnerable Transforms the Way We Live, Love, Parent, and Lead**, Brené Brown explains, based on her own qualitative studies, that "we love seeing raw truth and openness in other people, but we are afraid to let them see it in us. . . . Vulnerability is courage in you and inadequacy in me."

Anna Bruk and her team at the University of Mannheim in Germany wondered if they could replicate Brown's findings quantitatively. They asked subjects to imagine themselves in a variety of vulnerable situations—such as being the first to apologize after a big fight and admitting that you made a serious mistake to your team at work. When people imagined themselves in those situations, they tended to believe that showing vulnerability would make them appear "weak" and "inadequate." But when people imagined someone else in the same situations, they were more likely to describe showing vulnerability as "desirable" and "good." Bruk concluded that honesty about mistakes is good for relationships, health, and job performance.

On the other hand, there is also research showing that if someone is already viewed as ineffective, they only deepen that opinion by highlighting their own mistakes. In 1966, psychologist Elliot Aronson ran an experiment. He asked students to listen to recordings of candidates interviewing to be part of a quiz-bowl team. Two of the candidates showed how smart they were by answering most of the questions correctly, while the other two answered only 30 percent right. Then, one group of students heard an explosion of clanging dishes, followed by one of the smart candidates saying, "Oh my goodness—I've spilled coffee all over my new suit." Another group of students heard the same clamor, but then heard one of the mediocre candidates saying he spilled the coffee. Afterward, the students said they liked the smart candidate even more after he embarrassed himself. But the opposite was true of the mediocre candidate. The students said they liked him even less after seeing him in a vulnerable situation.

This tendency has a name: the pratfall effect. The pratfall effect is the tendency for someone's appeal to increase or decrease after making a mistake, depending on his or her perceived ability to perform well in general. In one study conducted by Professor

Lisa Rosh from Lehman College, a woman introduced herself, not by mentioning her credentials and education, but by talking about how she'd been awake the previous night caring for her sick baby. It took her months to reestablish her credibility. If this same woman was first presented as a Nobel Prize winner, the exact same words about being up all night with the baby would provoke reactions of warmth and connection from the audience.

When you combine the data with Reed's advice, this is the takeaway: a leader who has demonstrated competence and is liked by her team will build trust and prompt risk-taking when she widely sunshines her own mistakes. Her company benefits. The one exception is for a leader considered unproven or untrusted. In these cases you'll want to build trust in your competency before shouting your mistakes.

THE FIFTH DOT

If you have the best employees on the market and you've instituted a culture of open feedback, opening up company secrets increases feelings of ownership and commitment among staff. If you trust your people to handle appropriately sensitive information, the trust you demonstrate will instigate feelings of responsibility and your employees will show you just how trustworthy they are.

▶ **TAKEAWAYS FROM CHAPTER 5**

- To instigate a culture of transparency, consider what symbolic messages you send. Get rid of closed offices, assistants who act as guards, and locked spaces.

- Open up the books to your employees. Teach them how to read the P&L. Share sensitive financial and strategic information with everyone in the company.

- When making decisions that will impact your employees' well-being, like reorganizations or layoffs, open up to the workforce early, before things are solidified. This will cause some anxiety and distraction, but the trust you build will outweigh the disadvantages.

- When transparency is in tension with an individual's privacy, follow this guideline: If the information is about something that happened at work, choose transparency and speak candidly about the incident. If the information is about an employee's personal life, tell people it's not your place to share and they can ask the person concerned directly if they choose.

- As long as you've already shown yourself to be competent, talking openly and extensively about your own mistakes—and encouraging all your leaders to do the same—will increase trust, goodwill, and innovation throughout the organization.

Toward a Culture of Freedom and Responsibility

Now that you have high talent density, candor, and organizational transparency in place, and you've experimented a little with symbolic freedoms (like removing vacation limits and lifting travel and expense policies), you're ready to ramp up the freedom to a serious level. The topic of the next chapter—"No Decision-making Approvals Needed"—cannot be implemented unless you have already addressed the topics in the previous chapters. Assuming you've done the groundwork, this coming chapter is the one most likely to increase innovation, speed, and employee satisfaction throughout the organization.

NOW RELEASE MORE CONTROLS . . .

6

NO DECISION-MAKING
APPROVALS NEEDED

 In 2004, we were still exclusively a DVD-by-mail company, and Ted Sarandos was responsible for buying all the DVDs. He decided whether we should order sixty copies of a new movie title or six hundred. These DVDs would be sent to our customers.

One day, some new movie about aliens had come out and Ted thought it would be hot. He and I were having a cup of coffee while he worked on his ordering form, so he asked me, "How many of these do you think we should order?"

I responded, "Oh, I don't think that's going to be popular. Just get a few." Within a month, the title was in crazy demand and we were out of stock. "Why didn't you buy more of that alien movie, Ted?!" I exclaimed.

"Because you told me not to!" he protested.

That was when I began to understand the dangers

of the standard decision-making pyramid. I'm the boss and I have strong opinions, which I share freely, but I am not the best person to decide how many movies to order or to make a slew of other critical daily decisions at Netflix. I told him:

"Ted, your job is **not** to try to make me happy or to make the decision you think I'd most approve of. It's to do what's right for the business. You are not allowed to let me drive this company off a cliff!"

At most companies, the boss is there to approve or block the decisions of employees. This is a surefire way to limit innovation and slow down growth. At Netflix, we emphasize that it's fine to disagree with your manager and to implement an idea she dislikes. We don't want people putting aside a great idea because the manager doesn't see how great it is. That's why we say at Netflix:

DON'T SEEK TO PLEASE YOUR BOSS.
SEEK TO DO WHAT IS BEST FOR THE COMPANY.

There's a whole mythology about CEOs and other senior leaders who are so involved in the details of the business that their product or service becomes amazing. The legend of Steve Jobs was that his micromanagement made the iPhone a great product. The heads of major networks and movie studios sometimes make many decisions about the creative content of their projects. Some executives even go so far as to boast about being "nanomanagers."

Of course, at most companies, even at those who have leaders who don't micromanage, employees seek to make the decision the boss is most likely to support. The popular notion is that the boss knows more because she made it to that higher rung in the ladder. If you value your career and don't want to be accused of insubordination, listen carefully to what she thinks is the best and follow that course of action.

We don't emulate these top-down models, because we believe we are fastest and most innovative when employees throughout the company make and own decisions. At Netflix, we strive to develop good decision-making muscles everywhere in our company—and we pride ourselves on how few decisions senior management makes.

Awhile back, Sheryl Sandberg of Facebook spent a day shadowing me at work. She attended all of my meetings and one-on-ones. It's something I do occasionally with other Silicon Valley executives, so we can learn from watching one another in action. Afterward, when Sheryl and I debriefed, she said, "The amazing thing was to sit with you all day long and see that you didn't make one decision!"

I felt great—because that's exactly what we are going for. Our dispersed decision-making model has become a foundation of our culture and one of the main reasons we have grown and innovated so quickly.

When we first began working on this book, I asked how Reed would find the time to collaborate. He replied, "Oh, I can give this pretty much whatever time you think it will need."

I was surprised. Given the growth rate of Netflix, how could he be anything but overwhelmed? Yet Reed believes so deeply in dispersed decision-making that, by his model, only a CEO who is not busy is really doing his job.

Dispersed decision-making can only work with high talent density and unusual amounts of organizational transparency. Without these elements, the entire premise backfires. Once those elements are in place, you are ready to remove controls that are not just symbolic (such as vacation tracking) but also have the power to dramatically increase the speed of innovation across your business. Paolo Lorenzoni, a marketing expert who worked for Sky Italy before joining Netflix in Amsterdam, demonstrates the principle by comparing his old and new workplaces:

> Sky is the sole Italian provider for **Game of Thrones**. At Sky, my boss asked me to come up with promotional ideas for the show. I came up with a great one.
>
> If you've watched **Game of Thrones**, you know about the big ice wall protecting the country. A

lot of the show is filmed up on the wall, and it is very, very cold up there. That gave me the idea for the ad.

Four friends are having a drink outside on a warm evening in Milan. The sun is setting, and they are sipping pink Bellini cocktails from champagne glasses. They are dressed in T-shirts and they are outside in the courtyard. You can see the reflection of the TV screen from the house windows behind them. One of the friends checks his watch. Seeing that **Game of Thrones** is about to start, he laughs, "We'd better go inside. Winter is coming" (wink-wink). Two of the friends grab their stuff. They don't want to miss the show either. But the fourth friend doesn't understand. "What do you mean? It's warm out!" The other three laugh at his ignorance. He apparently doesn't have Sky TV and doesn't know about that wall of ice. "You have to get it to get it!" they tell him.

Everyone we tested the idea on loved it. But at Sky, everything had to be approved by the CEO. The CEO was the one person who didn't get it. He killed that idea in about three and a half minutes.

Paolo was hired at Netflix to promote shows to Italians. The popular Netflix original **Narcos** was one series he was sure would be a big hit. It's the story of the Colombian drug lord Pablo Escobar.

Pablo is handsome, with 1980s coiffed hair and a bushy mustache. "Despite all the deplorable things he does you find yourself rooting for him," explains Paolo. "Italians—who love Mafia shows—were going to love it. Over dozens of wakeful evenings pacing in my flat, I developed a plan for how to get all of Italy hooked. It was so clear to me I could taste it. It would be expensive, and I'd need to use all of the Italy marketing budget."

But Paolo wondered if his new boss, vice president of marketing Jerret West, an American living in Singapore, would agree with his idea. Would he get management approval to move ahead?

Jerret was coming to Amsterdam. I'd spent weeks now on this proposal and, if he shot it down, it would all be a waste. Monday, Tuesday, Wednesday, I worked day and night writing the most convincing argument I could put to paper. Noon on Thursday I put it in an email addressed to Jerret. Before I sent the email, I whispered to my computer, "Please let Jerret say yes."

The day of the meeting I was so nervous I had to put my hands in my pockets to stop them shaking. But Jerret spent most of the meeting talking about hiring challenges. I could barely listen I was so stressed. I took a big breath and jumped in. "'Jerret, I want to make sure we have time to discuss my **Narcos** proposal."

Paolo couldn't believe Jerret's response:

"Did you have elements you wanted to discuss? It's your decision, Paolo. Is there something I can do to help?" It was one of those light bulb moments: I got it! At Netflix, if you share all the context of your decision, you've done the groundwork. You don't need approval. It's up to you. You decide.

People desire and thrive on jobs that give them control over their own decisions. Since the 1980s, management literature has been filled with instructions for how to delegate more and "empower employees to empower themselves." The thinking is exactly what we've heard from Paolo. The more people are given control over their own projects, the more ownership they feel, and the more motivated they are to do their best work. Telling employees what to do is so old-fashioned, it leads to screams of "micromanager!" "dictator!" and "autocrat!"

But at most organizations, no matter how much autonomy is given to employees to set their own objectives and develop their own ideas, nearly everybody agrees that it's the boss's job to make sure his team doesn't make stupid decisions that waste money and resources. And if you happen to be the boss, Reed's mantra, "Don't seek to please the boss," can be not just odd but downright frightening.

YOU'VE GOT HIGH TALENT DENSITY AND CANDOR: ARE YOU READY TO REALLY RELEASE CONTROLS?

Imagine this scenario. You land a plum management position at a fast-paced, cutting-edge company. You're paid well, and you're handed a team of five highly experienced, hardworking direct reports. It's all good . . . except for one small caveat. This company is known for hiring only the very best and for firing those who don't do great work. You feel immense pressure to succeed.

Now, you are not a micromanager. You know how to get things done without leaning over your team members' shoulders and telling them which pen to pick up and which phone call to make. In fact, you were celebrated for your empowering leadership style in your last job.

One morning a team member, Sheila, comes to you with a proposal. She's got an innovative idea for how to move the business forward and she wants to abandon the project you've suggested for her. You've been impressed with Sheila, but this idea, you believe, is going to flop. If you allow her to spend four months working on a project you feel is likely to fail, how's that going to make you look to your own boss?

You explain, with passion, all the reasons you're against the idea. But you've been trying to empower your staff more, so you leave the decision in Sheila's lap. She thanks you and says she will consider all your points. A week later Sheila sets up another meeting. This time she says, "I know you disagree, but I'm going to follow this new idea because I think it will lead to greater gains. Let me know if you want to specifically override my decision." What are you going to do?

At this point, the plot of the imaginary scenario thickens. After a couple of days, another employee comes to you with an idea he wants to spend half of his time working on. You are certain that this too is going to bomb. And then, a few days later, a third person pops up with a similar request. You care about your own career and you care about the careers of your employees, so you can't help but feel the very strong tug to tell them these are not the initiatives they are going to be working on.

 Our mantra is that employees don't need the boss's approval to move forward (but they should let the boss know what's going on). If Sheila comes to you with a proposal you think is going to fail, you need to remind yourself why Sheila is working for you and why you paid top of the market to get her. Ask yourself these four questions:

- Is Sheila a stunning employee?
- Do you believe she has good judgment?
- Do you think she has the ability to make a positive impact?
- Is she good enough to be on your team?

If you answer NO to any of these questions, you should get rid of her (see the next chapter where we'll learn that "adequate performance gets a generous severance"). But if your answer is yes, step aside and let her decide for herself. When the boss steps out of the role of "decision approver," the entire business speeds up and innovation increases. Remember all the time Paolo spent preparing to get Jerret's approval to implement his new idea? If Jerret had nixed the initiative, Paolo would have had to kill a proposal he believed in and start exploring other paths. All the time he'd invested, not to mention a great idea, would have been wasted.

Of course, not all decisions your people make will succeed. And when the boss moves aside from vetting judgment calls, it's likely they'll fail more often. That's precisely why it's so hard to let Sheila go ahead with her idea, when you think it won't work.

WHAT WE DRINK AT NETFLIX

A few years ago I was attending a conference in Geneva. Sitting at the bar, I overheard two CEOs chatting about the challenge of innovation. One was a Swiss guy who runs a sporting goods company. "One of my managers suggested putting a Rollerblade lane in our stores to pull young clients away from online competitors," he said. "We need this type of fresh thinking in our company. But no sooner had she made the suggestion than she began to retract it. We wouldn't have space! It would be too expensive! It might be dangerous! In two minutes, she'd completely dismissed the entire idea. She never brought it to her boss for input. Everyone in our company is so risk-averse! Innovation doesn't have a chance."

The other CEO, an American fashion retailer, nodded: "We have banners hanging in our cubicles that read **Ten minutes to innovate**. Our problem is that we're all working too hard to have time to think up new ways to do things. So I'm trying to give everyone time to just think. We're going to start 'Innovation Fridays' when, one day a month, all employees will do nothing but come up with great ideas. We work all day long in the world of Google, we buy stuff from Amazon, listen to music from Spotify, take Uber rides to Airbnb apartments, and spend our evenings watching Netflix. But we can't figure out how these Silicon Valley companies move so fast and innovate so quickly."

"Whatever they're drinking at Netflix," he concluded, "that's what we need to be drinking."

That was a funny thing to overhear. What **are**

we drinking at Netflix? Our employees are good, but when they enter the company they are just as concerned about minimizing failure as the woman with the roller-rink idea. We don't have innovation Fridays, or innovation banners. And our employees are busy, just as busy as that guy from the fashion retail business.

The difference is the decision-making freedom we provide. If your employees are excellent and you give them freedom to implement the bright ideas they believe in, innovation will happen. Netflix does not operate in a safety-critical market, like medicine or nuclear power. In some industries, preventing error is essential. We are in a creative market. Our big threat in the long run is not making a mistake, it's lack of innovation. Our risk is failing to come up with creative ideas for how to entertain our customers, and therefore becoming irrelevant.

If you hope for more innovation on your team, teach employees to seek ways to move the business forward, not ways to please their bosses. Coach your staff to challenge their managers exactly like Sheila did: "I know you disagree, but I'm going to follow this new idea because I think it will lead to greater gains. Let me know if you want to specifically override my decision." At the same time, teach your leaders **not** to override decisions like Sheila's, even in the face of their own skepticism and long experience of what has worked in the past. Sometimes the employee will fail, and the boss will feel like saying, "I told you so" (but, she won't!). Sometimes the employee will succeed despite the boss's reservations.

A great example comes from Kari Perez, a director in our communications department responsible for building Netflix brand awareness across Latin America. Kari is from Mexico but lives in Hollywood:

> It was late 2014 and Netflix was still pretty unknown in Mexico. I had a vision for how to change that. I wanted to present Netflix as the champion of local Mexican content, even though we didn't have any original Mexican shows yet.
>
> The idea was to nominate ten big Mexican movies from that year—with famous Mexican directors and starring local celebrities. We would also select a ten-person, all-Mexican jury of celebrities like Ana de la Reguera (the telenovela star turned **Narcos** actress) and Manolo Caro (the superstar director who had recently appeared on the cover of **Vanity Fair** in a wrinkled tuxedo, lying between two beautiful actresses) with the goal of making our brand more relevant to the audiences that these celebrities influenced.
>
> The celebrities from the movies and jury panel would lobby on social media for their favorite movies, encouraging everyone to vote on Twitter, Facebook, and LinkedIn. The two films with the most votes would win a one-year international

distribution contract with Netflix. We would finish up with a big party inviting all the who's who of Mexico.

But my boss Jack hated the idea. Why spend all that time and money on movies that Netflix hadn't even made? Worse, we'd tried something similar in Brazil, partnering with film festivals, and that hadn't gotten any real traction. Jack kept stating publicly, in meetings, that if the buck stopped with him, we would do it over his dead body.

But I believed in it. I was ready to make that bet and, if it failed, I'd be responsible. I listened carefully to Jack's concerns and decided to work with local influencers and vendors instead of film festivals, to avoid a repeat of the Brazil fiasco. Of course it's scary to move forward when you know your boss thinks you're making a bad decision.

I needn't have worried. The press conference for the launch and closing events of the contest were packed with press and Twitter exploded with the competition in the weeks leading up to the event. The celebrity jury panel pushed the message like crazy via Facebook and Twitter. Producers, directors, and actors also launched their own campaigns, which positioned Prêmio Netflix as a critical platform for the independent Mexican film industry.

Ana De La Reguera ✔ **@ADELAREGUERA** · 4 Mar 2015 ⌄
#PremioNetflix Mexico. Entra a premionetflixmx.com **para votar y apoyar al cine independiente Mexicano !!**

Thousands of people voted. It was a pivotal moment for us. Suddenly everyone knew the Netflix brand. I knew it had been a success at the awards party when high-profile influencers arrived, including the Mexican president Enrique Peña Nieto's daughter, and then one of the most famous Mexican actresses alive, Kate Del Castillo, showed up on the red carpet—brought in on a private plane hired by none other than my (no longer reticent) manager!

Jack stood up in front of everyone at the next team meeting and announced that he'd been absolutely wrong: that had been one great campaign.

In order to encourage our employees like Kari and their managers like Jack to shift their mind-set in the direction of experimentation, we use the image of placing bets. This motivates employees to think of themselves as entrepreneurs—who typically don't succeed without some failures. The examples of Kari and (from a few pages back) Paolo reflect everyday life at Netflix. We want all employees taking bets they believe in and trying new things, even when the boss or others think the ideas are dumb.

When some of those bets don't pay off, we just fix the problems that arise as quickly as possible and discuss what we've learned. In our creative business, rapid recovery is the best model.

STEPS TO TAKE BEFORE (AND AFTER) YOU PLACE YOUR BET

 Bet-taking has been linked to entrepreneurship for decades. In 1962, Frederick Smith wrote a paper for his economics class at Yale outlining the idea for an overnight delivery service. The idea was that you could put a package in the mail in Missouri on Tuesday and, if you paid enough, it would arrive in California on Wednesday. According to legend, Smith received a C on the paper and his professor told him that in order to get a better grade, the idea had to be feasible. If Smith's professor had been Smith's boss, he would certainly have put the kibosh on the whole innovation.

Smith, however, was an entrepreneur, and that Yale paper became the basis for FedEx, which he founded in 1971. He was also a betting man: once, in the early days of FedEx, after a bank had refused to extend a crucial loan, he took the company's last $5,000 to Las Vegas and won $27,000 playing blackjack to cover the company's $24,000 fuel bill. Of course,

Netflix doesn't encourage its staff to go to casinos, but it does seek to instill some of Fredrick Smith's spirit into the workforce. As Kari remembers:

> When I started at Netflix, Jack explained to me that I should consider I'd been handed a stack of chips. I could place them on whatever bets I believed in. I'd need to work hard and think carefully to ensure I made the best bets I could, and he'd show me how. Some bets would fail, and some would succeed. My performance would ultimately be judged, not on whether any individual bet failed, but on my overall ability to use those chips to move the business forward. Jack made it clear that at Netflix you don't lose your job because you make a bet that doesn't work out. Instead you lose your job for not using your chips to make big things happen or for showing consistently poor judgment over time.

Jack explained to Kari, "We don't expect employees to get approval from their boss before they make decisions. But we do know that good decisions require a solid grasp of the context, feedback from people with different perspectives, and awareness of all the options." If someone uses the freedom Netflix gives them to make important decisions without soliciting others' viewpoints, Netflix considers that a demonstration of poor judgment.

Then Jack introduced Kari to the Netflix Innovation Cycle, a framework she could follow in order to make the bets most likely to succeed. The principle of "don't seek to please your boss" works best if employees follow this simple four-step model.

The Netflix Innovation Cycle

If you have an idea you're passionate about, do the following:

1. "Farm for dissent," or "socialize" the idea.
2. For a big idea, test it out.
3. As the informed captain, make your bet.
4. If it succeeds, celebrate. If it fails, sunshine it.

INNOVATION CYCLE STEP 1: FARM FOR DISSENT . . .

 The premise of farming for dissent came out of the Qwikster debacle, the biggest mistake in Netflix history.

In early 2007, we offered one service for ten dollars that was a combination of mailing DVDs and streaming. But it was clear that streaming video would become of increasing importance while people would watch fewer and fewer DVDs.

We wanted to be able to focus on streaming, without DVDs distracting us, so I had the idea to separate the two operations: Netflix would stream, while we created a new company, Qwikster, to handle the DVD market. With two separate companies, we would charge eight dollars for each service separately. For customers who wanted both DVDs and streaming, it meant a price hike to sixteen dollars. The new arrangement would allow Netflix to focus on building the company of the future without being weighed down by the logistics of DVD mailing, which was our past.

The announcement provoked a customer revolt. Not only was our new model way more expensive, but it also meant customers had to manage two websites and two subscriptions instead of one. Over the next few quarters, we lost millions of subscribers and our stock dropped more than 75 percent in value. Everything we'd built was crashing down because of my bad decision. It was the lowest point in my career—definitely not an experience I want to repeat. When I apologized on a YouTube video, I looked so stressed that **Saturday Night Live** made fun of me.

But that humiliation was a valuable wake-up call, because afterward dozens of Netflix managers and VPs started coming forward to say they hadn't believed in the idea. One said, "I knew it was going to be a disaster, but I thought, 'Reed is always right,' so I kept quiet." A guy from finance agreed,

"We thought it was crazy, because we knew a large percentage of our customers paid the ten dollars but didn't even use the DVD service. Why would Reed make a choice that would lose Netflix money? But everyone else seemed to be going along with the idea, so we did too." Another manager said, "I always hated the name Qwikster, but no one else complained, so I didn't either." Finally, one VP said to me, "You're so intense when you believe in something, Reed, that I felt you wouldn't hear me. I should have laid down on the tracks screaming that I thought it would fail. But I didn't."

The culture at Netflix had been sending the message to our people that, despite all our talk about candor, differences of opinion were not always welcome. That's when we added a new element to our culture. We now say that it is disloyal to Netflix when you disagree with an idea and do **not** express that disagreement. By withholding your opinion, you are implicitly choosing to not help the company.

 Why did everyone keep quiet when they saw Reed piloting the ship into the Qwikster storm?

Part of the reason is our natural human desire to conform. There's a funny candid-camera-style video that shows three actors riding an elevator with their faces turned toward the back, away from the door. A woman enters the elevator and, at first, she looks confused. Why are these people facing the wrong way? But then, slowly, although she obviously thinks what they are doing is weird, she also starts to turn around. Humans are much more comfortable when going along with the herd. In many areas of life, this is not bad. But it may push us to go along with or even actively support an idea that our instinct or experience tells us is crazy.

The other part of the reason is that Reed's the founder and CEO. That makes things more complicated because it is also deeply ingrained in all of us to follow and learn from our leaders. In Malcolm Gladwell's book **Outliers,** we learn that a major plane crash was caused when Korean Air staff refrained from telling the lead pilot that there was a problem because they wanted to show respect for his authority. This tendency is human.

A few months after the Qwikster crisis had passed, at the end of a weeklong executive staff retreat, everyone sat in a circle and went around the room taking turns saying what they had learned. Jessica Neal, a VP in Human Resources who today is chief talent officer, recalls, "Reed went last and just started crying, talking about how bad he felt that he put the company in the situation he did, how much he learned and how appreciative he was of all of us for sticking through it with him. It was a very moving moment that likely doesn't happen with most CEOs at other companies."

I can't make the **best** decisions unless I have input from a lot of people. That's why I and everyone else at Netflix now actively seek out different perspectives before making any major decision. We call it **farming for dissent.** Normally, we try to avoid establishing a lot of processes at Netflix, but this specific principle is so important that we have developed multiple systems to make sure dissent gets heard.

If you are a Netflix employee with a proposal, you create a shared memo explaining the idea and inviting dozens of your colleagues for input. They will then leave comments electronically in the margin of your document, which everyone can view. Simply glancing through the comments can give you a feeling for a variety of dissenting and supporting viewpoints. For a sample, see the memo on the next page, which discusses Android Smart downloads.

In some cases, an employee proposing an idea will distribute a shared spreadsheet asking people to rate the idea on a scale from −10 to +10, with their explanation and comments. This a great way to get clarity on how intense the dissent is and to begin the debate.

Before one big leadership meeting, I passed around a memo outlining a proposed one-dollar increase in the price of a Netflix subscription along with a new tiered-pricing model. Many dozens of managers weighed in with their ratings and comments. Here are a few of them in abridged format:

A more aggressive idea is to couple My List buttons with Smart Downloads. Given that both My List and Downloads are conceptually about saving something for later viewing, could an add to My List trigger a Smart Download?

Such a feature could apply across devices. For example, see something you like tonight while browsing Netflix on your SmartTV? Add it to My List and it will be downloaded on your phone ready to go for your morning commute.

We will be bringing such ideas forward to future product strat meetings. If you have ideas of your own, please add them below.

_____

IDEAS

- Aggressively auto-download the first episode of new content with a high PVR score and we know member watches on mobile. [Eddy]
- Aggressively auto-download episodes from Continue Watching not just actively downloaded titles (or Watchlist in the future). [Stephen]
- Auto-download Mobile Previews for easy access viewing. [Stephen]
- Create a different section for auto-downloads of things I'm not watching, so there are "My downloads" - what I manually download and what was tested here - and recommended downloads - the ideas listed above like PVR & CW titles. [Cathy]
- "Long Flight" one-click download -- recommend a few things for my kid/s or me to watch and give me a one-click affordance to make it happen (e.g., downloads a popular movie, a few episodes of something novel, and something rewatched a lot). [Pat]

● ⬤⬤⬤⬤
Apr 2, 2018   Resolve
I don't think we need to give them a proactive option to opt out. Goal would be to lightly introduce the feature so Show more

Show all 7 replies

👤 Sharon Williamson
   Apr 4, 2018
ah ok - so it's not as if all the other download settings are there but this one? thx

👤 Todd Yellin
   Apr 3, 2018   Resolve
Perhaps the copy should show a bit more excitement to make it clear that we're giving members an improvement.

Show all 3 replies

👤 Zach Schendel
   Apr 5, 2018
What if any episode that we smart

Alex	-4	Making two changes at once is a bad idea.
Dianna	8	Timing is perfect just before big market launch.
Jamal	-1	Certain tiering is right move. Don't think amount is right for this year.

The spreadsheet system is a super-simple way to gather assent and dissent, and when your team consists entirely of top performers, it provides extremely valuable input. It's not a vote or a democracy. You're not supposed to add up the numbers and find the average. But it provides all sorts of insight. I use it to collect candid feedback before making any important decision.

The more you actively farm for dissent, and the more you encourage a culture of expressing disagreement openly, the better the decisions that will be made in your company. This is true for any company of any size in any industry.

. . . OR SOCIALIZE THE IDEA

For smaller initiatives, you don't need to farm for dissent, but you'd still be wise to let everyone know what you're doing and to take the temperature of your initiative. Let's go back to your employee, Sheila, the woman who came to you with an idea you're against. After explaining why you don't agree, you can suggest that she socialize the idea with her peers and other leaders in the company. This means that she sets up multiple meetings, where she outlines her proposal and enters into discussions in order to stress-test her thinking and collect numerous opinions and data points before making her decision. Socializing is a type of farming for dissent with less emphasis on the dissent and more on the farming.

In 2016, I had a personal experience where socializing an idea led me to change my own opinion.

Up until then I believed strongly that kids' TV shows and movies would not bring new customers to Netflix or even retain the customers we had.

Who signs up to Netflix for a children's show? I was convinced adults choose Netflix because they love our content. Their kids will just watch whatever we have available. So when we began producing original programs, we focused on adult content only. For kids, we continued to license shows from Disney and Nickelodeon. And when we did release our own Netflix kids shows, we didn't put much money into them, not in the way Disney did. The kid's content team disagreed with this approach: "These are the next generation of Netflix customers," they argued. "We want them to love Netflix as much as their parents do." They wanted us to start producing original kids' content as well.

I didn't think that was a great idea but I socialized it anyway. At our next QBR meeting we placed our top four hundred employees at sixty round tables in groups of six or seven. They received a small card with this question to debate: Should we spend more money, less money, or no money on kids' content?

There was a tsunami of support for investing in kids' content. One director who is also a mom got up onstage and passionately declared, "Before working here I subscribed to Netflix exclusively so my daughter could watch **Dora the Explorer**. I care a lot more about what my kids watch than what I watch myself." A father came up and announced, "Before coming to Netflix I only subscribed because I could trust the content for my children." He explained why: "My wife and I don't watch TV but my son does. On Netflix there's no advertisements like on cable and no dangerous rabbit holes for my son to fall down like when he surfs on YouTube. But if he hadn't been crazy about what Netflix was offering, he'd have stopped watching and we'd have canceled the subscription." One after another our employees were stepping onto that stage and telling me I was wrong. They believed kids shows were critical to our customer base.

Within six months we'd hired a new VP of kids and family programming from DreamWorks and started making our own animated features. After two years we'd tripled our kids' slate, and in 2018 we were nominated for three Emmys for our original kids shows **Alexa and Katie**, **Fuller House**, and **A Series of Unfortunate Events.** To date, we've won over a dozen Daytime Emmys for children's programs like **The Mr. Peabody and Sherman Show** and **Trollhunters: Tales of Arcadia.**

If I hadn't taken the time to socialize the idea, none of this could have happened.

INNOVATION CYCLE STEP 2: FOR A BIG IDEA, TEST IT OUT

 Most successful companies run all sorts of tests in order to find out how and why customers behave the way they do—and the results of those tests usually influence the corporate strategy. The big difference at Netflix is that the tests take place even when those in charge are dead set against the initiative. The history behind Netflix and downloading is a clear example.

In 2015, if you were taking an airplane and wanted to watch your favorite Netflix show during the trip, you were out of luck. There was no way to download the content onto your phone or any other device. Netflix was all live internet streaming. If you didn't have the internet, you didn't have Netflix. Amazon Prime did offer downloading, as did YouTube in some countries, so the topic was a hot one at Netflix.

Neil Hunt, chief product officer at the time, was against offering downloads. It would be a big, time-consuming project and would distract from the core mission of making streaming work better, even on poor connections. Also, the internet would become faster and more ubiquitous, so the feature would become less useful every month. Neil is quoted in the British press explaining that downloading adds considerable complexity to your life: "You have to remember that you want to download this thing. It's not going to be instant, you have to have the right storage on your device, you have to manage it, and I'm just not sure people are actually that compelled to do that, and that it's worth providing that level of complexity."

Neil wasn't the only one against downloading.

Reed was frequently asked at employee gatherings why the feature was absent. Here are his replies to questions in a 2015 document accessible to all Netflix employees:

> Employee question: Now that other services are ramping up off-line downloads, do you think Netflix refusing to offer this service will have a negative impact on perceived brand quality?

> Reed's response: No. Soon we'll be announcing our first airline free Wi-Fi streaming deals with full Netflix. We are focused on streaming, and as the Internet expands (planes, etc.) the consumer desire for downloading will go away. Our competitors will be stuck with supporting a shrinking downloading use case for years. We'll end up far ahead on brand quality sentiment on this issue.

> Employee question: There is an earlier comment in this doc about not offering download-and-watch capabilities due to content costs. Could we buy this right for just the top shows and movies and offer it only to the top tier?

> Reed's response: We think streaming will get everywhere, including planes, over time. The UX [user experience] complexities of downloading

are material for a one percent use case, so we are avoiding this approach. It's our judgment call for utility against complexity.

The big guys, Neil and Reed, were set against the idea publicly and privately. At most places this would be end of discussion. But Todd Yellin, VP of product, (who worked for Neil) had doubts. He discussed with Zach Schendel (senior user experience researcher) about running some tests to find out if Neil and Reed's claims were accurate. Zach remembers it like this:

I thought, "Neil and Reed are against this idea. Is it okay to test it out?" At any of my past employers, that would not have been a good move. But the lore at Netflix is all about lower-level employees accomplishing amazing things in the face of hierarchical opposition. With that in mind I went ahead.

YouTube was not available for download in the US but it was in a few places like India and Southeast Asia. That was interesting because Netflix was getting ready for a massive international expansion in January 2016 and these countries would all be important to us. We decided to run interviews in India and Germany to find out what percentage of customers used the download feature. In India we would interview YouTube users, in Germany Watchever users (a similar type of German platform), and in the US we would interview Amazon Prime users (because Amazon Prime offered downloads).

In the United States, 15 to 20 percent of Amazon Prime users used the downloading function according to our findings. That was a lot higher than the one percent Reed estimated, though clearly a minority of customers.

In India, our research revealed that over 70 percent of YouTube consumers used the download function. That number was enormous! Common responses included: "I have a ninety-minute commute and I ride to work in a car pool so I spend an hour and a half in traffic each day. Cell phone streaming isn't fast enough in Hyderabad, so I download everything I watch." Another case, unheard of in the US: "The Internet at my office is fast enough for streaming but at my house it's not. So I download all my shows at the office and watch them at home in the evening."

Germans have neither the traffic problems nor the commute distances of Indians. But the internet isn't as ubiquitously reliable as in the US either. "When I watch a show in my kitchen it stops every few minutes to spool," one German explained, "so I download it in the living room, where the Internet is faster, in order to watch while I'm cooking." Germany came between the US and India.

Zach pushed his findings up to his boss, Adrien Lanusse, who pushed this up to his boss, Todd Yellin, who pushed this up to his boss, Neil Hunt, who pushed this up to his boss, Reed, who said he and Neil had been wrong—and in the face of its international expansion Netflix had better get to work on the downloading functionality.

"Let me be clear," Zach concludes, "I am nobody in the company. I'm just some researcher. Yet I was able to push back against a strong and publicly stated opinion from the top leadership to rally excitement for this feature. This is what Netflix is all about."

Netflix now provides downloads.

INNOVATION CYCLE STEP 3: AS THE INFORMED CAPTAIN, PLACE YOUR BET

Farm for dissent. Socialize the idea. Test it out. This sounds a lot like consensus building, but it's not. With consensus building the group decides; at Netflix a person will reach out to relevant colleagues, but does not need to get anyone's agreement before moving forward. Our four-step Innovation Cycle is individual decision-making with input.

For each important decision there is always a clear informed captain. That person has full decision-making freedom. In Erin's scenario, Sheila is the informed captain. It's not for her boss or any of her colleagues to decide. She collects opinions and chooses for herself. She is then solely responsible for the outcome.

In 2004, Chief Marketing Officer Leslie Kilgore introduced a practice to emphasize that the informed captain is solely responsible for the decision. At most companies all important contracts are signed by someone high up in the organization. With Leslie's encouragement, one of her employees, Camille, had begun signing all of the media agreements for which she was the informed captain. One day our General Counsel went to Leslie and said: "You didn't sign this huge contract with Disney! Why is Camille's name on it?" Leslie responded:

The person who is living and breathing the contract needs to be the person who owns and signs the contract, not a head of a function or a VP. That takes responsibility of the project away from the person who should be responsible. Obviously, I look at those contracts too. But Camille is proud of what she accomplished. This is her thing, not mine. She is psychologically invested, and I want to keep her that way. I'm not going to take ownership away from her by putting my name on the deal.

Leslie was right, and we follow her example across Netflix today. At Netflix you don't need management to sign off for anything. If you're the informed captain, take ownership—sign the document yourself.

 When you read about Freedom and Responsibility at Netflix, it's easy to get lost in the lovely idea of Freedom without properly considering the accompanying weight of Responsibility. Being the informed captain and signing off on your own contracts is a case in point. Although Reed certainly doesn't intend to induce fear and trembling in his workforce, part of the reason that F&R works so well is because people do feel the burden of the responsibility that comes with the freedom and make extra efforts accordingly.

Among the many people who told me about the pressures of signing their own contracts is Omarson Costa, one of the first employees at Netflix Brazil. His story is about his early days in the company when he was a business development director:

> I had been with Netflix for just a few weeks when I received an email from the legal department. The message said, "Omarson, you have the authority to sign contracts and agreements for Netflix in Brazil."

I thought they'd left off part of the email. I replied immediately. "Up until what amount of money? If I need to go beyond that, whose approval should I get?"

The response was, "The limit is your judgment."

I didn't understand. Were they saying that I could sign deals worth millions of dollars? How can they grant so much power to one employee in Latin America, who they've only known for a few weeks?

I was amazed and scared! They trusted me, so my judgment should be very sharp and my decisions impeccably researched. I would be making decisions for my boss, for the boss of my boss, for the boss of my boss of my boss and for all of Netflix, on my own, no approvals needed. I felt responsibility mixed with fear like I had never felt before! That feeling catapulted me to work harder than I have in my life, to assure each contract I signed would be a blessing for the entire company.

The feeling of responsibility felt by Netflix employees is often intense. Diego Avalos, director of international originals, didn't know what had hit him when he joined the Beverly Hills office of Netflix from Yahoo in 2014:

I was new to Netflix and my manager asked me to finish the acquisition of a film we were buying for $3 million. At Yahoo even a $50,000 commitment required the signature of the CFO or the General Counsel. Even though I was a director at Yahoo, I didn't sign any deal myself.

I got the negotiations all figured out, but when my boss said, "Sign the deal yourself," I was plagued with anxiety. This was mind-boggling. What if it goes wrong? What if I lose my job because I made a mistake? Netflix believed in me as a stunning colleague and now it had put a noose around my neck, which I might be using to unintentionally hang myself. I had to step out of the office and go for a walk because my heart was palpitating.

Later, after Legal had reviewed the document and handed it to me to sign, my hands got clammy when I saw my name under the signature line. I pulled out my pen and it was shaking. I couldn't believe I was being given so much responsibility.

Somehow, at the same time, I also felt liberated. One of the reasons I left Yahoo was that I didn't feel ownership for anything. Even though I might have come up with an idea and started an initiative, by the time it got approved by everyone and his mother it didn't feel like mine any more. If it crashed, I'd feel: "Well, thirty other people agreed! It's not my fault!"

It took me about six months to get used to this at Netflix. I learned that getting it perfect doesn't matter. What matters is moving quickly and learning from what we're doing. I'm at a place where I can take responsibility for my own decisions. I've prepared my entire career for this. I signed a 100-million-dollar multilevel deal recently—and it doesn't feel scary anymore. It feels great.

Often talented people find it liberating to be the informed captain—and many join Netflix because of this freedom. Some, like Diego, also find it more terrifying than comfortable. If so, they learn to adjust or move on.

INNOVATION CYCLE STEP 4: IF IT WINS, CELEBRATE IT; IF IT FAILS, SUNSHINE IT

 If Sheila's initiative succeeds, make it clear you're delighted. You might pat her on the back, offer her a glass of champagne, or take the entire team out to dinner. How you celebrate is up to you. The one thing you **must** do is show, ideally in public, that you are pleased she went ahead despite your doubts and offer a clear "You were right! I was wrong!" to show all employees it's okay to buck the opinion of the boss.

If Sheila's initiative fails, the way you, the boss, respond is even more critical. After a failure, everyone will be watching to see what you do. One possible course of action would be to punish, scold, or shame Sheila. In 800 BC, Greek merchants whose businesses had failed were forced to sit in the marketplace with a basket over their heads. In seventeenth-century France, bankrupt business owners were denounced in the town square and, if they didn't want to go straight to prison, had to endure the shame of wearing a green bonnet every time they went out in public.

In today's organizations, people tend to be more discreet about failure. As the boss, you could look at Sheila sideways, sigh, and whisper, "Well, I knew this would happen." Or you could put an arm around her shoulder, and say in a friendly voice, "Next time, take my advice." Alternatively, you could give her a short lecture about all the things the company needs to accomplish and what a shame it is to have wasted time on a failure that was so clearly predictable. (From Sheila's point of view, a basket on the head or a green bonnet is beginning to look quite appealing.)

If you adopt any of these strategies, one thing is certain. No matter what you say in the future, everyone on the team will know that "don't seek to please your boss" is a joke, that all your talk about chips and placing bets is a charade, and that you care more about error prevention than innovation after all.

We suggest instead a three-part response:

1. Ask what learning came from the project.
2. Don't make a big deal about it.
3. Ask her to "sunshine" the failure.

1. ASK WHAT LEARNING CAME FROM THE PROJECT

Often a failed project is a critical step in getting to success. Once or twice a year, at our product meetings, I ask all of our managers to complete a simple form outlining their bets from the last few years, divided into three categories: bets that went well, bets that didn't go well, and open bets. Then we break up into smaller groups and discuss the items in each category and what we've learned from each bet. This exercise reminds everyone that they are expected to implement bold ideas and that, as part of the process, some risks won't pay off. They see that making bets is not a question of individuals' successes and failures but rather a learning process that, in total, catapults the business forward. It also helps newer people get used to admitting publicly that they screwed up on a bunch of stuff—as we all do.

2. DON'T MAKE A BIG DEAL ABOUT IT

 If you make a big deal about a bet that didn't work out, you'll shut down all future risk-taking. People will learn that you preach but don't practice dispersed decision-making. Chris Jaffe, who was hired as a director of product innovation in 2010, clearly remembers a time Reed did not make a big deal after Chris wasted hundreds of hours of talent and resources on a failed bet of his own:

Back in 2010 you could stream TV shows to computers but there weren't many smart TVs. If you wanted to stream a Netflix show to your television, you needed to do that through a PlayStation or a Wii.

I wanted people to reach into their closets, pull out their old Wii devices and start streaming Netflix. That would bring the Internet to the living room in a way most of our customers had never experienced. I decided to use a team of my designers and engineers to improve the Netflix interface on the Wii. The current interface was super-basic. Under my supervision, my group devoted thousands of hours to developing something more complex, and, I believed, attractive to users. The team worked on it full time for over a year. We named the project "Explorer."

At completion we tested the new interface out on two hundred thousand Netflix users. The news we got made me feel sick. The new interface was driving consumers to use the Wii interface LESS! We thought it must be a bug in the system, so we checked everything and launched the test again. Same thing. The users preferred the more basic original version.

I was still pretty new at Netflix. Before this project I'd had one successful innovation, and now this massive flop. We had a quarterly meeting with Reed called "Consumer Science." The product managers would get up onstage and give an update on their product bets. What had worked? What hadn't? What had we learned? All of my peers were there as well as all of my managers (my boss, Todd Yellin; his boss, Neil Hunt; and Reed).

I didn't know what would happen. Would Reed rail at me for having wasted thousands of hours and hundreds of thousands of dollars? Would Neil cringe? Would Todd wish he'd never hired me?

We talk about sunshining our failed bets at Netflix, which means talking openly and publicly about things that go wrong. I'd seen leaders speak about their mistakes with such force and transparency that I decided to shine not just some sun on my failure, but a big fat strobe light.

I got up onstage. The room was dark. I put up my first slide. In red capital letters it said:

EXPLORER: A BIG BET FOR ME THAT FAILED

I talked about the project, detailing every part that had and hadn't worked and explaining that this had been one hundred percent my bet. Reed asked some questions and we talked about which parts of the project led to the flop. Then he asked what we'd learned. I told him we'd learned that complexity kills consumer engagement. That, by the way, is a lesson that the entire company now understands as a result of the Explorer project.

"Okay, that's interesting. Let's remember that," Reed concluded. "Well that project's over. What's next?"

Eighteen months later, with a few successes under his belt, Chris was promoted to vice president of product innovation.

Reed's reaction is the only type of leadership response that encourages innovative thinking. When a bet fails, the manager must be careful to express interest in the takeaways but no condemnation. Everyone in that room left with two major messages in mind. First, if you take a bet and it fails, Reed will ask you what you learned. Second, if you try out something big and it doesn't work out, nobody will scream—and you won't lose your job.

3. ASK HER TO "SUNSHINE" THE FAILURE

 If you make a bet and it fails, it's important to speak openly and frequently about what happened. If you're the boss, make it clear you expect all failed bets to be detailed out in the open. Chris could have brushed the failure under the table, blamed someone else, or pointed fingers defensively. Instead he showed great courage and leadership capacity by addressing the failed bet head-on.

In so doing, he helped not just himself but all of Netflix. It's critical that your employees are continually hearing about the failed bets of others, so that they are encouraged to take bets (that of course might fail) themselves. You can't have a culture of innovation if you don't have this.

At Netflix, we try to shine a bright light on every failed bet. We encourage employees to write open memos explaining candidly what happened, followed by a description of the lessons learned. Here's an abridged example of one such communication. By chance, it was also written by Chris Jaffe but several years later, in 2016, about another project that didn't pay off called "Memento." This document is often passed around Netflix as an example of how to sunshine a failed bet in writing.

When you sunshine your failed bets, everyone

Memento update – Product Management Team: Chris J

Around 18 months ago, I brought a memo to the product strategy meeting outlining an idea to include supplemental title-level metadata such as actor bios and related titles into our second screen playback experience.

Following a vibrant debate, I decided to pursue the project. We moved forward building the Memento experience on Android mobile. This project took more than a year. Last September we had a release build that we launched in a small test.

In February, I concluded that we should not move forward and ended the project.

It is important to underscore that the decision to pursue Memento and continue investing in it throughout was solely mine. This outcome and the resulting cost are my complete responsibility. Having invested in this for over a year and then decided not to launch has wasted time and resources and also brought learning. Some of my takeaways:

- There was real opportunity cost in pursuing this project which, as a result, slowed us down on important mobile innovation. This was a big miss from me on leadership and focus.

- I should have more thoughtfully considered the limited ability to gain insight from the small second screen population. I assumed that it would grow larger, but I was wrong.

- I should have considered more deeply the suggestion from the initial strategy meeting that Darwin would be a better test platform for this idea. This reminds me to be open to challenging my own preconceived notions.

- When I decided to pursue this after the product strategy meeting, I should have come back with a memo to debate the notion of launching with a flat holdback. This was misaligned with how we approach product innovation—not how we do things here.

- As I got into the project I should have realized its declining value and shut it down months ago. The crash rates in September should have been a clear signal to me to halt our work on it. The end always seemed near, which was an illusion. As it often is.

wins. You win because people learn they can trust you to tell the truth and to take responsibility for your actions. The team wins because it learns from the lessons that came out of the project. And the company wins because everyone sees clearly that failed bets are an inherent part of an innovative success wheel. We shouldn't be afraid of our failures. We should embrace them.

And sunshine mistakes even more!

 Using the terminology of the last chapter, a calculated bet that fails at Netflix is not so much an SOS (stuff of secrets) as an actual mistake is. When Chris spoke about his failed bets, Explorer and Memento, he had nothing to be embarrassed about. He was doing exactly what Netflix asked of him: thinking boldly and placing his chips on ideas he believed in. In this context, it's not so hard to stand up onstage or send out a memo saying: "Look I made this bet, and the results were not as I'd hoped."

But when you make an actual mistake it can be highly embarrassing, especially when that mistake suggests a serious lapse of judgment or negligence.

When the embarrassing mistake is a big one, the temptation to distance yourself from it is great. This is not recommended at Netflix. To survive a big mistake, you must lean all the more into the sunshine. Talk openly about it and you will be forgiven, at least the first few times. But if you brush your mistakes under the rug or keep making them (which you're more likely to do if you're in denial about them), the end result will be much more serious.

Yasemin Dormen, a Turkish social media expert living in Amsterdam, showed clearly that she understood this expectation when she described a mistake she had made promoting season 4 of the Netflix hit show **Black Mirror:**

> In **Black Mirror** there is a character named Waldo who is a blue cartoon bear. The fourth season was due for release on December 29, 2017, so I dreamed up a holiday scheme to promote it.
>
> We would send a mysterious promotional message to hundreds of subscribers to the Turkish equivalent of Reddit from "iamwaldo." The content would be cryptic and alluring: "We know what you're up to. Watch and see what we will do." I hoped people would respond by tweeting their friends: "Is Waldo back?" "Is **Black Mirror** season 4 out?" I was looking forward to the positive buzz it would cause.
>
> My big mistake was that I didn't socialize the idea with anybody. I was busy getting ready for a week off with my family. I didn't inform my PR colleagues in other countries. I didn't farm for dissent with the Netflix communications team. I just set it up and went on vacation with my dad to Greece.

On December 29, Dad and I were in an Athens museum listening to a tour guide when my phone started buzzing like mad. My colleagues around the world were going berserk about the "iamwaldo" message coming out of Turkey and the media firestorm it was causing. "Is this us?" one text read. I started a frantic search on my phone and saw Turkish media was going crazy.

Technology blog **Engadget** explained what happened like this:

'Tis the season for ominous, intrusive internet promotional campaigns. Netflix has spooked users on a Turkish equivalent to Reddit, Ekşi Sözlük, by sending them promotional direct messages meant to hype up the debut of **Black Mirror**'s fourth season. The messages from "iamwaldo" (a reference to **Black Mirror** season two's "The Waldo Moment") came in the middle of the night and sounded almost like a threat: "we know what you're up to," they read, "watch and see what we will do."

The snafu even made the mainstream British media: "Black Mirror season 4: Viewers RAGE over 'creepy marketing' stunt. 'Not cool!'" shouted the headline from the news site **Express**. Yasemin recalled the whole painful experience:

My heart sunk into my socks. I felt my stomach turn. This mistake was one hundred percent mine. I'd set up this campaign and hadn't socialized it with anyone. My colleagues were mad and my boss was mystified.

My father took me aside. I was practically in tears as I explained what had happened. "Do you think you'll get fired?" he gasped. And that made me laugh. "No, Dad! We don't get fired at Netflix for things like that. We get fired **for not** taking risks, for **not** making bold moves. Or for not talking openly about it when we screw up."

Of course, I won't make the mistake of not socializing another media event. That **might** get me fired.

I spent the rest of my holiday outlining for everyone what mistake I'd made and what I'd learned from the mistake. I wrote memos and made dozens of calls. I spent that entire vacation sunshining—and not the kind you normally do on the beach in Greece.

Yasemin has gone on to have a great career at Netflix. Five months after the "iamwaldo" blunder she was given a position of senior marketing manager, increasing her responsibility 150 percent, and eighteen months after she was promoted to director of marketing.

Most important were the lessons that not just Yasemin, but the entire Netflix Marketing team learned from her mistake. "When we hire new marketing people, we have a series of historic cases we cover with them to teach what not to do. The Turkey **Black Mirror** campaign is one of our favorite teaching cases and everyone talks about it." Yasemin explains. "It demonstrates so clearly the importance of socializing and what happens when you don't do it. But it also helped all of us in marketing to remember our goal at Netflix is to create moments of joy. So don't run a campaign that's a little creepy. Don't try to spook the public into watching our shows. Instead, a good campaign should be exciting, joyful, and just plain fun."

THE SIXTH DOT

If you have high talent density and organizational transparency firmly in place, a faster, more innovative decision-making process is possible. Your employees can dream big, test their ideas, and implement bets they believe in, even when in opposition to those hierarchically above them.

▶ TAKEAWAYS FROM CHAPTER 6

- In a fast and innovative company, ownership of critical, big-ticket decisions should be dispersed across the workforce at all different levels, not allocated according to hierarchical status.

- In order for this to work the leader must teach her staff the Netflix principle, "Don't seek to please your boss."

- When new employees join the company, tell them they have a handful of metaphorical chips that they can make bets with. Some gambles will succeed, and some will fail. A worker's performance will be judged on the collective outcome of his bets, not on the results from one single instance.

- To help your workforce make good bets, encourage them to farm for dissent, socialize the idea, and for big bets, test it out.

- Teach your employees that when a bet fails, they should sunshine it openly.

Toward a Culture of Freedom and Responsibility

Your company is now benefiting heavily from a culture of Freedom and Responsibility. You're moving faster, innovating more, and your employees are happier. But as the organization grows, you may find that it's difficult to maintain these cultural elements in which you have so carefully invested.

This is what happened to us at Netflix. Between 2002 and 2008 we laid the foundation for most of the aspects outlined in the first six chapters of this book. But when we had dozens of new employees joining us from other companies every week, it became more challenging to shift people's mind-sets to working in the Netflix way.

For this reason, we have introduced a set of techniques for all managers in the company to use in order to assure that the critical elements of talent density, candor, and freedom persist despite change and growth. These techniques are the topic of section 3.

SECTION THREE

TECHNIQUES TO REINFORCE A CULTURE OF FREEDOM AND RESPONSIBILITY

Max up talent density...
7 ▸ The Keeper Test

Max up candor...
8 ▸ A Circle of Feedback

And eliminate most controls...!
9 ▸ Lead with Context, Not Control

This section focuses on practical techniques you can implement in your team or organization in order to reinforce the concepts we've covered in the first two sections. In chapter 7 we'll explore the Keeper Test, the primary device used at Netflix for encouraging managers to maintain high talent density. In chapter 8 we'll look at two processes encouraging plentiful and ongoing feedback between bosses, employees, and peers. In chapter 9 we'll consider exactly how to adjust your management style to provide greater decision-making freedom to the people you lead.

MAX UP TALENT DENSITY . . .

7

THE KEEPER TEST

It was the week between Christmas and New Year 2018, and at Netflix we had a lot to celebrate. The past six weeks had been some of the most successful in the history of the company. I was feeling great when I called up Ted Sarandos to congratulate him.

In November Ted's team released **Roma**, a film written and directed by Alfonso Cuarón, following the life of a live-in housekeeper for a middle-class Mexican family. **Roma** was called a "masterpiece" by **The New York Times** and hailed as the best Netflix original movie ever. The film went on to win Best Director and Best Foreign Language Film at the Oscars.

A few weeks later Ted's team released **Bird Box**, a thriller starring Sandra Bullock as a woman who must take a perilous journey with her children—blindfolded down a raging river—to save their lives.

Bird Box was released on December 13 and within a week over forty-five million Netflix accounts had watched it, the best first seven days ever for any Netflix original.

"Pretty amazing six weeks you've had!" I told Ted. He responded, "Yes, we've all picked well!" I must have looked puzzled because he clarified. "Well you picked me, and I picked Scott Stuber. Scott picked Jackie and Terril. Jackie and Terril picked **Roma** and **Bird Box**. That's great picking!"

Ted was right. With our dispersed decision-making model, if you pick the very best people and they pick the very best people (and so on down the line) great things will happen. Ted calls this the "hierarchy of picking" and it's what a workforce built on high talent density is all about.

Picking sounds primarily like it's about hiring. Ideally, an organization could just pick carefully, and these well-chosen employees would flourish forever. The reality is tougher. No matter how careful you are, sometimes you will make hiring mistakes, sometimes people won't grow as much as you had hoped, and sometimes your company's needs change. To achieve the highest level of talent density you have to be prepared to make tough calls. If you're serious about talent density, you have to get in the habit of doing something a lot harder: firing a good employee when you think you can get a great one.

One of the reasons this is so difficult in many companies is because business leaders are continually telling their employees, "We are a family." But a high-talent-density work environment is not a family.

A FAMILY IS ABOUT STAYING TOGETHER REGARDLESS OF "PERFORMANCE"

For many centuries, almost all businesses were run by families, so it's no surprise that today the most common metaphor CEOs use for their companies is the family. The family represents belonging, comfort, and commitment to helping one another over the long term. Who wouldn't want their employees to feel a deep fondness for and loyalty to the company they work for?

The people greeters at Walmart were encouraged for decades to think of themselves as part of the "Walmart family." When trained how to greet customers, they were told they should welcome everyone as if they were receiving a guest in their own home.

Former Netflix vice president of engineering, Daniel Jacobson, worked at National Public Radio (NPR) for a decade in Washington, DC, before working at Netflix for a decade. He explained the benefits of the family ethos at NPR like this:

I began at NPR in late 1999 as the first full-time software engineer hired online. When I got there, I was super-pumped. People who want to work at NPR believe in the mission and love the organization's dedication to news and information. That shared purpose resulted in a culture that at times felt more like a family than a workplace. It was very appealing, and I developed a lot of close relationships at work.

NPR had such a strong family culture that many people turned it into their real family. One of the "founding mothers" of NPR, Susan Stamberg, maintained a "Met and Married List" for NPR employees. NPR is a relatively small organization and the list of couples who had met there was pretty long.

Daniel also remembers some of his colleagues saying, "If you're at NPR for three years, you're at NPR for life."

Of course families aren't just about love and loyalty. In families we cut each other slack and put up with quirks and crankiness because we are committed to supporting one another for the long term. When people behave badly, don't pull their weight, or aren't able to fulfill their responsibilities, we find a way to make do. We don't have a choice. We are stuck together. That's what family is all about.

The second part of Daniel's NPR story illustrates the problem with treating a workforce like a family:

The culture at NPR has a lot of advantages and works for them. But after a while, I started to see the problems of having a family ethos at work. There was a software engineer on my team, Patrick. Although he was an experienced engineer, he didn't have the skills to accomplish his job well. He would continually need extra time to complete his projects and would often have significant bugs or problems in his code. Sometimes other engineers needed to be included in his projects to ensure that we could get the work done effectively.

Patrick had a great attitude, which added complexity. He was eager to do the right thing and wanted to prove that he could operate independently. We all yearned for him to succeed and we would seek out opportunities that would fit well with his limited skills. But his work quality didn't compare to that of his colleagues. Every day I needed to worry about him and I didn't need to worry about them. He was a lovely person, but the deliverables weren't there.

Patrick took up so much of my time—and so much of the team's time correcting his mistakes—that it became a real problem. The best engineers on the team were often frustrated and looking for me to intervene. I worried that some of them were becoming so irritated they might look for jobs elsewhere.

I could see that the team would have been considerably more effective without Patrick. Even if I couldn't replace him with someone else.

I spoke to my boss, who encouraged me to seek out different kinds of work that would take advantage of Patrick's strengths while shielding others from his weaknesses. Firing him wasn't even part of the discussion. We didn't have cause. He hadn't done anything wrong. The organization was such a family the response was: "He's one of us. We're all in this together. We'll work around him."

FROM FAMILY TO TEAM

 In the early Netflix days, our managers also worked to foster a family-like environment. But, after our 2001 layoffs, when we saw the performance dramatically improve, we realized family is not a good metaphor for a high-talent-density workforce.

We wanted employees to feel committed, interconnected, and part of a greater whole. But we didn't want people to see their jobs as a lifetime arrangement. A job should be something you do for that magical period of time when you are the best person for that job and that job is the best position for you.

Once you stop learning or stop excelling, that's the moment for you to pass that spot onto someone who is better fitted for it and to move on to a better role for you.

But if Netflix wasn't a family, what were we? A group of individuals looking out for ourselves? That definitely wasn't what we were going for. After a lot of discussion Patty suggested that we think of Netflix as a professional sports team.

Initially this didn't sound very profound. The metaphor of team for company is just about as tired as the metaphor of family. But as she kept talking, I started to see what she meant:

I just watched **Bull Durham** with my kids. On a pro baseball team, the players have great relationships. These players are really close. They support one another. They celebrate together, console one another, and know each other's plays so well that they can move as one without speaking. But they are not a family. The coach swaps and trades players in and out throughout the year in order to make sure they always have the best player in every position.

Patty was right. At Netflix, I want each manager to run her department like the best professional teams, working to create strong feelings of commitment, cohesion, and camaraderie, while continually making tough decisions to ensure the best player is manning each post.

A professional sports team is a good metaphor for high talent density because athletes on professional teams:

- Demand excellence, counting on the manager to make sure every position is filled by the best person at any given time.
- Train to win, expecting to receive candid and continuous feedback about how to up their game from the coach and from one another.
- Know effort isn't enough, recognizing that, if they put in a B performance despite an A for effort, they will be thanked and respectfully swapped out for another player.

On a high-performing team, collaboration and trust work well because all the members are exceptionally skilled both at what they do and at working well with others. For an individual to be deemed excellent she can't just be amazing at the game; she has to be selfless and put the team before her own ego. She has to know when to pass the ball, how to help her teammates thrive, and recognize that the only way to win is for the team to win together. This is exactly the type of culture we were going for at Netflix.

This is when we started saying that at Netflix:

WE ARE A TEAM, NOT A FAMILY

If we are going to be a championship team, then we want the best performer possible in every position. The old notion is that an employee has to do something wrong, or be inadequate, to lose their job. But in a pro, or Olympic, sports team, the players understand the coach's role is to upgrade—if necessary—to move from good to great. Team members are playing to stay on the team with every game. For people who value job security over winning championships, Netflix is not the right choice, and we try to be clear and nonjudgmental about that. But for those who value being on winning teams, our culture provides a great opportunity. Like any team successfully competing at the highest level, we form deep relationships and care about each other.

THE KEEPER TEST

Of course, managers at Netflix, like good people anywhere, want to feel positive about their actions. To get them to feel good about cutting someone they like and respect requires them to desire to help the organization and to recognize that everyone at Netflix is happier and more successful when there is a star in every position. So we ask the manager: Would the company be better off if you let go of Samuel and looked for someone more effective? If they say "yes," that's a clear sign that it's time to look for another player.

We also encourage all managers to consider each of their employees regularly and make sure they've got the best person in every spot. To help managers on the judgment calls, we talk about the Keeper Test:

IF A PERSON ON YOUR TEAM WERE TO QUIT TOMORROW, WOULD YOU TRY TO CHANGE THEIR MIND? OR WOULD YOU ACCEPT THEIR RESIGNATION, PERHAPS WITH A LITTLE RELIEF? IF THE LATTER, YOU SHOULD GIVE THEM A SEVERANCE PACKAGE NOW, AND LOOK FOR A STAR, SOMEONE YOU WOULD FIGHT TO KEEP.

We try to apply the Keeper Test to everyone, including ourselves. Would the company be better off with someone else in my role? The goal is to remove any shame for anyone let go from Netflix. Think of an Olympic team sport like hockey. To get cut from the team is very disappointing, but the person is admired for having had the guts and skill to make the squad in the first place. When someone is let go at Netflix, we hope for the same. We all stay friends and there is no shame.

Patty McCord herself is one example. After working together for over a decade, I started feeling that it would be best for us to have someone new in the role. I shared these thoughts with Patty, and we talked about what was leading me there. As it turned out, she wanted to work less, so she left Netflix and it was very amicable. Seven years later we remain close friends and informal advisers to one another.

In another case, Leslie Kilgore was incredible for us as chief marketing officer, and she was instrumental in our culture, our battle with Blockbuster, and our growth overall. She was, and is, a great business thinker. But with **House of Cards** launching, and a future of marketing titles rather than making offers, I knew we needed someone with deep Hollywood studio experience, partially to make up for my own lack of showbiz knowledge. So I let go of Leslie, but she was willing to serve on our board, so she has become one of my bosses and has been a great company director for many years.

So the Keeper Test is real and all our managers at all levels in the company use it consistently. I tell my bosses, the board of directors, that I should be treated no differently. They shouldn't have to wait for me to fail to replace me. They should replace me once they have a potential CEO who is likely to be more effective. I find it motivating that I have to play for my position every quarter, and I try to keep improving myself to stay ahead.

 At Netflix, you might be working your hardest to do your very best, giving your all to help the company succeed, managing to deliver pretty good results, and then you walk into work one day and boom . . . you're unemployed. Not because there was some unavoidable financial crisis or big unforeseen layoffs, but because your deliverables are not as amazing as your boss had hoped they'd be. Your performance is merely adequate.

In the introduction we looked at some of the most controversial slides of the Netflix Culture Deck that explains Reed's philosophy:

These slides pose tough questions. In order to make sure Reed answers those questions, we'll set the rest of this chapter up like a Q and A:

The other people should get a generous severance now,
so we can open a slot to try to find a star for that role

The **Keeper Test** Managers Use:

Which of my people,
if they told me they were leaving,
for a similar job at a peer company,
would I fight hard to keep at Netflix?

NETFLIX   26

AN INTERVIEW WITH REED

Question 1

According to former chief product officer, Neil Hunt, "We are a team, not a family" has caused controversy at Netflix since the early days. He remembers:

> Back in 2002 Reed organized a leadership offsite meeting in Half Moon Bay, where he emphasized that we must continually go through the same rigorous exercise that he and Patty had gone through preparing for the layoffs. We must ask ourselves on an ongoing basis which employees were no longer the best choice for their positions and, if they were not able to become "best choice" after receiving feedback, we would need to have the courage to let them go.

I was taken aback. I spoke to the group about the difference between penguins and elephants. Penguins abandon those in the group that are weak or struggling, while elephants rally around them and nurture them back to health. "Are you telling me we are going to choose to be penguins?" I asked.

Reed, are you not concerned about Netflix being the callous penguins in Neil's story? Losing your job is a big deal. That job loss will impact that person's financial situation, reputation, family dynamics, and career. Some people are on immigration status and, without a job, might be deported. You, of course, are very wealthy, so losing your salary would be no skin off your back. But that's not the case for most of your employees.

Is it even ethical to let go of people who are doing their best but failing to deliver amazing results?

Answer 1

 We pay our employees top of their personal market, so they are all paid very well. Part of that agreement is that they will play on the team as long as they are the best player for the spot. They understand that the needs of our company change quickly and that we expect outstanding performance. So, each employee who chooses to join the Netflix team opts in to our high-talent-density approach. We are transparent about our tactics and many employees are delighted to be surrounded by such high-quality colleagues and happy to put up with some job risk in return. Other people may prefer long-term job security and they choose not to join Netflix. So yes, I believe our approach is ethical. It is also highly popular with most of our employees.

That said, since our performance bar is so high, it seems only fair that, if we take away people's jobs, we should give them enough money to get started on their next projects. We give everyone we dismiss a big severance—enough to take care of themselves and their families until they move on to another job. Each time we let go of someone, we offer several months' salary (from four months for an individual contributor to nine months for a vice president). That's why we say:

ADEQUATE PERFORMANCE GETS A GENEROUS SEVERANCE

To some people, this will sound prohibitively expensive. And it probably would be, if it weren't for our efforts to eliminate unnecessary control processes.

In many companies in the US, when a manager decides to let go of someone, he is required to put in place a process called a performance improvement plan (PIP). This means that the manager documents weekly discussions with the employee over a period of months, demonstrating in writing that the employee has not managed to succeed despite feedback. PIPs rarely help employees improve and they delay the firing by many weeks.

PIPs were invented for two reasons. The first is to protect employees from losing their job without getting constructive feedback and the opportunity to improve. But with our culture of candor at Netflix, people get loads of feedback every day. Before any employee is let go, he should have heard clearly and regularly what he needs to do in order to improve.

The second is to protect the company from a lawsuit. We ask exiting employees, in order to receive the generous severance we are offering, to sign an agreement that they won't sue us. Almost all accept the offer. They get a big chunk of money and can focus on the next step of their careers.

PIPs are of course expensive. If you put someone on a four-month PIP, that's four months you have to pay an underperformer and countless hours spent by the line manager and HR enforcing and documenting the process. Instead of pouring that capital into a prolonged PIP, give it to the employee in a nice, big, up-front severance package, tell him you're sorry it didn't work out, and wish him well in his next adventure.

Question 2

There is a scene in the movie **The Hunger Games** in which the teenage protagonist Katniss, played by Jennifer Lawrence, stands on a small platform dressed in camouflage gear and surveys her competition. Twenty-four young people between the ages of twelve and eighteen have been drafted for a televised event pitting youth against each other. Only one of the players will win and all the others will die. If you want to live, you have to kill the competition.

When I began interviews at Netflix I expected that it would feel a lot like **The Hunger Games** around the office. Every professional team-sports player knows that for someone to win others have to lose: you have to compete for your seat.

I'd also read about similar-sounding practices used in the past by companies like Microsoft that are now generally considered to have incited harmful internal competition. For example, until 2012, Microsoft managers were asked to rank their employees on a scale from top to bottom performers and encouraged to let go of those at the bottom.

In a **Vanity Fair** article titled, "Microsoft's Lost Decade," journalist Kurt Eichenwald quoted a former employee:

> If you were on a team of ten people, you walked in the first day knowing that, no matter how good everyone was, two people were going to get a great review, seven were going to get mediocre reviews, and one was going to get a terrible review. It leads to employees focusing on competing with each other rather than competing with other companies.

One Microsoft engineer reportedly said:

> People will openly sabotage other people's efforts. One of the most valuable things I learned was to give the appearance of being courteous while withholding just enough information from colleagues to ensure they didn't get ahead of me in the rankings.

Why should the team-not-a-family at Netflix be any different? I expected to find Netflix employees scratching and backstabbing to keep their spots too. In truth, I didn't find this during my interviews.

Reed, given how tough it is to get and maintain a spot on the Netflix team, how do you manage to stave off internal competitiveness?

Answer 2

 Accidentally inciting internal competition is a real concern for organizations like ours that seek to increase their talent density. Many have implemented processes and rules to encourage their managers to get rid of mediocre employees and have fallen into systems that accidentally stoke internal competition. The worst is so-called stack ranking, also known as the "vitality curve" or, more colloquially, as "rank-and-yank."

The Vanity Fair article Erin quotes above outlines one version of stack ranking. GE and Goldman Sachs have also tried stack-ranking systems to increase talent density. Jack Welch, perhaps the first CEO to use the method, famously encouraged managers at GE to rank their employees every year and to let go of the bottom 10 percent in order to keep performance levels high.

In 2015, The New York Times reported that GE had, like Microsoft in 2012, dropped the evaluation method. As one might expect, stack ranking sabotages collaboration and destroys the joy of high-performing teamwork.

We encourage our managers to apply the Keeper Test regularly. But we are very careful to not have any firing quotas or ranking system. Rank-and-yank or "you must let go of X percent of your people" is just the type of rule-based process that we try to avoid. More important, these methods get managers to let go of mediocre employees, but they kill teamwork at the same time. I want our high-performing employees to compete against Netflix's competitors, not one another. With rank-and-yank what you gain in talent density you lose in reduced collaboration.

Fortunately, there is no reason to choose between high talent density and strong collaboration. With the Keeper Test we can achieve both. That's because there is one critical way we are not like a professional sports team. On the Netflix team there is no fixed number of slots. Our sport isn't being played to a rule book and we don't have limits on how many people we play with. One employee doesn't have to lose for the other to win. On the contrary, the more excellence we have on the team, the more we accomplish. The more we accomplish, the more we grow. The more we grow, the more positions we add to our roster. The more positions we add, the more space there is for high-performing talent.

Question 3

A November 2018 issue of **The Week** magazine ran an article titled, "Netflix's Culture of Fear." It quotes Rhett Jones of the tech website Gizmodo, who calls out Netflix for "brutal honesty, insider lingo, and constant fear." Less than a month earlier, Shalini Ramachandran and Joe Flint wrote in a **Wall Street Journal** article based on interviews with Netflix employees: "At a meeting in late spring of Netflix public-relations executives, one said every day he comes to work he fears he is going to get fired."

I too found in my interviews that some Netflix employees spoke openly of an ongoing fear that they will lose their jobs. One was Marta Munk de Alba, a recruiter in the Amsterdam office. She is a licensed psychologist who moved from Spain to the Netherlands in 2016 to join the Netflix Human Resources team. Here is her story:

> My first months on the job, I was filled with terror that my colleagues would discover I was not worthy of their dream team and I would lose my job. I saw firsthand the quality of my colleagues. I would think, "Do I really belong here? How long will it take for them to figure out I'm a fake?" Every morning, I would get into the elevator at eight a.m., and as I hit the elevator button, it was like a

trigger. The air would catch in my chest. I was sure that when the doors slid open my boss would be standing on the other side waiting to fire me.

I felt that if I lost my job, I would be losing the most important opportunity of my life. I worked like crazy—deep into the night—and pushed myself harder than I had ever done before. But the fear continued.

Derek, now a director at Netflix, provided another example:

During my first year at Netflix, I thought every day about whether I would be let go. For nine months I didn't unpack my boxes, because I was sure the day I unpacked would be the day I lost my job. It wasn't just me. My coworkers talked constantly about the Keeper Test. When we were in a cab or having lunch, the number one topic of conversation was always losing our jobs—those who had recently been let go, those who we thought would be let go, whether WE might be let go. It was only when my boss promoted me to director that I saw how misplaced my fears had been.

It's clear that the Keeper Test increases talent density, but it also creates worry. Employees report feelings ranging from "mildly concerned" to "occasionally terrified" that they will be cut from the team.

Reed, what are you doing to mitigate a culture of fear at Netflix?

Answer 3

 In white-water kayaking they teach you to look at the clear, safe water next to the dangerous hole you want to avoid. Experts have found that if you stare at what you are desperate to avoid, you are actually more likely to paddle into it. Similarly, at Netflix, we tell all employees it is best to focus on learning, teamwork, and accomplishment. If a person gets obsessed by their risk of being let go (or an athlete becomes obsessed with the risk of being injured) they can't play light and confident, and this can bring about the very troubles they were trying to prevent.

THE KEEPER TEST PROMPT

There are two steps we take at Netflix to minimize fear around the office.

The first step is that any employee who is feeling the type of anxiety that Marta and Derek discussed is encouraged to use what we call the "Keeper Test Prompt" as soon as possible. That almost always improves the situation.

During your next one-to-one with your boss ask the following question:

"IF I WERE THINKING OF LEAVING, HOW HARD WOULD YOU WORK TO CHANGE MY MIND?"

When you get the answer, you'll know exactly where you stand. Chris Carey is a senior tools engineer at the Netflix Silicon Valley office and one of many who ask the question on a regular basis:

> When you ask your boss the Keeper Test Prompt question, there are three possible outcomes. One, your boss might say he would fight hard to keep you. In that case any fear you've had about your performance will immediately go away. That's good.
>
> Two, your boss might give you an uncertain response with clear feedback about how to improve. That's good too because you hear what you need to do to excel in your role.
>
> Three, if your boss feels he would not fight hard to keep you, you may have caused him to notice something negative about your performance that wasn't previously in the forefront of his mind. This makes asking the question a little scary. But it is

still good because it sparks a clear discussion about whether this job is the right fit for your skill set and ensures you won't be blindsided to hear one morning that you've lost your job.

When Chris started at Netflix, he vowed to use the Keeper Test Prompt each year in November, so he'd never be taken by surprise.

I'm a software coder. I'm happiest spending 95 percent of my time head down in code. A year into my tenure at Netflix, I was pleasantly coding my life away. I asked my boss: "Paul, would you fight to keep me if I told you I was leaving?" His answer was a loud yes. That felt great.

Later I inherited a project that was also coding, but we had employees at Netflix who were using the tool I was developing. Paul suggested on several occasions that I set up focus group interviews with internal users. But I have some social anxiety, so instead of holding meetings, I chose to use my own intuition about how to improve the product.

November rolled around. I asked Paul the Keeper Test Prompt question again. This time his answer was less positive: "At this moment, I don't know if

I would fight to keep you. You can go back to your previous job, where you were excelling. But this role requires that you interact more with our users. If you want to keep this job, you'll have to lead focus groups and give presentations. It will take you out of your comfort zone and I don't know if you will succeed."

I decided to take the risk. I worked hard. I took a presentation class online and practiced in front of my neighbors. The day of my first Netflix presentation I got up at six a.m., unicycled for four hours, took a shower, and walked directly into the meeting room for my eleven a.m. presentation. My goal was to work out all my anxiety and not give myself time to get too nervous. For the focus group meetings I tried other methods like pre-discussion videos to minimize the amount of time I'd have to speak in front of the group.

It was only May, but I put the Keeper Test on the agenda again. I needed to understand if I was at risk of losing my job. "Would you fight to keep me?" I asked Paul.

Paul looked right in my eyes and said: "You are outstanding at ninety percent of this job. You are innovative, meticulous, and hardworking. For the other ten percent you've been able to incorporate feedback and you are now doing fine. You can continue to push yourself to interact more with our internal users. But you are doing high-level work. If you told me you were leaving, I would fight really hard to keep you."

All three times Chris asked the question, he got important information. The first answer felt good, but it didn't add much value. The second was the most stressful but provided him with a straightforward plan of action. The third reassured Chris his efforts were paying off.

The second technique that we use to abate the fear of job loss is the "post-exit Q and A."

POST-EXIT Q & A

There is nothing more ominous than people on your team disappearing from the roster with no word about how the decision was made or how much warning that person received. The biggest worry people have when they learn a colleague has been let go is whether that person had feedback or whether the termination came out of the blue.

Yoka, a content specialist in our Tokyo office, tells this story. Her anecdote is particularly potent because Japanese companies traditionally offer employment for life. Even today, firing a worker is rare in Japan. Many of our employees there have no previous experience of a colleague losing his job:

My closest colleague, Aika, worked for a man named Haru, who was really not a good boss. Aika and her entire team were suffering under Haru's management. I was hoping something would happen, but when Haru lost his job my own reaction surprised me.

One morning I came to the office a little later than usual. It was January and there was snow on the road. Aika raced to my desk, her face flushed. "Did you hear what happened?" Haru's boss Jim had flown from California and met with Haru early in the morning, before anyone else arrived at work. By the time Aika arrived Haru had been let go and was already packing his boxes and preparing to say goodbye. Now Haru was gone and we wouldn't see him again. I burst into tears. I didn't feel close to him, but I couldn't help thinking, "What if I came into work and someone was waiting to fire me?" The one thing I needed to know was did Haru get feedback? If so, what had he been told? Did he see this might be coming?

The best response after something difficult happens is to shine a bright light on the situation so everyone can work through it in the open. When you choose to sunshine exactly what happened, your clarity and openness will wash away the fears of the group. Let's pick up Yoka's story again:

I learned that there would be a meeting at 10:00 a.m. for Haru's team and for anyone else who had worked with Haru or had questions. About twenty people came together around a big oval table. The group was really quiet. Jim detailed Haru's strengths and struggles and explained why he felt he was no longer the best choice for his position. We sat silently for a while. Jim asked if there were questions. I raised my hand and asked how much feedback Haru had received and whether he had been surprised. Jim outlined the discussions he and Haru had had in the previous weeks. He said Haru was very upset and, despite all the feedback, did seem a little surprised.

Having information helped me calm down and also think about how to manage my own emotions. I called my own boss in California and told her that, if it ever crosses her mind that she might need to let me go, I wanted her to tell me plainly. I made her promise that if she ever has to let me go, I won't be surprised at all.

Meetings like the one organized by Jim help those who worked directly with a parting employee to process what happened and get their questions answered.

THE FINAL COUNT

 Most companies do what they can to minimize employee turnover. It costs money to find and train new people, so the traditional wisdom goes that it's cheaper to hold on to your current team members than to find new ones. But Reed doesn't pay much attention to turnover rate, believing that replacement costs are not as important as ensuring the right person is in every position.

So, given all the focus on Keeper Tests, just how many employees DOES Netflix let go of annually?

According to the Society for Human Resource Management's "Human Capital Benchmarking Report," the average annual turnover rate for American companies the past few years has been around 12 percent voluntary turnover (people choosing to leave the company of their own accord) and 6 percent involuntary (people who were fired), which adds up to a total average annual turnover of 18 percent. For technology companies, the total average annual turnover is more like 13 percent, and in the media/entertainment business it's 11 percent.

Over the same period, voluntary turnover at Netflix has remained steady at 3–4 percent (considerably below the 12 percent average—meaning not many choose to leave) and 8 percent involuntary (meaning 2 percent more people get fired at Netflix than the 6 percent average), equaling a grand total of 11–12 percent annual turnover . . . or just around the average for the sector. It seems there aren't actually that many people Netflix managers wouldn't fight to keep.

THE SEVENTH DOT

 The Keeper Test has helped to elevate the talent density at Netflix to a level rarely seen in other organizations. If each manager considers carefully, on a regular basis, whether every employee on the team is indeed the best choice for that position and replaces anyone who isn't, performance across the organization soars to new heights.

▶ TAKEAWAYS FROM CHAPTER 7

- In order to encourage your managers to be tough on performance, teach them to use the Keeper Test: "Which of my people, if they told me they were leaving for a similar job at another company, would I fight hard to keep?"

- Avoid stack-ranking systems, as they create internal competition and discourage collaboration.

- For a high-performance culture, a professional sports team is a better metaphor than a family. Coach your managers to create strong feelings of commitment, cohesion, and camaraderie on the team, while continually making tough decisions to ensure the best player is manning each post.

- When you realize you need to let someone go, instead of putting him on some type of PIP, which is humiliating and organizationally costly, take all that money and give it to the employee in the form of a generous severance payment.

- The downside to a high-performance culture is the fear employees may feel that their jobs are on the line. To reduce fear, encourage employees to use the Keeper Test Prompt with their managers: "How hard would you work to change my mind if I were thinking of leaving?"

- When an employee is let go, speak openly about what happened with your staff and answer their questions candidly. This will diminish their fear of being next and increase their trust in the company and its managers.

Toward a Culture of Freedom and Responsibility

You've implemented the Keeper Test. Congratulations! You now have a full-fledged high-performing workforce, which is the envy of your competitors. With such high talent density, your company is bound to grow, and when new people join the team you'll need to help them adjust to your way of working. As we've grown at Netflix, we've found it has been especially difficult to maintain the high level of candor that is one of the key foundations to our success. Candor is like going to the dentist: a lot of people will avoid it if they can. In the next chapter, we'll look at a couple of simple tactics to help keep candor levels at your company continually high.

MAX UP CANDOR . . .

8

A CIRCLE OF FEEDBACK

 There is one Netflix guideline that, if practiced religiously, would force everyone to be either radically candid or radically quiet: "Only say about someone what you will say to their face." The less we talk about people behind their backs, the more we eliminate the gossip that creates inefficiency and bad feelings—and the more we can wash our hands of the unpleasantness generally referred to as "office politics." While at Netflix, I tried to play within the rules of the culture. This particular rule was harder than it sounded.

I was conducting interviews in Silicon Valley. Briefed by PR manager Bart, most interviewees were bursting with stories and viewpoints. Heidi was the exception. She was standing in front of her desk talking to two colleagues when I arrived and looked away, as if she wasn't expecting me, forcing me to try and get her attention. Her demeanor went beyond aloof, edging toward hostile. She answered my questions with one-syllable answers. I ended the interview early.

While waiting with Bart for the elevator, we debriefed. "That was useless. She clearly wasn't prepared and didn't want to talk to me," I complained. Midsentence, I saw, in my peripheral vision, Heidi pass through an adjoining corridor not five feet from us. I don't know if she heard what I'd said, but that didn't stop the neon words that flashed across my brain: "ONLY SAY ABOUT SOMEONE WHAT YOU WILL SAY TO THEIR FACE." This Netflix culture thing was proving complicated. Most people do spend large parts of their day talking behind someone else's back. Myself included, apparently.

I asked Bart what the correct "Netflix" reaction would have been. I could hardly have ended the meeting by saying to Heidi, "Thank you for the eight minutes you gave me, but you clearly hadn't prepared and seemed as if you couldn't be bothered."

Bart looked at me like I was a goose pretending to be a duck: "You don't work for Netflix, plus you're conducting only one interview with Heidi, so your feedback wouldn't help the project. If you worked for Netflix and you were meeting with her again, you would aim to give her the input before the next interview, probably by putting a feedback meeting on her calendar." Then Bart showed who the real duck was: "I'll need her to interview with other writers in the future. I'll give her the feedback."

But not everyone at Netflix is as comfortable as Bart in initiating feedback.

GOING TO THE DENTIST

Saying that the company values candor is one thing. Maintaining it while the organization grows, new people join, and relationships become more numerous is more challenging. The problem became obvious to me during a one-on-one meeting with a director who had been at Netflix for almost a year. He said, "When I was hired, everyone said I would receive loads of feedback. But I've been at Netflix a while now, and I haven't received any."

I was worrying about that when I made a routine visit to my dentist. She poked me sharply on one of my molars. "You need to come in for more regular checkups, Reed. There are some spots in the back you're not getting when you brush."

Candor is like going to the dentist. Even if you encourage everyone to brush daily, some won't do it. Those who do may still miss the uncomfortable spots. I can't ensure the candor we encourage is happening every day. But I can ensure that we have regular mechanisms in place so that the most critical feedback gets out. In 2005, we became focused on finding tools that employees could rely on to get and receive candid feedback that didn't come out naturally in the course of day-to-day business.

The obvious choice would have been annual performance reviews. These days it's become trendy to ditch them, but in 2005 just about every company used performance reviews. With this system, the boss puts in writing the employee's strengths and weaknesses, along with an overall performance rating, and holds a one-on-one meeting to go over the assessment.

We've been against performance reviews from the beginning. The first problem is that the feedback goes only one way—downward. The second difficulty is that with a performance review you get feedback from only one person—your boss. This is in direct opposition to our "don't seek to please your boss" vibe. I want people to receive feedback not just from their direct managers but from anyone who has feedback to provide. The third issue is that companies usually base performance reviews on annual goals. But employees and their managers don't set annual goals or KPIs (Key Performance Indicators) at Netflix. Likewise, many companies use performance reviews to determine pay raises, but at Netflix we base salaries on the market, not performance.

We searched for a mechanism that would encourage everyone to give feedback to any colleague they wished, that reflected the level of candor and transparency we were trying to cultivate, and that was consistent with our Freedom and Responsibility culture. After a great deal of experimenting, we now have two processes we use regularly.

1: STATE YOUR NAME: A DIFFERENT KIND OF WRITTEN 360

When we first tested annual written 360s, we ran them like everyone else. Each employee selected a handful of people she wanted to receive feedback from, and those people filled out the report anonymously, rating the employee on a scale of 1 to 5 across a series of categories and leaving comments. We used a "Start, Stop, Continue" format for the comments to ensure that people didn't just pat each other on the back but gave concrete, actionable feedback.

Some on the management team felt that, given our culture of candor, we didn't need to offer anonymity, but I believed it was important. Amid all the candor in the office, if someone opted not to give a colleague open feedback during the year, there must be a reason. Perhaps people were concerned there would be retribution. Offering anonymity, I felt, would provide a safer format and make people more comfortable leaving comments.

But the first time we ran the 360s, something

funny happened. Our culture took over. A bunch of people, including Leslie Kilgore, felt too uncomfortable to leave comments **without** putting their names. "It just seemed backward to tell our employees all year long to give feedback directly to one another and then at 360 time to pretend the comments were coming from a secret source," Leslie explained. "Everything I was writing I had told them anyhow. I just did what felt natural given our climate. I put the feedback in writing and signed my name."

When I logged on to leave my own feedback for others, I also felt uncomfortable, knowing that I could say whatever I wanted and no one would see that the feedback was coming from me. It all had an air of dishonesty and secretiveness that was contrary to the culture I was trying to cultivate.

After we received our completed 360 reports that year and I started reading the comments our employees had left for me, my discomfort with the anonymity magnified. People were perhaps worried that if they left feedback that was too specific or concrete I would recognize the author, so they masked their observations in obliqueness. Some comments were so vague I barely understood them:

"Stop: sending mixed messages on certain issues."

"Stop: coming across as insensitive when turning down an idea that doesn't resonate."

I had no idea what these people were referring to. The feedback certainly wasn't actionable. How could this possibly help me? Since I didn't know who the comments were from, I couldn't follow up and ask for clarification. In addition, the anonymity encouraged a few people to vent in nasty and sarcastic ways that weren't helpful for anyone. One manager showed me a comment she'd received: "You have less enthusiasm than Eeyore." Eeyore is the ever-depressed donkey from the children's book **The House at Pooh Corner**. How is that remark useful?

Leslie's approach caught on. The second time Netflix ran the 360, a majority of employees, on their own initiative, chose to add their names. This meant that the minority who elected to remain anonymous were easy to recognize. "If you asked seven people to give you feedback and five of them left their names, it was pretty easy to guess who from the remaining two had said what," Leslie recalled.

By the third round, everyone was choosing to leave their names. "It just felt better," Leslie claimed. "People would walk right over to the desk of the feedback provider and start a conversation. These discussions ended up being much more valuable than anything that was written on the actual 360 report."

Leslie, Reed, and the management team saw no apparent loss of frankness when feedback ceased to be anonymous. Leslie feels that's "because Netflix had already invested so much time in building a culture of candor." Many claim the quality of the feedback was higher, as people knew the comments would be recognized as their work.

Here is a 360 comment Reed received from a recent round. It's essentially the same complaint he received in 2005, but this time the person provides examples and leaves his name, which makes his observations concrete and actionable:

> You can be overly confident—even aggressive— in advocating for a position, and dismissive of differing perspectives. I felt this was the case when you were advocating for relocating to Japan our Singapore-based folks working on Korea. It is hugely valuable that you ask the question and are open to making radical shifts, but throughout the due diligence process, it seems you are predetermined to get to a certain outcome and dismissive of counterarguments.—Ove

 I can remember exactly the conversations that Ove is referring to, which means I can adapt favorably in future situations. Most important, knowing who left the feedback, I was able to follow up with Ove and get further information.

We now do the 360 written feedback every year, asking each person to sign their comments. We no longer have employees rate each other on a scale of 1 to 5, since we don't link the process to raises, promotions, or firings. The goal is to help everyone get better, not to categorize them into boxes. The other big improvement is that each person can now give feedback to as many colleagues as they choose at any level in the organization—not just direct reports, line managers, or a few teammates who have invited input. Most people at Netflix provide feedback for at least ten colleagues, but thirty or forty is common. I received comments from seventy-one people on my 2018 report.

Most important, the open 360 feedback instigates valuable discussion. I systematically share the comments I receive with my direct reports, and my reports share their feedback with their teams, all the way down the line. This not only strengthens the sense of transparency but also creates "reverse accountability" whereby the team feels encouraged to call the boss out for recurrent bad behavior.

Ted Sarandos likes to tell this story about bungee jumping to demonstrate the value:

Back in 1997, when I worked in Phoenix before Netflix, I went to a work event, the kind where you have some meetings but there are also activities encouraging the group to bond and have fun.

Behind the restaurant in the parking lot, there was a bungee jumping station. For fifteen bucks you could jump off of a crane in full sight of everyone. No one was doing it, but I decided to try. Afterward the guy running the station said to me, "Why not go again? I'll give you a second jump for free?" That made me curious. "Why would you do that?" I asked. He responded, "Because I want all your colleagues gawking at you from the restaurant to see that you're happy to do it again. If they see it's not so scary, they'll be ready to try it also."

That's exactly why you as the leader need to share your 360 evaluations with your teams, especially the really candid stuff about all the things you do poorly. It shows everyone that giving and receiving clear, actionable feedback isn't so scary.

 This is a regular practice for Netflix managers today. Larry Tanz, VP of content (he went to interview with Facebook after Ted told his team to take recruiters' calls), has another story about a surprising meeting with Ted during his first few weeks at Netflix in 2014:

For the past five years I'd been working for ex-Disney CEO Michael Eisner. Let's just say those of us on Michael's staff weren't giving him a lot of direct negative feedback. Where I came from the boss might be candid with you but any feedback in the reverse direction was pretty much unheard of.

In my second T-staff (Ted's staff) meeting, Ted began by reminding the twelve of us that the written 360 was coming up in a few months, and that we all needed to be in the habit of giving frank feedback to one another. "Even if you don't work together," he said, "you need to be close enough to give candid criticism on an ongoing basis. We just finished a round of 360s with R-staff (Reed's staff). I'll just read to you the feedback I received."

I was confused. What was Ted doing? In my entire life I'd never had a boss tell me what his peers and superiors were saying about him. My immediate thought was that he would cherry-pick what he told us and we'd hear a sanitized version. Then he proceeded line by line to read through the feedback from Reed, David Wells, Neil Hunt, Jonathan Friedland, and all those folks. He didn't read many positive comments, although there must have been some. Instead he detailed all of his developmental comments including the following:

- When you don't respond to emails from my team, it feels hierarchical and discouraging, even though I know this is neither how you work nor how you think. Perhaps it is because we need to establish more trust, but I need you to be more generous with your time and insights, so my team can serve your organization better.

- Your "old married couple" disagreements with Cindy are not the best role model of exec interchange. There should be more listening and understanding on both your parts.

- Stop avoiding overt conflict within the team; it simply festers elsewhere and comes back bigger. The seeds of Janet's flaming out and the drama of Robert's role were planted well over a year ago. It would have been better to address both directly and head-on a year ago rather than have everyone suffer, and morale drop.

Ted read these items just like he was reading a list of food to buy at the supermarket. I thought, "Wow, could I be brave enough to share my feedback with my own staff?"

Apparently, Larry could: "Ever since that meeting I try hard to model what Ted did with us for my own team, not just at written 360 time but any time someone provides me with developmental feedback. And I've suggested that those leaders who work for me, do the same thing with their own teams."

Although the 360 written exercise established regular candid feedback, and many chose to discuss the feedback after the reports came out, it didn't ensure that those open discussions were actually happening. If Chris-Ann gives written 360 feedback to Jean-Paul that his whispering in client meetings is hurting his sales, but Jean-Paul never talks to Chris-Ann or anyone else about the comment, it turns into the stuff of secrets. Reed's next process was put in place in order to address that problem.

2: LIVE 360S

 By 2010, we had firmly instituted our version of the written 360 process with a lot of success. But, given the other steps we'd taken to increase transparency throughout the company, I felt that we could go further. So I began to run some experiments to see if increasing transparency in my own executive team would help it trickle down to the rest of the organization. The first thing I tried was an activity with my direct reports.

We met in the old Silicon Valley Netflix building at 100 Winchester in a little bird's nest perch of a room called The Towering Inferno. Leslie and Neil paired up and went to one corner of the room, Ted and Patty went to another, and so on. The exercise was a little like speed-dating except it was speed-feedback. Each pair had a few minutes to give one another feedback following the "Start, Stop, Continue" method and then we rotated, creating new pairs. Afterward, we came back into a circle as a group of eight and reported back what we'd learned. The pair exercise went fine, but the group discussion was by far the most important part of the session.

So the next time, we jumped right into the group discussion. I decided to do this second experiment over dinner with nothing else on the agenda, so we wouldn't feel rushed. We met at a restaurant called the Plumed Horse in Saratoga, a quaint little village just a short drive from the office. When we pulled up, the trees were lined with lights, like fireflies in a forest. We walked in and the seemingly small restaurant opened up into a big cavern, leading to a quiet, reserved room.

Ted volunteered to go first. We went around the circle and each person gave him feedback using Start, Stop, Continue. At that time Ted was one of just a few employees based in Los Angeles and he would commute up to Silicon Valley one day a week. Every Wednesday he'd race into the office and try to cram in three days' worth of discussions into six hours. David, Patty, and Leslie all gave Ted feedback about how hectic his one day in the office was for everybody else. "When you leave on Wednesday afternoon it feels like a jet boat came through and left a massive wake behind it," Patty explained. "It's stressful and disruptive for the entire office."

I'd been meaning to talk to Ted about this, but now I didn't have to. After that session he reorganized his schedule to come to Silicon Valley for longer trips and to handle more over the phone before his visits. Ted saw how his actions were disturbing everyone and talking about it openly made him find a better way.

The live 360s are so useful because individuals become accountable for their behavior and actions to the team. Given how much freedom we grant employees, along with the general "don't seek to please your boss" climate, this co-responsibility provides a safety net. The boss doesn't tell the employee what to do. But if the employee acts irresponsibly, he will get feedback from the group.

Next it was Patty's turn. Neil told her, "During our meetings you speak so much, I can't get a word in edgewise. Your passion sucks up all the air." But, as we worked around the table, Leslie disagreed: "I'm surprised about Neil's comments. I think you're a great listener and you always make sure everyone has equal time to talk."

At the end of the evening each person presented a short synthesis of their main takeaways. Patty said, "When I'm in meetings with people who are more reserved, like Neil, I compensate for that person's quietness by talking more. When I'm with other

talkative people, like Leslie, I don't have that problem. On my own team I have many quieter people
who don't speak at all in our meetings. I'm going
to start leaving the last ten minutes of every thirty-
minute meeting for others to speak. If no one speaks
we'll sit in silence."

As a talkative person myself, I wasn't even aware
that some experienced Patty as hogging the airspace.
I wouldn't have known to give her this feedback,
because it doesn't characterize the interactions I have
with her. This demonstrated why it's so important
employees receive feedback, not just from their boss
but also from teammates. The session helped me—
and everyone in the group—to understand team
tensions in new and unexpected ways. I saw that the
dinner was a way for us all to better understand the
interpersonal dynamics that shaped our collective
effectiveness and to work together to improve our
collaboration.

Soon after, many on my staff conducted the same
exercise with their own teams, and eventually it
became a common activity throughout the company.
It's not obligatory. You may meet a Netflix employee
who has never gone through a live 360. But our
managers have found such value in the method
that today the vast majority of our teams conduct
something similar at least once a year. By now, we
understand the process pretty well, and it's actually
not that difficult to run, as long as you set the context

and have a strong moderator. If you'd like to try the live 360 for yourself, here are a few tips:

Length and location: A live 360 will take several hours. Do it over dinner (or at least include a meal) and keep the group small. We sometimes have sessions with ten or twelve people, but eight or fewer is more manageable. For a group of eight you'll need about three hours. A group of twelve could run to five hours.

Method: All feedback should be provided and received as an actionable gift following the 4A feedback guidelines outlined in chapter 2. The leader will need to explain this in advance and monitor it during the session.

Positive actionable feedback (continue to . . .) is fine, but keep it in check. A good mix is 25 percent positive and 75 percent developmental (start doing . . . and stop doing . . .). Any nonactionable fluff ("I think you're a great colleague" or "I love working with you") should be discouraged and stamped out.

Getting started: The first few feedback interactions will set the tone for the evening. Choose a feedback receiver who will receive tough feedback with openness and appreciation. Choose a feedback provider who will give the tough feedback, while following the 4A guidelines. Often the boss chooses to be the first to receive.

Live 360s work because of our high talent density and "no brilliant jerks" policy. If your employees are immature, have bad attitudes, or lack the self-confidence to show public vulnerability, you might not be ready to run these events. And even if you're in a state of perfect readiness, you'll need a strong moderator who makes sure all feedback falls within the 4A framework and steps in if someone says anything out of line.

Scott Mirer, VP of device partner ecosystem, shared an incident when someone stepped out of line during his team's live 360, but he failed to address it in real time. This type of situation is rare, but dangerous when it happens, so the leader needs to be on the ball:

I had my management team of nine people going through the Live 360 dinner. We have a very nice manager named Ian, and he was giving feedback to his colleague, a woman named Sabina. When it was Sabina's turn to receive feedback, Ian said, "The way you work reminds me of the movie, **Women on the Verge of a Nervous Breakdown.**" He said it with a smile and Sabina nodded her head and took notes. For some reason at that moment it didn't hit me—or I guess any of the others on the team—as to how inappropriate that statement was, because we all let it slide. I learned a week later that Sabina had been upset for days after that event. "It is not selfless or helpful to use gender-charged comparisons when giving feedback," she confided with a colleague.

If someone moves out of the 4A feedback guidelines to speak in a way that is sarcastic, aggressive, or generally unhelpful during the live 360, the leader needs to step in and correct the comment in real time. This situation is particularly important because we've been working extensively with our leaders to make sure that everyone feels included and to understand how off-the-cuff comments can feed bias even unconsciously. Scott missed his opportunity. But, in this case the company's culture of candor saved the situation:

I called Sabina and apologized for not catching the inappropriateness of Ian's comment. But Sabina told me she was no longer upset. She had already spoken to Ian, he had apologized, and they had met for over an hour to work through it. So although it was a car-crash 360 dinner moment, overall I believe it was good for their relationship. Since then I'm a lot more careful to jump any time a piece of feedback starts to step over the line.

Public humiliation? Group isolation? Communal shaming? If these words have been popping into your head as you read the last few pages, you're not alone.

A majority of Netflix employees do enter their first live 360 with trepidation. VP of content Larry Tanz (the guy who was shocked to hear Ted detail his 360 feedback to the team) explained the experience like this:

Getting publicly ripped apart sounds like torture. Each time I go to a live 360 I'm nervous. But after you get started, you see it will be fine. Because everyone is watching, people are careful to be generous and supportive in the way they give the feedback—with the intention of helping you succeed. No one wants to embarrass or attack you. If anyone steps out of line, they will almost always get immediate feedback about their feedback: "Hey—that's not helpful!" If the live session goes well, everyone gets a lot of tough advice, so you're not singled out. When your turn finally comes around, it might be difficult to hear what people have to say, but this is one of the greatest developmental gifts of your life.

Just about every Netflix employee has a story about how a live 360 helped them. Some think the evenings are an enjoyable way to build bonds with their colleagues. Others like them just about as much as Reed enjoys those annual trips to the dentist. They know it's useful, but they dread it until it's over. Sophie, a French communications manager working out of the Amsterdam office, fell into the second category:

Like most French people, I build an argument the way we are trained in school. I introduce the principle, build up the theory, address any challenges to the argument, then come to my conclusions. Introduction, thesis, antithesis, synthesis, that's how we French learn to analyze over many years in school.

Americans often learn "get to the point and stick to the point." To the French person it's like, "How can you come to the point when you haven't explained your argument?!" Netflix is of course an American company by origin. I have an American boss, and most of my teammates are American. Unbeknownst to me, my communication approach wasn't working for them as intended.

It was November 2016 and my boss led a live 360 event for the team. We were in a private room at the Waldorf Astoria hotel in Amsterdam for a four-course dinner. It was literally a "dark and stormy night," and we were in an ornate medieval style room where the only light was a big crystal chandelier hanging over a big wood rectangular table. I was nervous but had soothed myself by thinking about all I had accomplished in my short time at Netflix. I believed I was clearly a "stunning colleague."

When it was my turn to receive feedback, my colleague Joelle began by telling me that I need to improve my communication skills. She said I lose the listener's attention and take too long to get to the point. I was like, "Me? A poor communicator? I am a communications specialist! My greatest skill is my ability to communicate!" That feedback made no sense to me, so I prepared to discard it.

But then my other American colleagues, one after another, went around the room giving me feedback: a lot of nice things, but also "You're too theoretical," "Your messages aren't crisp enough," "Your writing loses the reader's attention." After the fifth person I was like, "Okay, I get it! No need to gang up on me." By the seventh person I started to feel defensive. I felt like saying, "Hey American dude, try working in a French company and see how they like your writing style!"

But even for Sophie receiving the feedback was worth the discomfort of the evening:

> That dinner happened two years ago and was the most important developmental moment for me in the past decade. I've made enormous strides with my adaptability. I've mastered moving back and forth between the American and French communication patterns, which is incredibly challenging, but my colleagues have congratulated me in more recent live 360 sessions. I hated that evening at the Waldorf, but without it eventually I would have failed the Keeper Test. I don't think I'd be at Netflix."

This is the classic type of answer you get when you ask Netflix people what it's like to have your "areas for improvement" dragged across the dinner table while everyone is listening. Sometimes it's embarrassing. Often it's uncomfortable. But ultimately it boosts your performance. And for Sophie, it may have saved her job.

THE EIGHTH DOT

If you're serious about candor at some point, you do need to implement mechanisms to assure candor happens. With just two institutional processes you can ensure that everyone gets candid developmental feedback at regular intervals.

▶ TAKEAWAYS FROM CHAPTER 8

- Candor is like going to the dentist. Even if you encourage everyone to brush daily, some won't do it. Those who do may still miss the uncomfortable spots. A thorough session every six to twelve months ensures clean teeth and clear feedback.

- Performance reviews are not the best mechanism for a candid work environment, primarily because the feedback usually goes only one way (down) and comes from only one person (the boss).

- A 360 written report is a good mechanism for annual feedback. But avoid anonymity and numeric ratings, don't link results to raises or promotions, and open up comments to anyone who is ready to give them.

- Live 360 dinners are another effective process. Set aside several hours away from the office. Give clear instructions, follow the 4A feedback guidelines, and use the Start, Stop, Continue method with roughly

25 percent positive, 75 percent developmental—all actionable and no fluff.

Toward a Culture of Freedom and Responsibility

After implementing the Keeper Test system, you will have achieved a high level of talent density in your office. Now, with the implementation of the written and live 360 feedback processes, you don't just have a climate of candor around the office; you have institutionalized tools to ensure employees are talking openly and honestly to each other. With this much talent and candor, you can now focus your time on teaching your leaders to let go of whatever controls they are holding on to. We spoke about decision-making freedom in chapter 6, so conceptually your workforce is ready. But to develop a true environment of Freedom and Responsibility you'll need to teach all managers in your company to lead with context, not control. That's the topic of the next chapter.

AND ELIMINATE MOST CONTROLS . . . !

9

LEAD WITH CONTEXT, NOT CONTROL

Adam Del Deo, Netflix's director of original documentary programming, felt queasy as he hung up the phone. Standing in the lobby of the Washington School House Hotel in Park City, Utah, he leaned against the wall, took a deep breath, and closed his eyes. When he opened them, his colleague, senior counsel Rob Guillermo, was standing next to him. "Hey, Adam, is everything okay? Did you get news on the **Icarus** bid?"

Adam and Rob were attending the Sundance Film Festival in January 2017. The previous day, they'd watched a documentary, **Icarus**, about the Russian doping scandal. According to Adam, it was one of the greatest documentaries he'd ever seen:

> It follows this crazy story of a Colorado-based journalist, Bryan Fogel, who is also a cyclist and

wants to run an experiment to see if he can dope himself, get away with it like Lance Armstrong did, and show the extreme progress the doping allows him to make in a bike race. Through a contact he reaches out to the head of Russia's anti-doping program, this guy Rodchenkov, who agrees to help. They become Skype friends. But partway through Bryan's experiment, Russia is accused of doping its Olympic athletes—and it's Rodchenkov who's been running that doping program (alongside his anti-doping program!). Rodchenkov flees Russia and hides out in Fogel's house, afraid Putin is going to have him killed.

You just can't make up a story like that. The movie is completely gripping.

Adam wanted desperately for Netflix to get that movie. News on the street was that Amazon, Hulu, and HBO all wanted it too. He'd bid $2.5 million for it that morning—a huge amount for a documentary—but had just learned the bid was too low. Should he bid $3.5 million? $4 million? No documentary had ever gone for that much. He and Rob were discussing the bid when Ted Sarandos entered the lobby from the adjoining breakfast room. They told him about the **Icarus** situation, and he asked what they were going to do. Adam remembers the conversation like this:

"Maybe we'll go up to $3.75 or $4 million, but that's a huge amount to offer for a doc. It would completely reset the market," I said, watching for Ted's reaction.

Ted looked me square in the eye and said, "Well, is it 'THE ONE?'" He made quote marks with his fingers, like it meant something important. That made me nervous. It was my ONE. But was it his ONE? I asked him, "What do you think, Ted?"

Ted started moving toward the door. Clearly, he was not going to answer that question. "Listen," he said. "It doesn't matter what I think. You're the doc guy, not me. We pay YOU to make these decisions. But ask yourself if it's THE ONE. Is this going to be a massive hit? Is it going to be an Oscar nominee like **Super Size Me** or **An Inconvenient Truth**? If it's not, that's too much to pay. But if it's THE ONE you should pay whatever it's going to take: $4.5 million, $5 million. If it's THE ONE, get the movie."

Ten years before, in 2007, Leslie Kilgore had coined a phrase, which is now used across Netflix to describe exactly what Ted was doing as he walked out through the lobby of the hotel: "Lead with context, not control." At just about any other company, with this much money on the table, the senior guy would get involved and control the negotiations. But that's not what leadership looks like at Netflix. As Adam explained: "Ted wasn't about to make that decision for me, but he set broad context to help align my thinking with the company's strategy. That context he set laid the foundation for my decision."

CONTROL VERSUS CONTEXT

Leadership with control is familiar to most. The boss approves and directs the initiatives, actions, and decisions of the team. Sometimes she may control employees' decisions through direct oversight— telling them what to do, checking in frequently, and correcting any work that isn't done as she desires. Other times she may seek to empower her employees more, avoiding direct oversight but putting control processes in place instead.

Many leaders frequently use control processes to give the employee some freedom to approach a task as he chooses, while still allowing the boss an opportunity to control what gets done and when. For example, the boss might put in place a process like Management by Objectives, when she works with the employee to set Key Performance Indicators (KPIs); then she monitors the progress at regular intervals, judging the individual's final performance based on whether he achieves the predetermined goals on time and within budget. She might also seek to control the quality of her employees' work by putting in place error-reduction processes, such as checking work before it goes to the client or approving purchases before orders are placed. These are all processes that allow a manager to give some freedom while still exerting a good deal of control.

Leading with context, on the other hand, is more difficult, but gives considerably more freedom to employees. You provide all of the information you can so that your team members make great decisions and accomplish their work without oversight or process controlling their actions. The benefit is that the person builds the decision-making muscle to make better independent decisions in the future.

Leading with context won't work unless you have the right conditions in place. And the first prerequisite is high talent density. If you've ever managed anyone, even your own children or a contractor in your house, you'll understand why.

Imagine, for instance, that you're the parent of a sixteen-year-old boy. He loves to draw Japanese-style anime, solve complex sudoku problems, and play the saxophone. Lately he's also started going to parties with older friends on Saturday nights. You've already told him you don't want him to drink alcohol and drive, or get in the car with a driver who has been drinking, but every time he goes out you worry. There are two different ways you might approach this problem:

1. You decide which parties your son can go to (and not go to) and monitor his actions while at the party. If he wants to go out on Saturday night, there is a process. First he has to explain to you who will be there and what they will be doing. Then you need to speak to the parent who owns the house where the party will be held. During that conversation you verify if there will be an adult chaperone and if alcohol will be available. From this information you decide whether or not your son can go. When you give approval, you still put a tracker on your son's phone to assure that this is indeed the only party he goes to. This would be leading with control.

2. The second would be to set context so that you and your son are aligned. You talk to your son about why teenagers drink and the dangers associated with drinking and driving. In the safety of your kitchen, you pour different types of alcohol into glasses and discuss how much of each you'd need to become tipsy, drunk, or blacked out and how that impacts your driving effectiveness (and overall health). You show him an educational film on YouTube about drinking and driving and all the ramifications. Once you see he clearly understands the severity of the dangers that come with drinking and driving, you let him go to whatever parties he likes without any process or over-

sight restricting his actions. This would be leading with context.

The choice you make will most likely depend on your son. If he's shown poor judgment in the past and you don't trust him, you might choose to parent with control. But if you know him to be sensible and dependable, you can set the context and count on him to behave safely. In doing so, you prepare him to make not just good decisions on Saturday nights but also responsible decisions in the myriad of seductive or peer-influenced situations he will face in the coming years.

If you have a responsible child, option 2 may sound like the obvious answer. Who wants to be an overbearing parent and why would you not want a teenager to assume responsibility for his own safety? But in many situations the choice is not so clear-cut. Consider this scenario:

You are the matriarch of a modern-day Downton Abbey (aristocratic family with snooty accents, loads of drama, and lots of money). Your adult children are coming to your house for a month of holidays and you have hired someone to cook dinner. Your family is complicated when it comes to food. One person is diabetic, another is a vegetarian, and a third is on a low-carbohydrate diet. You know how and what to cook for this crowd but how is this chef you've hired, who doesn't know your family, going to manage?

Once again, you have two choices:

1. You provide her with a cooking schedule and a set of recipes, specifying exactly what to cook each night. You outline how much to make of each dish and note when one ingredient should be replaced by another. You ask to taste each menu item before it is served to ensure she has the seasonings correct and that the dish is cooked to perfection. All she needs to do is follow your instructions. Of course, she is welcome to suggest her own recipe ideas too. She just needs to get your okay before cooking them. This would be leading with control.

2. You talk with her in detail about the various dietary requirements in your family. You explain the principles of a low-carb diet, and what a diabetic can and can't eat. You show her recipes you've used successfully in the past, those that have flopped, and common substitutes you've tried. You explain that each meal should include some protein for everyone, a salad, and at least one vegetable. The two of you become highly aligned on what will make each meal a success. Then you ask her to find recipes and choose what to cook herself. This would be leading with context.

With option 1, you know what you're going to be served and you're pretty sure your family will like it. You've squashed out most of the possibility for your cook to fail or really make any mistake at all. So if you have a cook with little experience, who seems uncomfortable taking initiative, doesn't seem to be enterprising enough to find good recipes, and there aren't any certifiably more talented people available, then option 1 will be the right choice for you. Option 2 is just too risky.

Option 2, however, becomes interesting if you trust the judgment and skill of the person you've hired. A high-performing chef will thrive on the freedom to select and try out recipes on her own. She'll be able to offer more innovative meal choices than you could. If she does make mistakes, she'll learn from them and at the end of the holiday your family will remember the fabulous banquets she provided.

Therefore, the first question you need to answer when choosing whether to lead with context or control is, "What is the level of talent density of my staff?" If your employees are struggling, you'll need to monitor and check their work to ensure they are making the right decisions. If you've got a group of high performers, they'll most likely crave freedom and thrive if you lead with context.

But deciding whether to lead with context or control isn't just about talent density. You also have to consider your industry, and what you are trying to achieve.

SAFETY FIRST?

Take a look at these clippings about two companies that have had success in recent years. Consider which organization would be more likely to profit from leadership by control (with oversight and/or error-reduction processes) and—assuming high talent density—which would benefit from leadership through context.

Let's begin with ExxonMobil. Here is a short extract from their website:

ExxonMobil

Since 2000, we have reduced our workforce lost-time incident rate by more than 80 percent. While this number is declining, safety incidents do occur. We deeply regret that two contract workers were fatally injured in separate incidents related to ExxonMobil operations in 2017. One incident occurred at an onshore drilling site and the other happened at a refinery during construction activities. We thoroughly investigated the causes and contributing factors associated with the incidents to prevent similar events in the future and to globally disseminate findings. We have also joined cross-industry working groups with representatives from the oil and gas and other industries, such as the Campbell Institute at the National Safety Council, to better understand the precursors to serious injuries and fatalities. We will continue to promote a safety-first mentality for ExxonMobil employees and contractors until we reach our goal of a workplace where *Nobody Gets Hurt.*

The second example is the American retail giant Target. In 2019, **Fast Company** ranked it the eleventh most innovative company in the world. The following excerpt is from the article:

Target

The retail apocalypse hit many big box retailers hard: J.C. Penney, Sears, and Kmart have all faltered as e-commerce has grown, driving down foot traffic to brick-and-mortar stores. But in the face of these challenges, Target has nimbly adapted to the preferences of the modern consumer. The company has a network of more than 1,800 stores across the United States that come in different formats, from the extra-large SuperTarget to the smaller flexible format stores in urban centers, that cater to the specific needs of those shoppers. The brand also has invested in its online presence, with a robust website, same-day and two-day shipping that allows it to compete with Amazon, and the option to order items online that you can pick up within the day.

When considering whether to lead with context or control, the second key question to ask is whether your goal is error prevention or innovation.

If your focus is on eliminating mistakes, then control is best. ExxonMobil is in a safety-critical market. Its sites need hundreds of safety procedures to minimize the risk of people getting hurt. Control mechanisms are a necessity when you're trying to run a dangerous operation profitably with as few accidents as possible.

Likewise, if you are running a hospital emergency room and give junior nurses the context to make decisions themselves with no oversight, people might die. If you are manufacturing airplanes and don't have plenty of control processes ensuring every part is assembled perfectly, the possibility of deadly accidents increases. If you are washing windows on skyscrapers, you need regular safety inspections and daily checklists. Leading with control is great for error prevention.

But if, like Target, your goal is innovation, making a mistake is not the primary risk. The big risk is becoming irrelevant because your employees aren't coming up with great ideas to reinvent the business. Although many brick-and-mortar retailers have gone out of business as increasing numbers of people shop online, Target has made a priority of imagining fresh ways to get customers into the stores.

There are many businesses that share Target's priorities. Whether you're in the business of inventing toys for children, selling cupcakes, designing sportswear, or running a restaurant with fusion cuisine, innovation is one of your primary goals. If you've got high-performing employees, leading with context is best. To encourage original thinking, don't tell your employees what to do and make them check boxes. Give them the context to dream big, the inspiration to think differently, and the space to make mistakes along the way. In other words, lead with context.

Or as Antoine de Saint-Exupéry, the author of **The Little Prince**, put it rather more poetically:

> If you want to build a ship,
> don't drum up the people
> to gather wood, divide the
> work, and give orders.
> Instead, teach them to yearn
> for the vast and endless sea.

 As much as I love this passage—we cite it at the end of our culture memo—I also realize that for some readers it may feel entirely impractical. And that brings me to the third necessary condition you need to have in place in order for leading with context to work. In addition to high talent density (that's the first condition) and a goal of innovation rather than error prevention (that's the second), you also need to work (here comes the third) in a system that is "loosely coupled."

LOOSELY OR TIGHTLY COUPLED?

I'm a software engineer and software engineers speak about "tight coupling" and "loose coupling" to explain two different types of system design.

A tightly coupled system is one in which the various

components are intricately intertwined. If you want to make a change to one area of the system, you have to go back and rework the foundation, which impacts not just the section you need to change, but the entire system.

By contrast, a loosely coupled design system has few interdependencies between the component parts. They are designed so that each can be adapted without going back and changing the foundation. That's why software engineers like loose coupling; they can make a change to part of the system with no repercussions for the rest of it. The entire system is more flexible.

Organizations are constructed a bit like computer programs. When a company is tightly coupled, big decisions get made by the big boss and pushed down to the departments, often creating interdependencies between the various areas of the business. If a problem occurs at the departmental level, it has to go back to the boss who oversees all of the departments. Meanwhile, in a loosely coupled company, an individual manager or employee is free to make decisions or solve problems, safe in the knowledge that the consequences will not ricochet through other departments.

If the leaders up and down your company have traditionally led with control, a tightly coupled system may have come about naturally. If you are managing a department (or a team within a department) in a tightly coupled system and you decide you'd like to begin to lead your people with context, you may find that the tight coupling gets in your way. Since all the important decisions get made at the top, you might wish to give your employees decision-making power, but you can't, because anything important has to be approved not just by you but by your boss and by her boss.

If you are already part of a tightly coupled system, you may have to work with the top leaders in the company in order to change the entire organizational approach before trying to lead with context at a lower level. Even with high talent density, and innovation as your goal, if you don't sort this out, leading with context may be impossible.

It should be pretty clear by now that at Netflix, with our Informed Captain model, we have a loosely coupled system. Decision making is highly dispersed, and we have few centralized control processes, rules, or policies. This provides a high degree of freedom to individuals, gives each department greater flexibility, and speeds up decision making throughout the company.

If you're starting up your own company and your goal is innovation and flexibility, try to keep decision-making decentralized, with few inter-dependencies between functions, in order to nurture loose coupling from the outset. It will be a whole lot trickier to introduce once your organization has settled into a tightly coupled structure.

All this said, tight coupling does have at least one important organizational benefit. In a tightly coupled system, strategic change is easily aligned throughout the organization. If the CEO wants all departments throughout the company to focus on sustainability and ethical sourcing, then she can control that through her centralized decision-making.

With loose coupling, on the other hand, the risk of misalignment is high. Who's to say one department won't put low cost ahead of protecting the environment or workers in sweatshops and pull the entire organization off course? If the head of the department has a fantastic vision for contributing to the new strategy, but each team member decides for himself what projects to take on, everyone may run off in his own direction. Good luck making that departmental vision a reality anytime soon.

This brings us to the fourth and final precondition for leading with context.

IS YOUR ORGANIZATION HIGHLY ALIGNED?

 If loose coupling is to work effectively, with big decisions made at the individual level, then the boss and the employees must be in lockstep agreement on their destination. Loose coupling works only if there is a clear, shared context between the boss and the team.

That alignment of context drives employees to make decisions that support the mission and strategy of the overall organization. This is why the mantra at Netflix is

HIGHLY ALIGNED, LOOSELY COUPLED

To understand what this involves, let's return to Downton Abbey, where your family members are waiting for their dinner. If you have spent enough time ensuring you and your cook are aligned on exactly what types of foods will make the family happy, who eats what and why, the portions she should make, and which types of foods should be cooked rare, medium, or well, your high-performing chef will be ready to select and cook her meals without oversight.

However, if you hire a high-performing chef and give her free range to cook what she wants, but you haven't shared that your family hates salt and that any salad dressing with sugar will be rejected by all, it's likely your household of fusspots won't like the meal delivered to their plates. In this case, it's not your chef's fault. It's yours. You hired the right person, but you didn't provide enough context. You gave your cook freedom, but you and your chef were not aligned.

Of course in a company, it's not about one chef cooking for one family. Instead there are layers of leadership, which makes creating alignment more complex.

In the following pages we will look at how context gets set effectively across the organization when all leaders are focused on building alignment. The CEO provides the first level of context, building an initial foundation of alignment across the company, so we'll start there with Reed.

ALIGNING ON A NORTH STAR

 I use a handful of methods for setting context across the company, but my primary platforms are our E-staff (Executive Staff) and our Quarterly Business Review (QBR) meetings. A few times a year we bring together all the leaders (top 10 to 15 percent of people) of the company from around the world. It starts with a long meeting or dinner with my half dozen direct reports—people like Ted and Greg Peters and our head of HR Jessica Neal. Then I spend a day with E-Staff (all VPs and above) and then we have two days of presentations, sharing, and debates at QBR (all directors and above—about 10 percent of the entire workforce).

The number one goal for these meetings is to make sure that all leaders across the company are highly aligned on what I call our North Star: the general direction we are running in. We don't need to be aligned on how each department is going to get where they are going—that we leave to the individual areas—but we do need to make sure we are all moving in the same direction.

Before and after QBR, we make available many dozens of pages of Google Docs memos to every employee, explaining all the context and content we shared at QBR. This information is read not just by QBR participants but also by people at all levels of the company, including administrative assistants, marketing coordinators, you name it.

Between QBRs, I hold ongoing one-on-one meetings to get a feel for how aligned we actually are and where context is lacking. I have one thirty-minute meeting with each director once a year. That makes about 250 hours of meetings with people who are three to five levels below me in the org chart. In addition, I meet with each vice president (two to three levels below me) for one hour every quarter. This results in another 500 hours of meetings annually. When Netflix was smaller, I met with each person more frequently, but I still spend about 25 percent of my annual time on all these meetings.

These one-on-one meetings help me to better understand the context in which our employees are working, and alert me to areas where our leadership is not aligned so that I can revisit key points at the next round of QBR meetings.

Here's an example from March 2018, when I visited our Singapore office. During a thirty-minute one-on-one with a director in the product development department, he casually mentioned that his team was developing, per request, a five-year head count plan. I was surprised. A five-year plan may sound like a natural endeavor for a company to be working on, but in our dynamic industry it's absurd. It's impossible to know where a business like ours will be five years from now. Trying to guess and plan around those guesses is sure to tie the company down and keep us from adapting quickly.

I looked into the issue and discovered that one of our facilities executives was asking people in several of our offices to submit predicted head count numbers for 2023. When I spoke with him he explained that, in some of our locations around the world, we'd grown out of our office space far faster than expected and that had meant financial waste. "If I had a five-year hiring plan, I could get the best space for the cheapest price and not make the same mistake we made last time. That's why I asked each of the various departments to develop one," he explained.

I felt like saying, "You bozo! Don't prioritize error prevention over flexibility! That is a total waste of time. There is no way we can have any accuracy with a plan like that. Call off this project right away." But that would be leading with control.

Instead I reminded myself of what I often tell leaders throughout Netflix:

WHEN ONE OF YOUR PEOPLE DOES SOMETHING DUMB DON'T BLAME THEM. INSTEAD ASK YOURSELF WHAT CONTEXT YOU FAILED TO SET. ARE YOU ARTICULATE AND INSPIRING ENOUGH IN EXPRESSING YOUR GOALS AND STRATEGY? HAVE YOU CLEARLY EXPLAINED ALL THE ASSUMPTIONS AND RISKS THAT WILL HELP YOUR TEAM TO MAKE GOOD DECISIONS? ARE YOU AND YOUR EMPLOYEES HIGHLY ALIGNED ON VISION AND OBJECTIVES?

In the case of the facilities executive, I said very little in the moment. This guy is the informed captain when it comes to selecting office space, not me.

But the conversation notified me that I needed to set better context across our organization. If one person is misaligned with our strategy, there must be fifty others who are in the same boat. I added this topic to an upcoming QBR meeting. There I spoke with all of our leaders about why at Netflix we almost always prefer to pay more for the option that gives us greater flexibility, knowing that we can't— and shouldn't—try to foresee what our business will look like down the road.

Of course, each situation is different and in every

business we need to think somewhat ahead. During that QBR we discussed to what lengths we should go to in order to remain flexible. I provided some pre-reading that showed how bad we had been at predicting our growth in the past and how the best opportunities often can't be predicted. We had break-out discussions looking at past cases where we could have paid more for an option that increased future choice or less for an option that reduced flexibility. We debated just how much flexibility we needed in our business and how much we should be ready to pay for it.

Those conversations didn't lead to a clear conclusion or rule, but through the debates all our leaders became clearly aligned on the idea that preventing errors or saving money with long-term plans is not our primary objective. Our North Star is building a company that is able to adapt quickly as unforeseen opportunities arise and business conditions change.

Of course, the CEO in any organization only provides the first layer of context setting. At Netflix just about every manager, at every level, has to learn how to lead with context on entering the company. Melissa Cobb, on Ted's team, provided an example that demonstrates how context setting works across the entire organization.

ALIGNMENT IS A TREE, NOT A PYRAMID

Melissa Cobb, vice president of original animation, worked for Fox, Disney, VH1, and DreamWorks before she joined Netflix in September 2017. At Dream-Works she was the producer of the Oscar-nominated **Kung Fu Panda** trilogy. After twenty-four years in leadership positions, she uses two metaphors—the pyramid and the tree—to help the managers who join her team to understand the difference between a traditional leadership role and leading with context at Netflix. She explains it like this:

Decision making at every organization I'd worked at before Netflix was structured like a pyramid. Since I worked for networks I've been in the business of making movies and television shows. At the bottom of our pyramids we had a bunch—maybe forty-five or fifty—of what we call creative executives. Each of these executives would have one or more shows they were responsible for. For example, while I was at Disney, we produced **Man of the House** starring Chevy Chase and the creative executive responsible for that show was on the set each day, approving the pages, the costumes, and all the little details. Many little details of each show would be taken care of at the bottom of the pyramid.

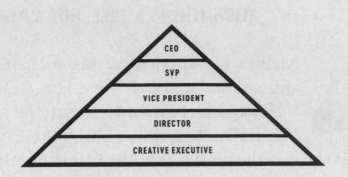

But if something important came up, like maybe someone wanted to change a sensitive piece of dialogue at the introduction of the show, that would need to be addressed at a higher level in the pyramid. The creative exec would say, "Oh, I'm not sure what my boss will think—let me give her a call."

The exec would call her manager, one of about fifteen directors at the next pyramid level. "What do you think boss? Can we make this dialogue change?" For most issues the director would endorse the change or sometimes refuse it.

But if the change was something bigger than just swapping a little dialogue, like maybe someone wanted to cut out an entire scene, then the director might say, "Well, I'm not sure what MY boss will say. I need to check with him." The issue would then be pushed up to the next level in the pyramid where we'd have half a dozen vice presidents. The director would call up his manager and say, "What do you think, boss? Can we cut out this scene?" That VP would then approve or decline the change.

Now if something even bigger happened—like one of the actors dropped out or the whole script had to be rewritten—that would need to go up to one of the few senior vice presidents at the next level. And for something really big—like the writer gets sick and a new writer needs to be approved posthaste—that might go all the way up to the CEO sitting in the tiny triangle at the top of the pyramid.

The pyramid decision-making structure Melissa experienced at her previous company is easily recognizable in the majority of organizations, regardless of industry or location. Either the boss makes the decision and pushes it down the pyramid for implementation, or those at lower levels make the smaller decisions but refer the bigger issues to the higher-ups.

But at Netflix, as we've discussed, the informed captain is the decision maker, not the boss. The boss's job is to set the context that leads the team to make the best decisions for the organization. If we follow this leadership system from the CEO all the way to the informed captain, we see that it works not so much like a pyramid but more like a tree, with the CEO sitting all the way down at the roots and the informed captain up at the top branches making decisions.

Melissa provided an in-depth example of how context setting works from the roots of the tree all the way out to the highest branches. In her tree exhibit, below, you can see the various levels of context being set from Reed, through Ted Sarandos, Melissa herself, Dominque Bazay (a director working for Melissa), and how all this context finally impacts the decision made by informed captain Aram Yacoubian. Let's look now at how the context setting at each point created alignment up and down the organization.

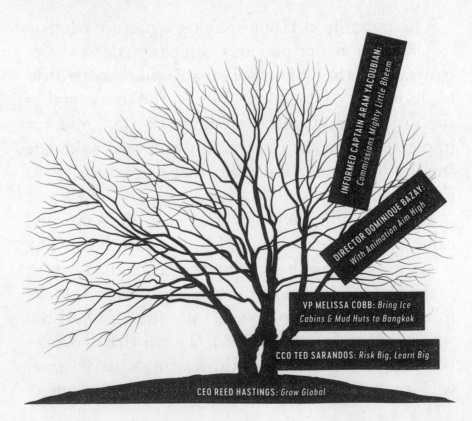

INFORMED CAPTAIN ARAM YACOUBIAN: *Commissions Mighty Little Bheem*

DIRECTOR DOMINIQUE BAZAY: *With Animation Aim High*

VP MELISSA COBB: *Bring Ice Cabins & Mud Huts to Bangkok*

CCO TED SARANDOS: *Risk Big, Learn Big*

CEO REED HASTINGS: *Grow Global*

REED AT THE ROOTS—GROW GLOBAL

In October 2017 Melissa attended her first QBR, where Reed presented information about the future global expansion of Netflix. She remembers it like this:

> I had been at Netflix for under a month. The second week of October we had my first QBR at the Langham Huntington Hotel in Pasadena. I had been trying to get a handle on how Netflix worked and everyone kept telling me that at QBR the pieces would come together. So I was listening carefully when Reed took the stage.
>
> During his fifteen-minute talk Reed explained, "In the past quarter, eighty percent of our growth came from outside of the US, and that is exactly where we should be focusing our energy. Over half our customers are now coming from other countries, and every year this number will increase. This is where the big growth lies. International growth is our priority."

Reed went on to detail which countries Netflix leaders should be focusing the most heavily on (including India, Brazil, Korea, Japan) and why (reasons to follow below). That message anchored much of Melissa's thinking on how to develop the strategy for her own department. Reed is not Melissa's direct boss, though. She works for Ted Sarandos. Shortly after the QBR, she had a one-on-one with Ted, where he added his own context to Reed's message.

TED SARANDOS AT THE TRUNK—RISK BIG, LEARN BIG

Before their one-on-one, Ted had already spoken with Melissa about some of the major international growth opportunities. India is a huge Netflix growth market. Japan and Korea have ecosystems that are particularly rich for content development. Brazil has only a very small Netflix office but over ten million viewers. But when Ted and Melissa sat down in late October 2017, Ted spoke not about what people at Netflix knew but about all the things they didn't know yet:

> Look, Melissa, we are at a turning point for Netflix. We have forty-four million members in the US. The big growth will be international and we have a lot to learn. We don't know if Saudi Arabians watch more or less TV during Ramadan. We don't know if Italians prefer documentaries or comedies. We don't know if Indonesians are more likely to watch movies alone in their bedrooms or around their family televisions. If we are going

to succeed, we need to become an international learning machine.

Melissa was already familiar with the language of bet-taking used at Netflix and the implication that some bets will succeed and others will fail. What the gambling analogy didn't capture was the critical aspect of learning from all that failing. This brings us to the context set by Ted:

As your team purchases and creates content around the world, we need to be laser-focused on learning. We should be ready to take bigger risks in high-growth-potential countries like India or Brazil so that we learn more about those markets. Let's have some wins. But let's also have some big messy losses where we learn how to succeed better the next time. We should always be asking, "If we purchase this show and it bombs, what will we learn from that?" If there is something big to learn, let's go ahead and take the bet.

Reed and Ted's context collectively helped Melissa to develop the context she set with her own Kids and Family content team at their next weekly meeting.

MELISSA COBB ON A BIG BRANCH—BRING ICE CABINS
AND MUD HUTS TO BANGKOK

Melissa's past employers like Disney and DreamWorks are known globally, and they deliver content watched everywhere on the planet. Yet Melissa believed that Netflix had a chance to differentiate itself, not just as a global brand, but as a truly global platform:

> Around the world most kids watch either content from their own country or shows and movies that originated in the US. But I felt that to be as international as Reed had outlined at QBR we could do better.
>
> I wanted the kids' slate of shows on Netflix to be like a global village. When ten-year-old Kulap, who lives in a Bangkok high-rise, wakes up on Saturday morning and turns on Netflix, I wanted her to see not just characters from Thailand (those are already on her local television channels) or from the US (those are on the Disney cable station) but a variety of TV and movie friends from around the world. She should be able to choose from shows based in ice-covered cabins in Sweden and others set in rural Kenya. The stories shouldn't just be **about** children from a wide array of countries. Disney can do that. They should have the look and feel that you only get when these shows actually **come from** around the world.

We had a lot of debates on my team about whether this strategy would work. Would children want to watch characters that were so dramatically different than they were? We didn't know.

That's where the context Ted set came in. As he had stressed, these were the questions we would seek to answer and we should be prepared for our bets to fail, provided they resulted in clear learning. We all came to an agreement. We would give it a try and learn along the way.

During this meeting Melissa found alignment with her six direct reports. Dominique Bazay, the director whose team acquires preschool content, was one of them.

DOMINIQUE BAZAY ON A MIDDLE-SIZE BRANCH— WITH ANIMATION AIM HIGH

After that meeting with Melissa, Dominique thought a lot about how to make Melissa's "global village" dream come true. To encourage Kulap to watch TV created in Sweden and Kenya, what types of shows should Netflix be offering? Dominique felt that animation was the best answer to this question. That led to the context she set with her own team:

Cartoon Peppa Pig speaks Spanish like a Spaniard, Turkish like a Turk, and absolutely perfect Japanese. Animation provides an opportunity for international programming that live-action can't. When actress Bella Ramsey's **Worst Witch** is shown in a new country, the viewer has to watch it dubbed or subtitled. Kids hate subtitles and Bella looks funny speaking Portuguese or German. The voices don't match the image and that impacts the quality of the viewing experience. But cartoon Peppa, like all animated characters, always speaks the language of the viewers. The Korean child and the Dutch child feel equally connected to Peppa.

If Netflix kids' programming was going to be the diverse platform Melissa spoke of, I believed that we needed to aim high. I discussed with my own team that for all animated shows we purchased, no matter what country they came from, the animation quality should be high enough to be considered top-notch by the most discerning nations in the world. If, for example, an animated show comes out of Chile, it shouldn't just be high enough quality for the most discerning Chilean viewer. It should be high quality enough to be a hit in anime-obsessed Japan.

It was with all of this context—from Reed, Ted, Melissa, and Dominique—that then manager of content acquisition, Aram Yacoubian, sitting in a small conference room in downtown Mumbai, considered the show he was being pitched: **Mighty Little Bheem**.

ARAM YACOUBIAN ON A SMALL BRANCH— MIGHTY LEARNINGS FROM LITTLE BHEEM

When Aram saw the original version of the adorable Indian animation series **Mighty Little Bheem**, he thought it would be a big hit in India:

> The main character is this little child in a small Indian village, whose boundless curiosity and extraordinary strength leads to all sorts of adventures. He's like a baby Indian Popeye. His character is based on Bheem, a mythical character in the Sanskrit epic Mahabharata, known across India. It seemed obvious to me, Indians would love this show.

But Aram had serious doubts about whether it was a good bet for Netflix. The first concern he had was with the animation quality.

> Indian shows tend to be low budget. The quality of the animation was good enough to be popular on

Indian TV. But I thought about what Dominique and I had agreed on. We wanted to make sure the quality was high enough to be successful not just in the country of origin but around the world. I knew that if we were going to purchase this show, we would have to invest two or three times what is normally spent on an Indian animation to get the quality we were looking for.

This led to Aram's second concern:

That was a lot of money to invest in an Indian show. To recoup the investment we'd have to get a lot of children all around the world to watch it. But very few Indian programs had ever been hugely popular outside of India—in all the history of television and streaming. This was due to low budgets but also to a belief that the storytelling was too locally specific for global audiences. There was a widely held belief that Indian series didn't travel well.

Aram's third concern was the lack of historical data on preschool shows—even within India:

Mighty Little Bheem is for young children and until now there had been practically no preschool shows made in India either for streaming or television. That's because Indian rating agencies don't measure preschool shows, so they can't be monetized. Was there even an audience in India for programming aimed at such young kids? History couldn't provide an answer.

On the face of it, all this made things look pretty bad for **Mighty Little Bheem**. "All of history and all these business reasons were telling me not to make this show," says Aram. But he also reflected on the context the Netflix leaders had set for him:

Reed made it clear that international expansion is our future and India is a key growth market. **Mighty Little Bheem** is a great show from a key Netflix growth market.

Ted made it clear that when it comes to countries like India, we have so much to learn that we should take big risks, as long as the learning potential is evident. With **Mighty Little Bheem** what we would learn from the bet was very clear. The context Ted had set was enough for me to say, "Okay, even if this show crashes and burns, I'm trying three different things, all of which are going to provide Netflix with really good information."

Melissa made it clear that we wanted children's shows from around the world that were deeply local

> in topic and texture to make up our programming slate. **Mighty Little Bheem** was deeply Indian and had the elements to appeal to children anywhere.
>
> Dominique and I had agreed that we should prioritize animation for our big international bets and that this animation should be of high quality. **Mighty Little Bheem** was an animated show that could achieve the high quality we needed with a financial investment.

With this context in mind Aram made his decision. He purchased **Mighty Little Bheem** and gave money to the local creators to upgrade the animation. The show launched mid-April 2019 and within three weeks became one of Netflix's most watched animated series from anywhere in the world. It has now been watched by more than twenty-seven million viewers.

When I interviewed him, Aram clarified the great advantage of dispersed decision-making when managers lead with context.

> I'm one of the best people at Netflix to decide what children's content to purchase in India, as I know the Indian animation market and Indian family-viewing patterns like the back of my hand. But it's only with organizational transparency, a ton

of context, and high alignment between me and the leadership that I can make the best decisions to benefit our organization and Netflix viewers around the world.

Aram's decision to purchase **Mighty Little Bheem** provides a clear example of how leading with context works at Netflix. Each leader from myself at the roots of the tree up through Dominique at the middle-branch level sets context informing Aram's decision. But Aram himself, as the informed captain, decides what shows to buy.

This case, you'll have noticed, is by no means unique. Throughout this book we've told stories about lower-level employees making multimillion-dollar financial decisions without getting approval from the boss. Outsiders are often puzzled about how this can work in a financially responsible organization. The answer is simple: it's because of the alignment.

Although Netflix gives employees a lot of financial freedom, the investment of money follows the same context tree that Melissa described. Ted and I are aligned on how much the content area will invest on purchasing films and shows over a specific quarter. Ted then cascades that down, providing context to Melissa on what amount her group should invest in kids and family programming. She then aligns with each of her directors about how much they should invest in each specific category. When Aram made the decision to bid for **Mighty Little Bheem** and also put a bunch of money into upgrading the animation, he wasn't spending money randomly. He was applying the financial context that Melissa and Dominique had set for him.

ICARUS—THE FINAL SCENE

 When we left Adam Del Deo, he was standing in the Washington School House Hotel trying to decide whether to bet big on a movie named after a man who flew so close to the sun that his wax wings melted.

Ted had set a clear context. If **Icarus** wasn't going to be a massive hit, Adam shouldn't bet massive money on it. He'd already bid $2.5 million and all the usual suspects, from Amazon to Hulu, were also sniffing around. If $2.5 million wasn't enough and this movie wasn't "the one," he should let it go. But if Adam believed **Icarus** was going to be a huge hit, then he should swing big—bet whatever it would take to get that movie on Netflix.

Adam did believe **Icarus** was going to be a massive hit, so he took the bet. Netflix paid a historic $4.6 million to get it. In August 2017, **Icarus** was released on Netflix.

In the first few months **Icarus** struggled to get off the ground. No one was watching. Adam was crushed:

> Ten days after the **Icarus** release, we had a team meeting where we went through the viewing data for new content and I was devastated by the poor numbers. My colleagues trust me to be able to predict the viewing of a movie, the public discussion that will result, and the yield at Oscars time. My reputation is built on that trust. I felt I had made a huge mistake that couldn't help but damage my colleagues' faith in me.

Then one event changed everything. In December 2017, the International Olympic Committee issued a report that Russia had been banned from the games. In that IOC report, **Icarus** was cited as the key piece of evidence. Rodchenkov went on **60 Minutes**, where he stated his belief that at least twenty countries were doping in the same way. Then Lance Armstrong came out publicly voicing his appreciation of **Icarus**. Suddenly everyone was talking about this movie and viewing figures skyrocketed.

In March 2018 **Icarus** was nominated for best documentary at the Oscars. Adam remembers the ceremony like this:

I was sure we wouldn't win. When actress Laura Dern was about to announce the winner, I whispered to my boss Lisa Nishamura, "We won't get it. **Faces Places** will get it." But then, like in slow motion, I heard actress Laura Dern say, "The winner is . . . **Icarus!**" Bryan Fogel was racing to the stage. Someone screamed out in delight from the balcony. I felt so overwhelmed that if I hadn't been sitting I would have fallen over.

On the way to the after-party Adam bumped into Ted, who congratulated him:

I asked, "Do you remember that conversation we had at Sundance, Ted?" He gave me a big grin and said, "Yep . . . it was 'THE ONE.'"

THE NINTH DOT

 In a loosely coupled organization, where talent density is high and innovation is the primary goal, a traditional, control-oriented approach is not the most effective choice. Instead of seeking to minimize error through oversight or process, focus on setting clear context, building alignment of the North Star between boss and team, and giving the informed captain the free-dom to decide.

▶ TAKEAWAYS FROM CHAPTER 9

- In order to lead with context, you need to have high talent density, your goal needs to be innovation (not error prevention), and you need to be operating in a loosely coupled system.

- Once these elements are in place, instead of telling people what to do, get in lockstep alignment by providing and debating all the context that will allow them to make good decisions.

- When one of your people does something dumb, don't blame that person. Instead, ask yourself what context you failed to set. Are you articulate and inspiring enough in expressing your goals and strategy? Have you clearly explained all the assumptions and risks that will help your team to make good decisions? Are you and your employees highly aligned on vision and objectives?

- A loosely coupled organization should resemble a tree rather than a pyramid. The boss is at the roots, holding up the trunk of senior managers who support the outer branches where decisions are made.

- You know you're successfully leading with context when your people are moving the team in the desired direction by using the information they've received from you and those around you to make great decisions themselves.

This Is Freedom and Responsibility

We've now explored how to build up the foundational elements of talent density and candor, and then to begin removing policies and procedures to offer employees more freedom, while also creating an environment that's increasingly fast and flexible. We've looked at over a dozen policies and processes that most companies have but that we don't have at Netflix. These include:

Vacation Policies
Decision-Making Approvals
Expense Policies
Performance Improvement Plans
Approval Processes
Raise Pools
Key Performance Indicators
Management by Objective
Travel Policies
Decision Making by Committee
Contract Sign-Offs

Salary Bands
Pay Grades
Pay-Per-Performance Bonuses

These are all ways of controlling people rather than inspiring them. It's not easy to avoid chaos and anarchy as you remove these controls, but if you develop every employee's sense of self-discipline and responsibility, help them develop enough knowledge to make good decisions, and develop a feedback culture to stimulate learning, you'll be amazed at how effective your organization can be.

This alone is enough reason to develop a culture of F&R. But these are not the only benefits. Beyond that:

- Some of the items on the list above squash innovation. Vacation policies, travel policies, and expense policies can lead to the type of high-rule environment that discourages creative thinking and scare off the most innovative employees.
- Other items on this list slow the business down. Approval policies, decision making by committee, and contract sign-offs all put hurdles in front of your employees so that they can't move quickly.
- Many of these items keep the organization from changing quickly when the

environment shifts. Pay-per-performance bonuses, Management by Objective, and Key Performance Indicators motivate employees to stay on a preset path, making it difficult to quickly dump one project and pick up another. Whereas Performance Improvement Plans (along with any hiring and firing processes) make it difficult to swap out and in employees quickly as business needs change.

If your goal is to build a more inventive, fast, and flexible organization, develop a culture of freedom and responsibility by establishing the necessary conditions so you can remove these rules and processes too.

We began this book with a couple of questions: Why do so many companies such as Blockbuster, AOL, Kodak, and my own first company, Pure Software, fail to adapt and innovate quickly as the environment morphs around them? How can organizations become more inventive and nimble in order to reach their goals?

In 2001 we began our journey at Netflix to what by the end of 2015 had become a highly tuned F&R culture. We had successfully transitioned Netflix from a DVD-by-mail enterprise to a streaming company that created award-winning television shows like **House of Cards** and **Orange Is the New Black**. Our stock price had risen from approximately $8 in

2010 to $123 by the end of 2015, and our user base had grown from 20 million to 78 million in the same time period.

After this remarkable success in the US, we then began our next cultural challenge: international expansion. Between 2011 and 2015 we began moving into a few countries one at a time. In 2016, we took the big leap, moving into 130 countries all in one day. Our culture had led us to achieve great things. But now we wondered: Would our corporate culture work around the world? That's what chapter 10 is about.

SECTION FOUR

GOING GLOBAL

10

BRING IT ALL TO THE WORLD!

 When I moved to rural Swaziland in 1983 as a Peace Corps volunteer, it was not my first international experience, but it was the one that taught me the most. It took only a few weeks for me to recognize that I understood and approached life very differently from the people around me.

One example came in my first month of teaching math to sixteen-year-old high school students. The kids in my class had been selected because of their strong mathematical abilities and I was preparing them for upcoming public exams. On a weekly quiz I provided a problem that, from my understanding of their skill set, they should have been able to answer:

A room measures 2 meters by 3 meters. How many 50-centimeter tiles does it take to cover the floor?

Not one of my students gave the accurate response and most of them left the question blank.

The next day in class I put the question on the blackboard and asked for a volunteer to solve it. Students shuffled their feet and looked out the window. I felt my face becoming flushed with frustration. "No one? No one is able to answer?" I asked incredulously. Feeling deflated, I sat down at my desk and waited for a response. That's when Thabo, a tall, earnest student raised his hand from the back of the class. "Yes, Thabo, please tell us how to solve this problem," I said, jumping up hopefully. But instead of answering the question Thabo asked, "Mr. Hastings, sir, please, what is a tile?"

My students lived mostly in traditional round huts, and their floors were either made of mud or concrete. They couldn't answer the question because they didn't know what a tile was. They just couldn't fathom what they were being asked to assess.

From this early experience—and many others that followed—I learned that I couldn't directly transfer my own way of life to the culture of another place. In order to be effective, I had to think about what adaptations I would need to make in order to get the results I was hoping for.

So in 2010, when Netflix began expanding internationally, I thought a lot about whether the organizational culture would also need to adapt to be successful around the world. By that time our management methods had developed so fully and were producing such good results that I was reluctant to make a significant change. But I felt uncertain if our candid feedback, low-rule ethos, and Keeper Test techniques would be effective in other countries.

I considered another company, which was already international and had taken a clear approach. Like us, Google was proud of having a strong corporate culture, but instead of adapting its culture to the countries it moved into, it focused on hiring for fit. It sought to hire employees throughout the world who were "Googlers": people with a personality that matched the corporate culture no matter what country they lived in or came from.

I also reflected on a situation I'd had in 1988, when I'd spent a year working for Schlumberger in Palo Alto. Schlumberger is a big French multinational, yet the corporate culture in the Silicon Valley office had clearly been imported from France. All the department leaders were French expats and, if you wanted to succeed, you needed to learn to navigate the decision-making systems and hierarchical patterns that originated from the headquarters in Paris. There were training programs for new employees on how to debate effectively and how to analyze situations using a principles-first approach—so typical of French culture.

Both Google and Schlumberger seemed to have had success keeping a uniform corporate culture around the world. So, with only a bit of trepidation, I felt we could do the same. Like Google, we would seek to hire for fit, selecting individuals in each country who were attracted to and comfortable with the corporate culture we had spent so long cultivating. And like Schlumberger, we would train our new employees in other countries to understand and work in the Netflix way.

At the same time, we would seek to be humble and flexible, tweaking our culture as we went and learning from each country we moved into.

In 2010, we began the internationalization process, first opening in neighboring Canada, and a year later in Latin America. Between 2012 and 2015, we made bigger moves into Europe and Asia Pacific. During this period, we opened our four regional offices in Tokyo, Singapore, Amsterdam, and São Paulo. Then, in 2016, we took a big international leap and made our platform available in a total of 130 new countries all in one day. The expansion was overwhelmingly successful and over the course of just three years we saw our non-US subscriber base skyrocket from forty to eighty-eight million.

During this same three years we doubled the number of Netflix employees overall, most of them still located in the United States, but of increasingly diverse backgrounds. We added inclusion as one of our cultural values, recognizing that our success would depend on how much our employees reflected the audiences we were trying to reach, and the ability of people to see their lives and passions reflected through the stories we told. In 2018, we added our first head of inclusion strategy, Vernā Myers, in order to help us identify and learn from our increasingly diverse employees.

As we grew our operations in other countries, and our employees became increasingly diverse, it didn't take long to recognize that some parts of our corporate culture would work well around the world. To my great relief, the freedom our employees thrive on in the US showed early signs that it would, without question, be successful everywhere. Some cultures had a little more difficulty getting in the swing of making decisions without checking a rule book or asking for approval, but once they get the hang of it, they love the autonomy and lack of rules as much as Californians do. It's not only Americans who love to be in control of their own lives and work. Nothing cultural about that.

Some of the other parts of our culture quickly proved less easy to export. One early example was the Keeper Test. We soon learned that, although we can follow our mantra "Adequate Performance Gets a Generous Severance" in every country, what is considered generous in the US is often seen as stingy—if not illegal—in some European countries. In the Netherlands, for example, the amount of severance required by law depends on how long the employee has been with the company. So we had to adapt. Now in the Netherlands, if firing someone who's been with us for a while, Adequate Performance Gets an **Even More** Generous Severance. The Keeper Test and all the elements that go with it can work internationally but require adaptation to the local employment practices and laws.

Beyond these quickly apparent elements, given how fast we were expanding around the globe and how important our corporate culture is to our success, I wanted to do all we could to understand the cultures of the countries we were moving into, and to find the similarities and potential challenges between the local culture and Netflix culture. I believed just being aware of that would prompt important discussions and ultimately improve our effectiveness.

ENTER THE CULTURE MAP

At about that time, a manager in our HR department lent me Erin's book, **The Culture Map**. The book outlines a system for comparing one national culture to another on a set of behavioral scales. It looks at issues like how much employees defer to the boss in different countries, how decisions are made in different parts of the world, how we build trust differently in different cultures, and most important for us at Netflix, how candid versus diplomatic people tend to be with critical feedback around the globe.

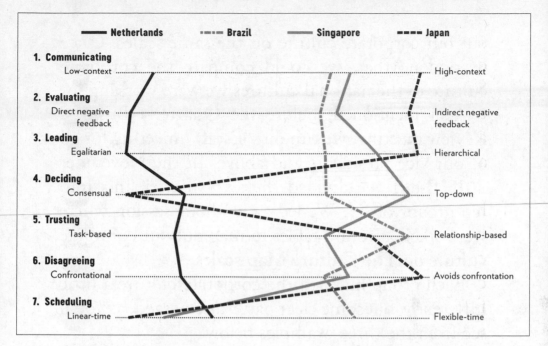

I did a bit of reading around the scales. The framework was based on an enormous amount of research and struck me as simultaneously robust and simple. I shared the book with our executive team and someone suggested that we look at the cultural "maps" for the various countries of our regional offices, compare them with one another, as per the chart above, and discuss what we felt the maps revealed.

The exercise was a revelation to many of us. The framework offered a convincing explanation for a number of things we had already encountered, such as why our experience with feedback in the Netherlands had been almost diametrically opposed to our experience in Japan (dimension 2 on the graph). We decided to get our executive team together to map out our corporate culture on the same scales. Once we'd done that, we could compare the corporate culture to the national cultures we were working in.

As I mentioned, before the Quarterly Business Review meeting, we run our "Estaff" meeting for all of our vice presidents and above. In the November 2015 Estaff, we divided the sixty participants into ten groups of six. We led a two-hour session where we worked at round tables to map out our corporate culture on **The Culture Map** scales.

Each group mapped the corporate culture a little differently, but some clear patterns emerged, as you'll see from the three examples below.

Group 1:

Group 2:

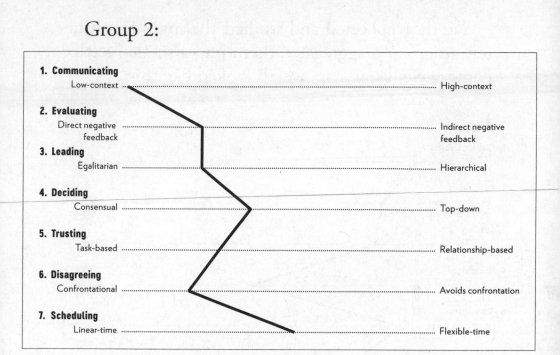

Group 3:

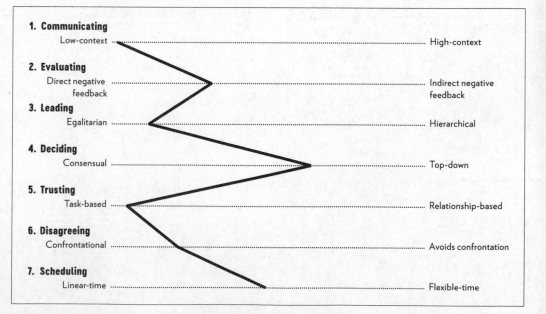

We then collected and studied the maps from the ten groups and aggregated them into a single Netflix corporate culture map, which looked like this:

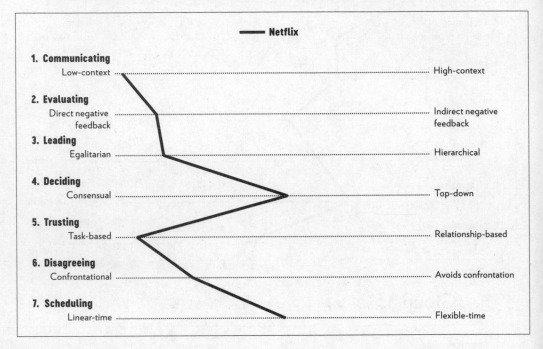

Next, using Erin's Country Mapping tool we compared our Netflix culture map to that of each of the countries where our regional hubs were located.

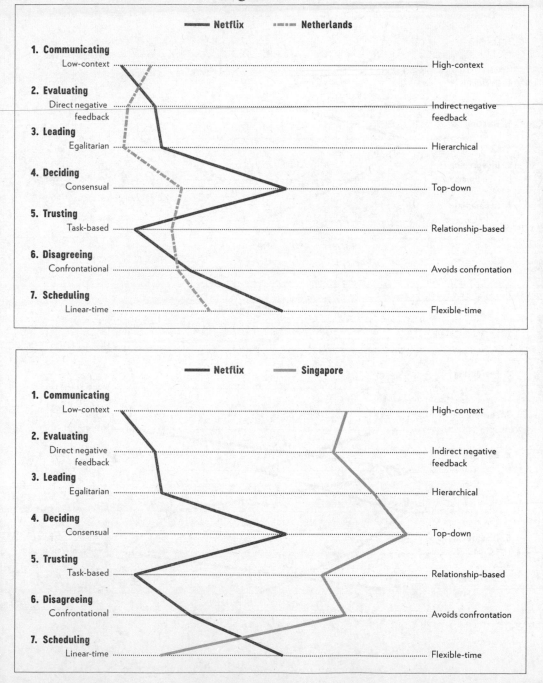

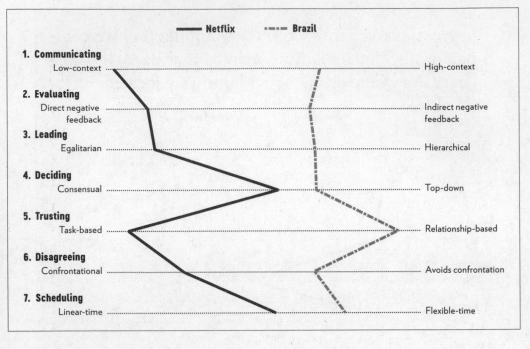

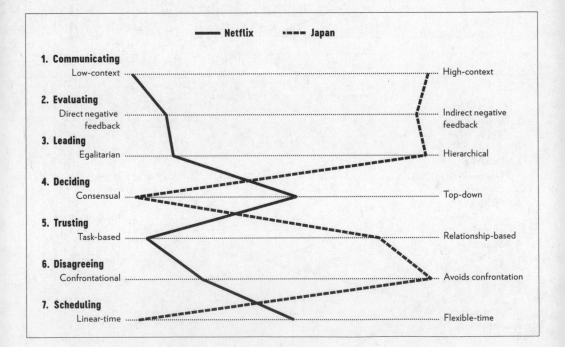

As we studied the maps, we realized that some of the issues we were having in our regional offices were due to cultural differences. For example, in comparison to Netflix culture, both the Netherlands and Japan fall to the consensual side of the decision-making scale (dimension 4) . That explained why many employees in our Amsterdam and Tokyo offices had been struggling with the Netflix Informed Captain model, where there is always one individual responsible for a decision (see chapter 6). As we looked at dimension 4, which measures how much a culture defers to authority, we saw Netflix falling to the right of the Netherlands (we learned that the Netherlands is one of the more egalitarian cultures in the world) and to the left of Singapore (more hierarchical). That helped us understand why our Dutch employees had no problem overruling their bosses' suggestions, while our Singaporean employees required more encouragement to make a decision if the boss didn't agree.

We were also struck by the trust dimension (dimension 5) where the Netflix culture was so clearly more task-oriented than almost every local culture we were moving into. The graph below zooms in on that specific dimension, so you can see the problem. We've added the US position for interest.

At Netflix, our emphasis had always been on watching the clock. The vast majority of meetings are thirty minutes long and we generally believe that

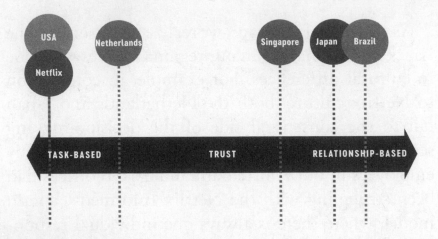

most topics, even important ones, can be settled in a half-hour time frame. We try to be friendly and helpful, but until this culture mapping exercise, we avoided spending much time on nonwork discussions. Our goal was efficiency and speed, not on spending time chatting over a cup of coffee. But as we increasingly hired employees around the world, we found that our obsession with investing every minute in the task was hurting us in myriad ways. Here is one pertinent example recounted by one of our very first employees in Brazil. Leonardo Sampaio, business development director for Latin America, joined Netflix in October 2015:

> After dozens of phone and video interviews, I came to Silicon Valley for a full day of face-to-face interviews. The recruiter set me up in a conference room and between nine and noon I had six thirty-minute interviews with all sorts of interesting

people, who would later become my colleagues. My agenda included just a half-hour lunch break.

In Brazil, lunch is a time to build friendships with your colleagues. It is a period to set the work aside each day and get to know one another beyond the tasks we have to complete. The trust we build during this time is critical to collaboration. It's also these relationships that, for a Brazilian, make coming to work enjoyable. I was surprised that lunch was scheduled for only thirty minutes and I wondered who would be coming to share this time with me.

A woman I didn't know came into the conference room where I was sitting. I stood up to greet her. Perhaps this was my lunch partner. She said in a friendly way, "Sarah asked me to bring you some lunch, I hope you like it." There was a nice meal in a bag including a couple of salads, a sandwich, and some fruit. She asked me if I needed anything else to feel comfortable. When I said no, she left, and I sat all alone eating my lunch. I understand now that to Americans, eating lunch during the work day is just a task to complete. But to a Brazilian, to be left alone eating lunch was shocking. I thought, "Isn't the guy who will be my boss at the very least going to come in and chat with me—ask how I'm feeling and ask about my life back in Brazil? I guess this is what Netflix means when they say, 'We are a team, not a family.'"

Of course, I wasn't alone for long because thirty minutes passes fast, and my next interviewer arrived.

When I heard this story, I was uncomfortable. "We are a team, not a family" is about insisting on high performance; it's not about investing every minute in the work, avoiding getting to know one another deeply, or not caring about the people you work with. Most Americans sitting for a full day of interviews would welcome thirty minutes alone over lunch to review their notes, but I understand now that to our Brazilian interviewees, leaving them alone over a meal just feels like bad manners. Now when our Brazilian colleagues come to visit, we remember the importance of investing more time in getting to know them at a personal level and we also know to ask our Brazilian colleagues to help us to adapt our own relationship-building approach when negotiating with providers in Brazil.

Having the Culture Map in front of us helped us to be more prepared and more effective, not just in this situation, but at many other important moments. Much of the awareness we developed from the culture mapping exercise led to critical discussions resulting in not-so-difficult solutions.

But not all of the elements highlighted on the culture maps were easy to address. The dimension linked to candor, what is referred to as the Evaluating scale on The Culture Map, has led to ongoing challenges big and small. It built our awareness of the differences, but what to do about those differences was anything but obvious.

IDEAS ABOUT CANDOR DIFFER GREATLY AROUND THE WORLD

 As anyone who has worked internationally will tell you, feedback that's effective in one country doesn't necessarily work in another. For instance, the direct corrective feedback given by a German boss might seem unnecessarily harsh in the US, while an American's tendency to give copious positive feedback might come off as excessive and insincere in Germany.

That's because employees in different parts of the world are conditioned to give feedback in dramatically different ways. The Thai manager learns never to criticize a colleague openly or in front of others, while the Israeli manager learns always to be honest and give the message straight. Colombians are trained to soften negative messages with positive words, while the French are trained to criticize passionately and provide positive feedback sparingly. Positions of the Netflix corporate culture and the local cultures where their primary offices are located looks something like this:

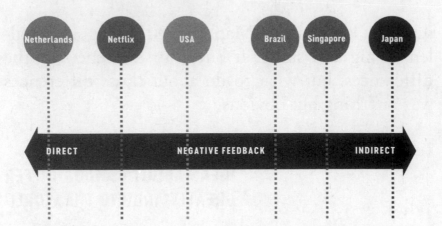

When it comes to delivering criticism, the Netherlands is one of the more direct cultures in the world. Japan is highly indirect. Singapore is one of the most direct of the East Asian countries, but still to the indirect side of a world scale. The US average falls a little left of center. Brazil (with strong regional differences) is just a bit more direct than Singapore. The Netflix positions come from the culture-mapping exercise Reed led in 2015.

One of the reasons for the country placements on this scale has to do with the language people use when they provide criticism. More direct cultures tend to use what linguists call **upgraders,** words preceding or following negative feedback that make it feel stronger, such as "absolutely," "totally," or "strongly": "This is absolutely inappropriate" or "This is totally unprofessional." In contrast, more indirect cultures use more **downgraders,** when giving negative feedback. These are words that soften the criticism, such as "kind of," "sort of," "a little," "a bit," "maybe," and "slightly". Another type of downgrader is a deliberate understatement, such as, "We are not quite there yet," when you really mean, "We are nowhere near our goal."

The Japanese, as the most indirect of the cultures where Netflix has an office, tend to use plenty of downgraders when giving negative feedback. But this isn't the only technique they use to make the criticism feel softer. Often feedback is passed implicitly and barely spoken at all. When Netflix opened in Japan in 2015, it didn't take long to see that the explicit, frequent, and often upward feedback expected by Netflix management was neither natural nor comfortable for the newly-hired local employees. Vice president of business and legal affairs Josephine Choy (an American) remembers one experience:

> I was one of the early employees in Tokyo and, as the then-General Counsel for Japan, my first duty was to hire a team of legal professionals. I sought Japanese people who were bilingual (Japanese/English) and seemed to embody—or at least be attracted to—the Netflix culture.

The hiring was successful, but challenges popped up early. One of the first was during those difficult moments when discussing a problem or a mistake, Josephine's staff appeared to discuss the situation openly, while simultaneously finessing the most important pieces of information between the lines. Josephine explains:

> In English we usually state the subject followed by a verb and an object. We rarely drop the subject, or the sentence doesn't make sense. In Japanese, however, the syntax is flexible. The subject, verb, and object are all optional. It is possible to have a sentence in Japanese with only a noun. Often the sentence might start with the main topic, followed by some content, and the verb at the end. Sometimes the speaker assumes everyone knows what the subject is, so he drops it. And this aspect of Japanese language lends itself nicely to a conflict-avoidant culture. At these moments, you have to consider what is being said in context in order to know who did what.

For example, on Josephine's team, when someone made a mistake or a deadline was missed, they would use Japanese-style linguistic techniques to avoid pointing fingers even while speaking English.

> In a meeting, when discussing something that had gone wrong, my team would often use the passive voice. They might say, "The assets didn't get created and therefore the commercial couldn't air," or "Approval wasn't given so there was surprise and

the bill didn't get paid." In this way they avoided embarrassing someone in the room or placing explicit blame, while having a completely open discussion amongst themselves.

It also meant that I—as the only non-Japanese—frequently would have to stop them in order to figure out what was going on. "Wait, who didn't create the assets? We didn't, or the agency didn't?" Sometimes a passive construction seemed to allude to something I had failed to do but no one dared mention. "Wait, was I supposed to give the approval? Was it my fault and how can I help?"

This tendency to speak and read between the lines is most common when giving corrective feedback, expressing disagreement, or communicating negative impressions. Conveying an unpleasant message indirectly allows the feedback giver to preserve a harmonious relationship with the feedback receiver. In Japanese culture, explicit constructive feedback is rarely voiced—and certainly not to someone further up the hierarchy. Josephine remembers the difficulties that arose the first time she solicited feedback from one of her Japanese employees:

One of my first hires in Tokyo was a director-level attorney named Miho. Once we got through our initial onboarding, I set up a weekly one-on-one meeting. For the first meeting I sent out an agenda and the last item was feedback. The one-on-one went very well until we got to that last item. I said, "As you know Netflix has a culture of feedback and candor. I would like to begin by asking for your feedback. How has the onboarding process been and are there any changes I can make in my approach to be a more effective manager to you?"

Having used this same method with dozens of employees in the US, Josephine didn't expect what happened next:

Miho looked at me and tears started running down her face. Not out of fear or anger. It was just like, "Oh my goodness, my boss is asking me to give her feedback. This is happening!" She said, "Oh. . . . I'm sorry. I'm crying. I really want to do this. I just don't know how. We don't give feedback to the boss like this in Japan."

I decided to start the process gently. "I'll go first this time. My feedback to you is that when I send out meeting agendas in the future, you can add anything you like to the list of topics to discuss." She dried her eyes and said, "Okay, that is helpful feedback. Let me think about it and I'll get back to you with my feedback at the next meeting."

For Josephine it was an eye-opener.

> Obviously, I know the Japanese are less direct than Americans and giving feedback to a superior might have added complications, but I wasn't prepared for that response. After some practice, Miho began giving me clear and actionable feedback in our one-on-ones, so that was a clear success.

But getting the Japanese employees to give one another ad hoc feedback in a meeting or during a presentation was proving more challenging. After trial and error, Netflix leaders learned a few key lessons for how to successfully implement a culture of candor, not just in Japan, but in many other less direct cultures around the world. The first lesson was to increase formal feedback moments when dealing with less direct cultures.

WITH LESS DIRECT CULTURES, INCREASE FORMAL FEEDBACK MOMENTS

 Given the feedback challenge in the Tokyo office, a group of US-based managers tried an experiment in their attempts to get their Japanese employees to give

4A-type feedback. They travelled from California to Japan to run a feedback clinic. Japanese content manager Yuka, who attended the clinic, remembers it like this:

> Four American Netflix leaders came to Tokyo to lead a session on how to give and receive feedback. They stood on stage and gave corrective feedback to one another and responded to the feedback they were receiving. They told stories about times they had received tough feedback from other American colleagues, how it had felt, and the positive impact it had made.
>
> Afterward we all clapped politely. But we agreed that this helped us not at all. One American giving feedback to another American in English isn't the challenge. This we've seen dozens of times. What we needed to see was one Japanese giving feedback to another Japanese (ideally in Japanese) in a way that is appropriate, respectful, and doesn't harm the relationship. That's the link we were missing.

It was chief product officer Greg Peters who identified a better approach. Greg is married to a Japanese woman and is a fluent Japanese speaker, which is part of the reason I asked him to move to Tokyo and open the regional office in 2015. He recalls:

I'd been in Japan for about six months and despite a lot of encouragement, there was very little impromptu feedback in the office. When the 360 process came around, I had low expectations.

We did the written 360s. Then we did a live 360 session, which is one of the most un-Japanese activities imaginable: giving frank feedback to a colleague and superior in front of a group. But I knew there were parts of the culture that might make this group feedback possible. Most Japanese are meticulous and dedicated preparers. If you set clear expectations, they will do everything they can to meet them. If you say, "Please prepare for this and these are the instructions we are going to follow," they almost always excel.

The results were remarkable. During the 360 process the Japanese on my team provided higher-quality feedback than my teams in the US had in previous years. The comments were frank and well-constructed. Their recommendations were actionable, and they didn't pull punches. They received the feedback with grace and appreciation.

Afterward, when I debriefed with several of them, they said, "You told us it was part of our job. You told us what to do and how to do it. We prepared and some of us even rehearsed. We wanted to make sure we met your and Netflix's expectations."

What we learned from this experience, and later found to be true not just in Japan but in most cultures where direct negative feedback is less comfortable and less common, was that asking employees to give ad hoc feedback to peers and superiors at informal moments doesn't usually work well. But if you run more formal events, putting feedback on the agenda, providing preparation instructions, and giving a clear structure to follow, you can get all the useful feedback out there just as effectively.

Josephine took this away from both her Netflix experience in Japan and later leading teams in Brazil and Singapore:

Now I tell my Netflix colleagues who are managing employees in any office where the culture is less direct than in the US: "Practice feedback early and often. Put feedback on the agenda in as many meetings as possible to take the stigma out of it. The first few times you provide feedback, gently mention small things that are easily actionable. Instead of decreasing the amount of formal feedback moments, increase them while also investing time in relationship-building. Informal spontaneous feedback is unlikely to happen much, but you can get many benefits from selfless candor by putting feedback on the agenda and allowing people the space to prepare for it."

Creating copious formal feedback moments is the first lesson Netflix managers learned for implementing a culture of candor around the world. The second lesson is . . .

LEARN TO ADJUST YOUR STYLE AND TALK, TALK, TALK

When Netflix moved to Japan, Josephine, Greg, and the rest of the management team were on high alert for the cultural differences that might impact their effectiveness; they knew going in that the Japanese culture would be different. But when Netflix moved to Singapore, the cultural differences were less apparent and therefore the leaders were less careful. Many found their Singaporean colleagues, with their perfect English and experience of working with Westerners, so familiar in their approach that they didn't give culture much thought at all. But then the differences started creeping in.

Marketing coordinator Karlyne Wang, who joined Netflix from HBO Asia in October 2017, provided a specific example:

> Our administrative assistant left, and I am temporarily filling in. Last week there was a call with an external partner scheduled on two of my senior

American colleagues' calendars. The call was scheduled by my predecessor, not me. The Americans
got up early, but the partner never dialed in.

The two Americans then pinged me separately.
Their text messages made me so angry that I ghosted
them. I didn't respond. I had to take a walk, during
which I told myself: try to be as open as possible.
Calm down, that's just how they write. Maybe they
don't realize that their messages feel rude. Maybe
they don't know how their words impact people.
These are good people. I know they are good people.

As Karlyne told this story I became increasingly
curious to see just how obnoxious these Americans
had been. Perhaps this wasn't a cultural misunderstanding but simply bad behavior. Karlyne dug up
one of the offensive text messages:

> Karlyne - We got up early for the call but
> the partners never dialed in. We could've
> used the slot for another call. Can you
> please try and double check all calls the day
> before and if not happening delete from
> calendar?

To my American eyes, this text message struck me
as neither rude nor inappropriate. Seeking to assist
the business, the sender laid out a problem and an
actionable solution. She didn't berate Karlyne. She

explained what behavior change she was hoping for, and said "please." I wondered if Karlyne's reaction was cultural or simply oversensitivity on her part.

So I showed a screenshot of the text to several other Netflix Singaporean employees to get their input. Seven out of eight echoed Karlyne's reaction: the message is rude. One of them was Programmatic Manager Christopher Low.

CHRISTOPHER: To a Singaporean person this text message is aggressive. It's very directive. Here's the situation. Do A. Do B. If I received this message I would feel this person was shouting at me. The worst part is where she writes, "We could have used the slot for another call." There is no need for that sentence. The first sentence already implies this to be true. Stating it openly feels unnecessarily harsh. I would think, "What could I have done to trigger such a nasty reaction?"

ERIN: Do you feel the sender is being selflessly candid?

CHRISTOPHER: I think the Westerner feels like, "I just need to do this quickly and make sure I am clear. I don't want to waste unnecessary minutes." But to a Singaporean it feels like a kick. It doesn't feel selfless. It's shocking.

ERIN: What could the sender have done to communicate the same message without coming off as rude or insulting?

CHRISTOPHER: She could have been more personal, maybe saying, "Hey, I know this was the middle of the night Singaporean time. Sorry to start your day with bad news." Or she could have removed the blame saying, "It's not your fault. You weren't the one to schedule the meeting." She could have framed it less like an order. "I know you're super busy. I wonder if you'd be able to help us out with this in the future?" It would have helped to add a relationship-oriented touch—like maybe a friendly emoji.

Christopher emphasized that it's not just the Americans who need to adapt:

Don't get me wrong! As employees who work for a company headquartered in the US, we also need to make an effort to adapt ourselves. The Singaporean's immediate reaction might be to feel paralyzed or angry. But to succeed at Netflix we need to adjust our reaction. We need to remind ourselves that in some other countries this behavior is appropriate and then start a dialogue. Karlyne should pick up the phone and talk openly with the woman who sent the message. She should say, "I get that this happened, and it was frustrating for you. But your message upset me." She could also explain the cultural differences: "Maybe this is cultural. I know in Singapore we are often less direct when giving feedback and more sensitive when receiving it." With open dialogue and transparent discussions, we can live the Netflix culture while becoming increasingly competent at giving and receiving feedback to our colleagues around the world.

 Chris's instructions encapsulate the second lesson we learned. Given the importance of candor for Netflix, employees in indirect cultures need to get used to both giving and receiving feedback with a frankness they may not be accustomed to. This requires emphasizing and re-emphasizing the 4A feedback model outlined in chapter 2. It requires talking openly about the cultural differences and coaching and supporting our global teams to take direct feedback not as a slap, but as a way to get better. For example, in our São Paulo office, there is a weekly meeting to discuss the corporate culture for all employees who'd like to attend. Giving and receiving feedback is one of the most frequent topics on the agenda.

But learning to foster candor around the world is not a one-way street. When collaborating with less direct cultures, we've learned at headquarters to be more vigilant and to try to calibrate our communication so that it feels helpful to the receiver and is not rejected simply because of form. Chris's advice was simple and anyone who needs to give feedback to a colleague in a less direct culture should take heed. Be friendlier. Work harder to remove the blame. Be careful to frame the feedback as a suggestion, not an order. Add a relationship-based touch like a smiling emoji. These are all things we can do to make our messages feel more appropriate in the context within which we are working.

The overarching lesson we've learned is that— no matter where you come from—when it comes to working across cultural differences, talk, talk, talk. One of the best ways to get better at providing feedback to an international counterpart is to ask questions and show curiosity about the other person's culture. If you need to give feedback to a counterpart in another country, ask another trusted colleague from that country first, "Does my message sound aggressive?" "What's the best approach in your culture?" The more questions we ask and the more curiosity we show, the better we all become at giving and receiving feedback around the world.

In order to ask the right questions and understand the answers we get from around the world, it's important to remember a final cross-cultural lesson. . . .

EVERYTHING IS RELATIVE

As with all the dimensions of culture, when it comes to giving feedback internationally everything is relative. The Japanese find the Singaporeans unnecessarily direct. The Americans find the Singaporeans opaque and lacking transparency. The Singaporeans who join Netflix are shocked at their American colleagues' bluntness. To many a Dutch person, the Americans at Netflix don't feel particularly direct at all.

Netflix, despite its multinational desires, continues to have a largely American-centric culture. And when it comes to giving negative feedback, Americans are more direct than many cultures but considerably less direct than the Dutch culture. Dutch director of public policy Ise, who joined Netflix Amsterdam in 2014, explains the difference like this:

The Netflix culture has succeeded in creating an environment where feedback is frequent and actionable. Yet when an American gives feedback, even at Netflix, they almost always start by telling you what's good about your work before telling you what they really want to say. Americans learn things like, "Always give three positives with every negative" and "Catch employees doing things right." This is confusing for a Dutch person, who will give you positive feedback or negative feedback but is unlikely to do both in the same conversation.

At Netflix, Ise quickly learned that the manner of giving feedback that would be natural and comfortable in her own Dutch culture was too blunt for her American collaborators:

Donald, my American colleague who had recently moved to the Netherlands, was hosting a meeting in Amsterdam. Seven non-Netflix partners had taken planes and trains from around Europe for the discussions. The meeting went very well. Donald was articulate, detailed, and persuasive. His preparation was evident. But several times I could tell other participants wanted to share their own perspective but didn't have the opportunity, because Donald talked so much.

After the meeting Donald said to me, "I thought that went great. What did you think?" This seemed to me like a perfect time to give that candid feedback Netflix leaders are always preaching about so I jumped in: "Stinne came all the way from Norway to attend the meeting but you spoke so much she couldn't get a word in edgewise. We asked these people to take planes and trains, and then they didn't get time to speak. We didn't hear all of the opinions that could have helped us. You talked for 80 percent of the meeting, making it difficult for anyone else to say anything at all."

She was about to move on to the part of the feedback where she gives actionable suggestions for future improvement when Donald did something that Ise feels is typical of Americans:

Before I'd even finished, he groaned and looked crestfallen. He took my feedback way too harshly, as Americans often do. He said, "Oh my gosh, I'm so sorry for having messed this all up." But he hadn't "messed it all up." That's not what I said. The meeting was a success and he showed he knew that by saying, "That went great." There was just this one aspect that was not good, and I felt understanding that could help him improve.

That's what frustrates me about my American colleagues. As often as they give feedback and as eager as they are to hear it, if you don't start by saying something positive they think the entire thing was a disaster. As soon as a Dutch person jumps in with the negative first, the American kills the critique by thinking the whole thing has gone to hell.

In her past five years at Netflix, Ise has learned a lot about giving feedback to international colleagues, especially Americans:

Now that I better understand these cultural tendencies, I give the feedback just as frequently, but I think carefully about the person receiving the message and how to adapt to get the results I'm hoping for. With more indirect cultures I start by sprinkling the ground with a few light positive comments and words of appreciation. If the work has been overall good I state that enthusiastically up front. Then I ease into the feedback with "a few suggestions." Then I wrap up by stating, "This is just my opinion, for whatever it is worth," and "You can take it or leave it." The elaborate dance is quite humorous from a Dutch person's point of view . . . but it certainly gets the desired results!

Ise's words sum up the strategies Netflix learned for promoting candor as they opened offices around the world. When you are leading a global team, as you Skype with your employees in different cultures, your words will be magnified or minimized based on your listener's cultural context. So you have to be aware. You have to be strategic. You have to be flexible. With a little information and a little finesse, you can modify the feedback to the person your speaking with in order to get the results that you need.

 Personally, I loved the frank approach Ise used when delivering her feedback to Donald. She aimed to help. She was clear about what behavior diminished the success of the meeting. The feedback was actionable.

What her approach was lacking was global sensitivity. Despite her candor, her feedback technique led to misunderstanding. Her intended message was that the meeting was great and Donald should shut up more to make the next meeting even better. The way she delivered the message led Donald to think the meeting had been a disaster. And if Donald had been Brazilian or Singaporean, he'd probably have left the meeting expecting to lose his job the next week.

This brings us to . . .

THE LAST DOT . . . FOR NOW

When giving feedback with those from your own culture, use the 4A approach outlined in chapter 2.

But when giving feedback around the world, add a 5th A:

The 4As are as follows:

- Aim to assist
- Actionable
- Appreciate
- Accept or decline

Plus one makes 5:

- Adapt—your delivery and your reaction to the culture you're working with to get the results that you need.

We still have a lot to learn about integrating our corporate culture into our growing number of offices around the world. At most QBRs, we have at least one discussion about corporate culture. As the majority of our future growth is outside the US, we increasingly focus these discussions on how to make our values work in a global context. What we've learned is that in order to integrate your corporate culture around the world, above all you have to be humble, you have to be curious, and you have to remember to listen before you speak and to learn before you teach. With this approach, you can't help but become more effective every day in this ever-fascinating multicultural world.

► **TAKEAWAYS FROM CHAPTER 10**

- Map out your corporate culture and compare it
  to the cultures of the countries you are expanding
  into. For a culture of F&R, candor will need extra
  attention.

- In less direct countries, implement more formal
  feedback mechanisms and put feedback on
  the agenda more frequently, because informal
  exchanges will happen less often.

- With more direct cultures, talk about the cultural
  differences openly so the feedback is understood as
  intended.

- Make ADAPTABILITY the fifth A of your candor
  model. Discuss openly what candor means in
  different parts of the world. Work together to
  discover how both sides can adapt to bring this
  value to life.

CONCLUSION

Near my childhood home in Minneapolis is a three-mile-round lake called Bde Maka Ska. On hot summer Saturdays, hordes of city-dwellers flock to the lake's running paths, docks, and beaches. Despite the mobs, it feels surprisingly peaceful because there are plenty of rules guiding everyone's actions. Walkers are not allowed on the bike paths. Bikes move only clockwise. No smoking anywhere. No swimming beyond the marked buoys. Rollerblades and scooters go on the bike path, not the walking path. Joggers use the walking path only. These regulations are widely known and rigorously followed, creating a haven of organization and calm.

If Netflix has a culture of freedom and responsibility, Bde Maka Ska has a culture of rules and process.

Peaceful as this rules-and-process culture may be, there are also some disadvantages. If you need to bike somewhere a short counterclockwise ride away, you can't. You have to go clockwise all the way around the lake. If you want to swim across the lake, you'll be stopped by a lifeguard in a boat and brought back to shore. It doesn't matter how well you swim; it's not allowed. The culture was developed to deliver peace and safety to the greater group, not freedom to the individual.

"Rules and process" is so familiar a paradigm for coordinating group behavior, it hardly needs any explanation at all. Starting in kindergarten when Mrs. Sanders sat all the other five-year-olds on the green rug and explained in detail what you were and weren't allowed to do, you were already learning rules and process. Later, when you took that first job bussing dishes at that noodle place by the mall and you learned what color socks you could and couldn't wear under your uniform and how much would be subtracted from your paycheck if you ate a biscuit during your shift, your apprenticeship in rules and process was progressing.

The rules-and-process approach has been the primary way of coordinating group behavior for centuries. But it isn't the only way, and it isn't only Netflix using a different method. For the past nineteen years, I've lived a nine-minute drive from the Arc de Triomphe in Paris. A short trip to the top of the monument provides spectacular views of the famed Avenue des Champs-Elysées, the Eiffel Tower and the Sacré-Cœur Basilica, but most impressive is the massive traffic circle in orbit around the Arc, known as "l'Etoile," or "the Star." Reed sometimes refers to Freedom and Responsibility as operating on the edge of chaos. For that, there's no clearer image than the traffic at l'Etoile.

Every minute, hundreds of cars spill from the twelve multilane boulevards that all converge on the unmarked ten-lane roundabout. Motorcycles whip between double-decker buses. Taxis merge aggressively to drop off tourists at the center. Cars plunge, often without turn signals, toward their boulevard of choice. Despite the masses of vehicles and people, there is one basic principle guiding all the traffic: once you are on the roundabout, you give right of way to those entering from any of the twelve incoming streets. Beyond that, know where you want to go, focus on your goal, and use your best judgment. You'll probably get there quickly and unharmed.

The first time you go to the top of the Arc de Triomphe and witness the turmoil below, the advantages to operating with so few rules seems unclear. Why not put a dozen traffic lights around the circle to make cars wait their turn? Why not mark the lanes and provide rigorous restrictions about who can move where at what moment?

According to my French husband, Eric, who has been driving around the Arc de Triomphe almost daily for decades, that would also slow everything down. "L'Etoile is incredibly efficient. There is no faster way for a skilled driver to get from point A to point B," he claims. "Plus the system provides extreme flexibility. You might get onto the round-about planning to exit at the Champs Elysées only to see a tourist bus blocking the street. No need to panic. You can change your route on the fly. You can exit on Avenue de Friedland or Avenue Hoche, or you can circle around Etoile a few more times until the bus has moved on. Almost no other traffic method allows you to change course mid-route so quickly."

Now that you've read this book you've seen that when you lead a team or manage a company, you have a clear choice. You can go the way of Bde Maka Ska, working to control the movements of your employees with rules and process. Or you can implement a culture of freedom and responsibility, choosing speed and flexibility, and offering more freedom to your employees. Each approach has its advantages. When you started this book you already knew how to coordinate a group of people through rules and process. Now you know how to do it through freedom and responsibility too.

WHEN TO CHOOSE RULES AND PROCESS?

 The Industrial Revolution has powered most of the world's successful economies for the past three hundred years. So it's only natural that the management paradigms from high-volume, low-error manufacturing have come to dominate business organizational practices. In a manufacturing environment, you are trying to eliminate variation, and most management approaches have been designed with this in mind. It really is a sign of excellence when a company manages to produce a million doses of penicillin or ten thousand identical automobiles with no errors.

Perhaps that's why, during the industrial era, many of the best companies operated like symphonic orchestras, with synchronicity, precision, and perfect coordination as the goal. Instead of a musical score and a conductor, it was processes and policies that guided their work. Even today, if you are running a factory, managing a safety-critical environment, or you want the same thing produced identically with great reliability, a rules-and-process symphony is the way to go.

Even at Netflix we have pockets of the company where safety and error prevention are our primary goals and there we fence off an area to build a little symphony orchestra that plays pitch-perfect rules-and-process.

Take, for example, employee safety and sexual harassment. When it comes to protecting our employees from injury or harassment, we invest in error prevention (training) and hotlines; we have strong processes to make sure all claims are properly investigated; and we use process-improvement principles to drive the incident rates down to zero.

Likewise, at other moments when making a mistake would lead to disaster, we choose rules and process. One example is the financial information we release to Wall Street every quarter. Imagine that we published our financials and then had to go back and say, "Wait, we were wrong. It's less revenue than we said." That would be a disaster. Another example is the privacy of our viewer data. What if someone hacked into our system, stole information about what our individual members were watching, and published it on the internet? That would be a catastrophe.

In select instances like these, where error prevention is clearly more important than innovation, we have loads of checks, processes, and procedures to ensure we don't screw anything up. In these moments, we want Netflix to be like a hospital where there are five people verifying the surgeon is operating on the correct knee. When a mistake would lead to a disaster, rules and process isn't just nice to have, it's a necessity.

With this in mind, you can consider your objective carefully before deciding when to opt for freedom and responsibility and when rules with process would be a better choice. Here are a set of questions you can ask in order to select the right approach:

- Are you working in an industry where your employees' or customers' health or safety depends on everything going just right? If so, choose rules and process.
- If you make a mistake, will it end in disaster? Choose rules and process.
- Are you running a manufacturing environment where you need to produce a consistently identical product? Choose rules and process.

If you're leading an emergency room, testing airplanes, managing a coal mine, or delivering just-in-time medication to senior citizens, rules with process is the way to go. This has been the go-to coordination model for the majority of organizations for centuries and, for some, will continue to be the best choice in coming years.

But for those of you who are operating in the creative economy, where innovation, speed, and flexibility are the keys to success, consider throwing out the orchestra and focusing instead on making a different kind of music.

IT'S JAZZ, NOT A SYMPHONY

Even during the industrial era there were pockets of the economy, such as advertising agencies, where creative thinking drove success, and they managed on the edge of chaos. Such organizations accounted for just a small percent of the economy. But now, with the growth in importance of intellectual property and creative services, the percentage of the economy that is dependent on nurturing inventiveness and innovation is much higher and continually increasing. Yet most companies are still following the paradigms of the Industrial Revolution that have dominated wealth creation for the last three hundred years.

In today's information age, in many companies and on many teams, the objective is no longer error prevention and replicability. On the contrary, it's creativity, speed, and agility. In the industrial era, the goal was to minimize variation. But in creative companies today, maximizing variation is more essential. In these situations, the biggest risk isn't making a mistake or losing consistency; it's failing to attract top talent, to invent new products, or to change direction quickly when the environment shifts. Consistency and repeatability are more likely to squash fresh thinking than to bring your company profit. A lot of little mistakes, while sometimes painful, help the organization learn quickly and are a critical part of the innovation cycle. In these situations, rules and process are no longer the best answer. A symphony isn't what you're going for. Leave the conductor and the sheet music behind. Build a jazz band instead.

Jazz emphasizes individual spontaneity. The musicians know the overall structure of the song but have the freedom to improvise, riffing off one another other, creating incredible music.

Of course, you can't just remove the rules and processes, tell your team to be a jazz band, and expect it to be so. Without the right conditions, chaos will ensue. But now, after reading this book, you have a map. Once you begin to hear the music, keep focused. Culture isn't something you can build up and then ignore. At Netflix, we are constantly debating our culture and expecting it will continually evolve. To build a team that is innovative, fast, and flexible, keep things a little bit loose. Welcome constant change. Operate a little closer toward the edge of chaos. Don't provide a musical score and build a symphonic orchestra. Work on creating those jazz conditions and hire the type of employees who long to be part of an improvisational band. When it all comes together, the music is beautiful.

ACKNOWLEDGMENTS

Throughout this book we have explored the value of talent density and candor. The creation of this book was also founded on these two elements.

Thank you to our fabulously talented dream team, beginning with literary agent Amanda "Binky" Urban, who saw promise in an early book outline and guided us in the creation of the book proposal and beyond. Thank you to our editor at Penguin, the legendary Ann Godoff, who believed steadfastly in this project and steered it along from first breath to completion.

Thank you for editorial help to David Champion, who loved this manuscript as if it were his own and edited every chapter, often multiple times, with the greatest care until it met his extremely high standards. Thank you to Des Dearlove and Stuart Crainer, who dared to provide tough, candid feedback at a time when we were struggling. Their frankness may very well have saved this book. Thank you to Elin Williams, who provided input on the earliest versions of book chapters, before we were ready to share them with anyone else, and who later polished up the writing, clearing away unnecessary paragraphs and helping us to keep our messages sharp. A special thanks to Patty McCord, who was instrumental in the development of the Netflix corporate culture and spent dozens of hours with us, telling and retelling stories from the early Netflix days.

A huge embossed thank you to the more than two hundred Netflix employees, past and present, who graciously shared their stories with us, which later became the foundation of this book. It is because of their generous, transparent, and colorful storytelling that this book has taken life. A special thanks to Netflix colleagues Richard Siklos, Bao Nguyen, and Tawni Argent, who have been an integral part of the project since the very early days.

 It is of course classic to thank one's family members at the end of a book, but a couple of mine took a more active role than most. Thank you to my mother, Linda Burkett, who painstakingly combed through each draft of each chapter throughout the development of the manuscript, removing run-on sentences, finding lost commas, and generally making the passages more readable. Thanks to my children, Ethan and Logan, who during the whole book-writing process kept each day joyful. A huge thank you to my husband and business partner, Eric, who has not just provided ongoing love and support throughout the book-writing process, but has spent hundreds of hours reading, rereading, and re-rereading each section, providing suggestions and counsel throughout.

Above all, thank you to the hundreds of Netflix leaders throughout the last twenty years, who have contributed to the development of Netflix culture. This book describes not something I discovered during deep quiet moments of thought, but something we all discovered together, through vigorous debate, endless exploration, and ongoing trial and error. It is due to your creativity, courage, and resourcefulness that Netflix culture is what it is today.

SELECTED BIBLIOGRAPHY

Introduction

Edmondson, Amy C. **The Fearless Organization: Creating Psychological Safety in the Workplace for Learning, Innovation, and Growth**. Hoboken, NJ: Wiley, 2019.

"Glassdoor Survey Finds Americans Forfeit Half of Their Earned Vacation/Paid Time Off." **Glassdoor**, About Us, May 24, 2017, www.glassdoor.com/about-us/glassdoor-survey-finds-americans-forfeit-earned-vacationpaid-time/.

"Netflix Ranks as #1 in the Reputation Institute 2019 US RepTrak 100." **Reputation Institute**, 3 Apr., 2019, www.reputationinstitute.com/about-ri/press-release/netflix-ranks-1-reputation-institute-2019-us-reptrak-100.

Stenovec, Timothy. "One Huge Reason for Netflix's Success." **HuffPost**, Dec. 7, 2017, www.huffpost.com/entry/netflix-culture-deck-success_n_6763716.

Chapter 1: A Great Workplace Is Stunning Colleagues

Felps, Will, et al. "How, When, and Why Bad Apples Spoil the Barrel: Negative Group Members and

Dysfunctional Groups." **Research in Organizational Behavior** 27 (2006): 175–222.

"370: Ruining It for the Rest of Us." This American Life, December 14, 2017, www.thisamericanlife .org/370/transcript

Chapter 2: Say What You Really Think (with Positive Intent)

Coyle, Daniel. **The Culture Code: The Secrets of Highly Successful Groups.** New York: Bantam Books, 2018.

Edwardes, Charlotte. "Meet Netflix's Ted Sarandos, the Most Powerful Person in Hollywood." **Evening Standard**. May 9, 2019. www.standard.co.uk/tech/ netflix-ted-sarandos-interview-the-crown-a4138071 .html.

Goetz, Thomas. "Harnessing the Power of Feedback Loops." **Wired**. June 19, 2011. www.wired.com/2011/ 06/ff_feedbackloop.

Zenger, Jack, and Joseph Folkman. "Your Employees Want the Negative Feedback You Hate to Give." **Harvard Business Review**. January 15, 2014. hbr .org/2014/01/your-employees-want-the-negative -feedback-you-hate-to-give.

Chapter 3a: Remove Vacation Policy

Bellis, Rich. "We Offered Unlimited Vacation for One Year: Here's What We Learned." **Fast Company**, November 6, 2015, www.fastcompany.com/3052926/ we-offered-unlimited-vacation-for-one-year-heres -what-we-learned.

Blitstein, Ryan. "At Netflix, Vacation Time Has No Limits." **The Mercury News**. March 21, 2007. www .mercurynews.com/2007/03/21/at-netflix-vacation -time-has-no-limits.

Branson, Richard. "Why We're Letting Virgin Staff Take as Much Holiday as They Want." Virgin. April 27, 2017. www.virgin.com/richard-branson/why-were -letting-virgin-staff-take-much-holiday-they-want.

Haughton, Jermaine. "'Unlimited Leave': "How Do I Ensure Staff Holiday's Don't Get out of Control? June 16, 2015, www.managers.org.uk/insights /news/2015/june/unlimited-leave-how-do-i-ensure -staff-holidays-dont-get-out-of-control.

Millet, Josh. "Is Unlimited Vacation a Perk or a Pain? Here's How to Tell." **CNBC**. September 26, 2017. www.cnbc.com/2017/09/25/is-unlimited-vacation-a -perk-or-a-pain-heres-how-to-tell.html.

Chapter 3b: Remove Travel and Expense Approvals

Pruckner, Gerald J., and Rupert Sausgruber. "Honesty on the Streets: A Field Study on Newspaper Purchasing." **Journal of the European Economic Association** 11, no. 3 (2013): 661–79.

Chapter 4: Pay Top of Personal Market

Ariely, Dan. "What's the Value of a Big Bonus?" **Dan Ariely** (blog). November 20, 2008. danariely. com/2008/11/20/what's-the-value-of-a-big-bonus/.

Gates, Bill quoted in chapter 6 in, Thompson, Clive. **Coders: Who They Are, What They Think and How**

They Are Changing Our World. New York: Picador, 2019.

Kong, Cynthia. "Quitting Your Job." Infographic. **Robert Half** (blog). July 9, 2018. www.roberthalf .com/blog/salaries-and-skills/quitting-your-job.

Lawler, Moira. "When to Switch Jobs to Maximize Your Income." **Job Search Advice** (blog). Monster. www.monster.com/career-advice/article/ switch-jobs-earn-more-0517.

Lucht, John. **Rites of Passage at $100,000 to $1 Million+: Your Insider's Strategic Guide to Executive Job-Changing and Faster Career Progress**. New York: The Viceroy Press, 2014.

Luthi, Ben. "Does Job Hopping Increase Your Long-Term Salary?" Chime. October 4, 2018. www.chimebank.com/2018/05/07/ does-job-hopping-increase-your-long-term-salary.

Sackman, H., et al. "Exploratory Experimental Studies Comparing Online and Offline Programing Performance." **Communications of the ACM** 11, no. 1 (January 1968): 3–11. https://dl.acm.org/ doi/10.1145/362851.362858.

Shotter, James, Noonan, Laura, and Ben McLannahan. "Bonuses Don't Make Bankers Work Harder, Says Deutsche's John Cryan." **CNBC**, November 25, 2015, www.cnbc.com/2015/11/25/ deutsche-banks-john-cryan-says-bonuses-dont-make -bankers-work-harder-says.html.

Chapter 5: Open the Books

Aronson, Elliot, et al. "The Effect of a Pratfall on Increasing Interpersonal Attractiveness." **Psychonomic Science** 4, no. 6 (1966): 227–28.

Brown, Brené. **Daring Greatly: How the Courage to Be Vulnerable Transforms the Way We Live, Love, Parent, and Lead**. New York: Penguin Random House Audio Publishing Group, 2017.

Bruk, A., Scholl, S. G., and Bless, H. "Beautiful Mess Effect: Self- other Differences in Evaluation of Showing Vulnerability. **Journal of Personality and Social Psychology**, 115 (2), 2018. https://doi.org/10.1037/pspa0000120.

Jasen, Georgette. "Keeping Secrets: Finding the Link Between Trust and Well-Being." **Columbia News**. February 19, 2018. https://news.columbia.edu/news/keeping-secrets-finding-link-between-trust-and-well-being.

Mukund, A., and A. Neela Radhika. "SRC Holdings: The 'Open Book' Management Culture." Curriculum Library for Employee Ownership (CLEO). Rutgers. January 2004. https://cleo.rutgers.edu/articles/src-holdings-the-open-book-management-culture/.

Rosh, Lisa, and Lynn Offermann. "Be Yourself, but Carefully." **Harvard Business Review**, August 18, 2014, hbr.org/2013/10/be-yourself-but-carefully.

Slepian, Michael L., et al. "The Experience of Secrecy." **Journal of Personality and Social Psychology** 113, no. 1 (2017): 1–33.

Smith, Emily Esfahani. "Your Flaws Are Probably More Attractive Than You Think They Are." **The Atlantic**. January 9, 2019. www.theatlantic.com/health/archive/2019/01/beautiful-mess-vulnerability/579892.

Chapter 6: No Decision-making Approvals Needed

Daly, Helen. "Black Mirror Season 4: Viewers RAGE over 'Creepy Marketing' Stunt 'Not Cool'." Express.co.uk, December 31, 2017, www.express.co.uk/showbiz/tv-radio/898625/Black-Mirror-season-4-release-Netflix-Waldo-Turkish-Viewers-RAGE-creepy-marketing-stunt.

Fingas, Jon. "Maybe Private 'Black Mirror' Messages Weren't a Good Idea, Netflix." **Engadget**, July, 18 2019, www.engadget.com/2017-12-29-maybe-private-black-mirror-messages-werent-a-good-idea-netfl.html.

Gladwell, Malcolm. **Outliers: Why Some People Succeed and Some Don't**. New York: Little Brown, 2008.

"Not Seen on SNL: Parody of the Netflix/Qwikster Apology Video." The Comic's Comic, October 3, 2011, http://thecomicscomic.com/2011/10/03/not-seen-on-snl-parody-of-the-netflixqwikster-apology-video.

Chapter 7: The Keeper Test

Eichenwald, Kurt. "Microsoft's Lost Decade." **Vanity Fair**. July 24, 2012. www.vanityfair.com/news/business/2012/08/microsoft-lost-mojo-steve-ballmer.

Kantor, Jodi, and David Streitfeld. "Inside Amazon: Wrestling Big Ideas in a Bruising Workplace." **The New York Times**, August 15, 2015, www.nytimes .com/2015/08/16/technology/inside-amazon -wrestling-big-ideas-in-a-bruising-workplace.html.

Ramachandran, Shalini, and Joe Flint. "At Netflix, Radical Transparency and Blunt Firings Unsettle the Ranks." **The Wall Street Journal**, October 25, 2018, www.wsj.com/articles/at-netflix-radical -transparency-and-blunt-firings-unsettle-the-ranks -1540497174.

SHRM. "Benchmarking Service." SHRM, December 2017, www.shrm.org/hr-today/trends-and-forecasting/ research-and-surveys/Documents/2017-Human -Capital-Benchmarking.pdf.

The Week Staff. "Netflix's Culture of Fear." **The Week**. November 3, 2018. www.theweek.com/ articles/805123/netflixs-culture-fear.

Chapter 8: A Circle of Feedback

Milne, A. A., and Ernest H. Shepard. **The House at Pooh Corner**. New York: E.P. Dutton & Company, 2018.

Chapter 9: Lead with Context, Not Control

Fast Company Staff. "The World's 50 Most Innovative Companies of 2018." **Fast Company**. February 20, 2018. www.fastcompany.com/ most-innovative-companies/2018.

Saint-Exupéry, Antoine de, et al. **The Wisdom of the Sands**. Chicago: University of Chicago Press, 1979.

"Vitality Curve." Wikipedia, Wikimedia Foundation, November 5, 2019, en.wikipedia.org/wiki/Vitality _curve.

Chapter 10: Bring It All to the World!

Meyer, Erin. **The Culture Map: Breaking through the Invisible Boundaries of Global Business.** New York: PublicAffairs, 2014.

To view the culture maps presented in this chapter as well as to create your own corporate culture maps, go to: www.erinmeyer.com/tools.

A

Academy Awards, xix, 245, 343

"accept or discard" feedback guideline, 46–47, 51

accidents and safety issues, management style and, 314–15, 396–99

"actionable" feedback guideline, 46, 47, 50, 54, 286, 378

"adapt" feedback guideline, 390

"aim to assist" feedback guideline, 45–46, 47, 50, 54

Airbnb, 203

Alexa and Katie, 218

alignment, 320–22, 341
  on a North Star, 322–26
  as tree, 327–42

Allmovie.com, 131

Amazon, 4, 123, 147, 203, 306, 342
  Prime, 219, 222

amygdala, 31–32

Anitta, 147

annual performance reviews, 282

Antioco, John, xi–xii

AOL, xxi, 348

Apple, xx, 116, 128

"appreciate" feedback guideline, 43, 46

Arc de Triomphe, 394–95

Ariely, Dan, 125–26

Armstrong, Lance, 306, 343

Aronson, Elliot, 188

Aspen Institute, 162–63

autonomy, 199
  see also decision-making; decision-making approvals, eliminating

Avalos, Diego, 226–28

B

Ballad of Buster Scruggs, The, xxi
Ballmer, Steve, 186
Baptiste, Nigel, 97–99, 102
Bazay, Dominique, 330, 335–42
Bde Maka Ska, 393, 396
Becker, Justin, 53–55
belonging cues, 36–37
bet-taking analogy, 208–10, 231–36, 332–35
Bird Box, 245–46
Blacklist, The, 39
Black Mirror, 237–38
Blitstein, Ryan, 78–79
Blockbuster, 3, 255, 348
  bankruptcy of, xiii, xxi
  late fees of, 3
  Netflix's offer to, xii–xiii
  size of, xi, xii
bonuses, 121–27
Booz Allen Hamilton, 123
brain:
  feedback and, 31, 32
  secrets and, 156
Branson, Richard, xxix, 76
Brazil, 206, 225, 331–33, 359, 364, 366–68, 378, 389
Brier, David, xxix
brilliant jerks, 51–55, 296
Brown, Brené, 187
Bruk, Anna, 187–88
Bull Durham, 251
Bullock, Sandra, 245
bungee jumping, 287–88

C

Canada, 356
candor, 26–31, 212, 260
  cultural differences around the world, 369–75, 383–84, 388–89
  culture of, 33–35
  dentist visits compared to, 281–83
  as disliked but needed, 31–33
  failure to speak up, 26–27, 42, 211
  increasing, xxiv, xxv, 1, 18–57, 109, 152–91, 278–303
  jerks and, 51–55
  misuse of, 44, 45, 54
  "only say about someone what you will say to their face," 23, 279–80
  performance and, 26–31
  and readiness to release decision-making controls, 200–202
  saying what you really think with positive intent, 19–57
  see also feedback; transparency
Carey, Chris, 268
Caro, Manolo, 205
Caruso, Rob, 172–73
Casa De Papel, La, xxi
celebrating wins, 210, 228
Chapman, Jack, 130

Chase, Chevy, 327
cheating, 94–96
Chelsea, 175
children's programming,
    216–18, 334–42
Choy, Josephine, 371–75, 378
Christensen, Nathan, 77–78
circle of feedback (360-degree
    assessments), 40–41,
    279–303
  benefits of, 299–300
  discussion facilitated by,
    286–87
  in Japan, 377–78
  live, 291–301
  stepping out of line during,
    296–98
  tips for, 295–96
  written, names used in,
    283–91
Cobb, Melissa, 326–35, 341
Coen, Joel and Ethan, xiii
Coherent Software, 153, 157
collaboration, 252, 264
Colombia, 369
Comparably, xx
competitiveness, internal,
    263–64
compliments and praise,
    32, 34
computer software, 116–18,
    318
conformity, 212–13
connecting the dots,
    xxix–xxx
  first dot, 15
  second dot, 55

third dot, 104–5
fourth dot, 149
fifth dot, 189
sixth dot, 240
seventh dot, 275
eighth dot, 301–2
ninth dot, 344–45
last dot, 389–90
consensus building, 223
contagious behavior,
    11–15
context, **see** leading with
    context, not control
contract signing, 224–28
control, leadership by, 308
  ExxonMobil example of,
    314
  leading with context versus,
    308–13
  see also leading with
    context, not control
controls, removing, xxiv–xxv,
    1, 58–110, 192–242,
    304–49
  decision-making approvals,
    193–242
  bet-taking analogy in,
    208–10, 231–36,
    332–35
  Informed Captain model
    in, 210, 223–28, 319,
    329, 330, 341, 365
  and picking the best
    people, 245–47
  readiness for, 200–202
  signing contracts,
    223–26

controls, removing (**cont.**):
  travel and expense
    approvals, 83–110
  cheating and, 93–96
  company's best interest
    and, 87–88, 90, 92,
    100, 103–4
  context and, 89–94
  Freedom and
    Responsibility ethos
    and, 91–94
  frugality and, 96–104
  vacation policy, xvii,
    59–80, 84, 105–6
  freedom and
    responsibility and,
    79–80
  Hastings' nightmares
    about, 61–62, 64, 67
  Hastings' vacations, 66,
    68, 71–72
  Japanese workers and,
    70–71
  leaders' modeling and,
    64–72
  loss aversion and,
    xvii–xviii
  and setting and
    reinforcing context
    to guide employee
    behavior, 72–75
  value added by, 75–79
  see also leading with
    context, not control
corporate culture, xiv
  of Netflix, xiv, xxvi,
    xxviii, 68

Netflix Culture Deck,
    xv–xviii, 256–57
Costa, Omarson, 225–26
coupling:
  alignment and, 321
  loose versus tight,
    317–20
Coyle, Daniel, 36–37
creative positions, 118–19,
    125–27
criticism (negative feedback),
    29–33, 34–35
  belonging cues and, 37
  brain and, 31, 32
  cultural differences around
    the world, 369–70,
    384
  as disliked but needed,
    31–33
  language used in, 370–71
  responding to, 36, 46–47
  upgraders and downgraders
    in, 370–71
  see also feedback
Crook-Davies, Danielle, 30
Crown, The, xix
Cryan, John, 125
Cuarón, Alfonso, xiii, 245
cultural differences around
    the world, **see** global
    expansion and cultural
    differences
Culture Code, The
    (Coyle), 36
culture map, 358–69
Culture Map, The (Meyer),
    xxvi, 28, 358–69

culture of freedom and responsibility, see Freedom and Responsibility

D

Daring Greatly: How the Courage to Be Vulnerable Transforms the Way We Live, Love, Parent, and Lead (Brown), 187

Dark, xix

days off, 59–61

    see also vacation policy, removing

decision-making:

    dispersed, 318–19

    innovation and, 194, 196, 202, 203–4

    and leading with context, 309, 319, 320

    to please the boss, 193–94, 200, 228–29

    pyramid structure for, 194, 327–29

    spreadsheet system and, 215–16

    talent density and, 196

    transparency and, 196

decision-making approvals, eliminating, 193–242

    bet-taking analogy in, 208–10, 231–36, 332–35

Informed Captain model in, 210, 223–28, 319, 329, 330, 341, 365

    and picking the best people, 245–47

    readiness for, 200–202

    signing contracts, 224–28

Del Castillo, Kate, 207

Del Deo, Adam, 305–8, 342

Disney, 217, 224, 288, 327, 334

dissent, farming for, 210–16, 237

diversity, 356–57

Dora the Explorer, 217

Dormen, Yasemin, 237–40

dot-com bubble, 5

dots, see connecting the dots

downloading, 219–23

dream teams, 115

DreamWorks, 218, 327, 334

driver feedback, 33

Dutch, Netherlands, 357, 359, 363, 366, 370, 385–88

DVDs, 4, 6, 193

    Qwikster and, 210–13

    shift to streaming from, xiii, xx, 210–11, 348

E

Edmondson, Amy, xv

Eichenwald, Kurt, 262

Eisner, Michael, 288–89

elephants, penguins versus, 258

Elite, xix
Emmy Awards, xix, 218
"Emperor's New Clothes"
    syndrome, 35–44
empowerment, 165, 199, 201
    see also decision-making;
        decision-making
        approvals, eliminating;
        Freedom and
        Responsibility
Engadget, 238
Enron, xiv
entrepreneurship, 208
error prevention, and
    management style,
    314–15, 324, 396–99
Escobar, Pablo, 197–98
Estaff meetings, 322, 360
Evening Standard, 38
Eventbrite, 76
expenses, **see** travel and
    expenses; travel and
    expense approvals,
    removing
experimentation, 207
Explorer project, 231–33, 236
Express, 238
ExxonMobil, 314–15

F

Facebook, xv, 116, 147, 195,
    205–6, 288
failures, 210, 228–40
    asking what learning came
        from the project, 230,
        234

not making a big deal
    about, 231–33
sunshining of, 230,
    234–40
family business metaphor,
    247–50
    moving to sports team
        metaphor from, 250–53,
        257–58
farming for dissent, 210–16,
    237
Fast Company, xxix, 315
fear of losing one's job, xvii,
    265–67, 271–73
Fearless Organization, The
    (Edmondson), xv
FedEx, 208
feedback, 21–26, 209, 260,
    280, 355
    annual performance
        reviews and, 282
    belonging cues and,
        36–37
    brain's response to, 31–32
    circle of (360-degree
        assessments), 40–41,
        279–303
        benefits of, 299–301
        discussion facilitated by,
            285
        in Japan, 377
        live, 291–301
        stepping out of line
            during, 296–98
        tips for, 295–96
        written, names used in,
            283–91

cultural differences and, 369–79, 382–83, 385–89

for drivers, 33–34

"Emperor's New Clothes" syndrome and, 35–44

failure to speak up with, 26–29, 42, 211–12

4A guidelines for, 45–55, 375–76, 389

  accept or discard, 46–47, 50–51

  actionable, 46, 47, 50, 54, 283, 378

  adding 5th A to (adapt), 390

  aim to assist, 45–46, 47, 50, 54

  appreciate, 46, 50

  cultural differences and, 383

  for giving feedback, 45–46

  for receiving feedback, 46–47

frequency of, 28

Hastings and, 40–44

honesty in, 28; **see also** candor

Japanese culture and, 370–78

loop of, 33–35

Meyer and, 29, 48

negative (criticism), 29–32, 34

  belonging cues and, 36–37

brain and, 31–32

cultural differences around the world, 369–70, 385

as disliked but needed, 31–33

language used in, 370–71

responding to, 36–37, 47

upgraders and downgraders in, 370–71

positive, brain and, 32

responding to, 36–37, 47

and speaking and reading between the lines, 373

spreadsheet system for gathering, 215–16

survey on, 32–33

teaching employees how to give and receive, 44–48

from teammates, 294

when and where to give, 47–51

see also candor

Felps, Will, 10–13

firing, **see** letting people go

Fisher Phillips, 76

five-year plans, 324

Flint, Joe, 265

flexibility, and leading with context or control, 324–25, 326

Fogel, Bryan, 305–6, 344

4K ultra high definition televisions, 98–100

Fowler, Geoffrey, 98–100

Fox, 327

France, 355, 369
  Paris, 394–96
Freedom and Responsibility
    (F&R), xxvi, 283, 348,
    393, 395
  expenses and, 91–94
  first steps to, 1–110
  Informed Captain model
      in, 210, 223–28, 319,
      329, 330, 341, 365
  next steps to, 111–242
  techniques to reinforce,
      243–349
  vacations and, 79–80
  weight of responsibility in,
      225–28
Friedland, Jonathan, 289
Fuller House, 218

G

Game of Thrones, 196–97
Garden Grove, Calif., 33
Gates, Bill, 117–18
General Electric (GE),
    263
Germany, 221–22, 369
Gizmodo, 265
Gladwell, Malcolm, 213
Glassdoor, xvii, 75
global expansion and cultural
    differences, 353–91
  adjusting your style for,
      379–85
  Brazil, 206, 225, 331–33,
      359, 364, 366–70, 378,
      389

candor and, 369–75, 384,
    388–89
culture map, 358–69
feedback and, 369–79, 383,
    385–89
Google and, 355–56
Japan, 70–71, 271, 331,
    332, 379, 385
  in culture map, 360, 363,
      364
  feedback and criticism in,
      360–79
  Japanese language,
      372–73
  360 process and, 377
Netherlands, 357–58, 359,
    363, 365, 366, 370,
    385–88
Schlumberger and, 355–56
Singapore, 359, 363, 365,
    366, 370, 379–83, 385,
    389
trust and, 365, 367
Golden Globe Awards, xix,
    115
Goldman Sachs, 263
Golin, 76
Google, xx, 116, 142–45,
    149, 203
  global expansion of, 355
gossip, 279
Guillermo, Rob, 305

H

Handler, Chelsea, 175–76
happiness, xx

Harvard Business Review,
    xxvii
Hastings, Mike, 131–32
Hastings, Reed:
    childhood of, 13–14, 19
    at Coherent Software, 153,
        157
    downloading issue and,
        220–22
    feedback and, 40–42
    interview with, 257–67
    in leadership tree, 331–32
    marriage of, 20–22
    Meyer contacted by,
        xxvi–xxviii
    Netflix cofounded by,
        xi–xii, 3–5
    in Netflix's offer to
        Blockbuster, xii
    in Peace Corps, xxvii,
        xxviii, 20–21, 153,
        353–54
    Pure Software company of,
        xxi–xxii, xxx, 3, 4, 8, 9,
        19–20, 83, 96–97, 108,
        153, 184–85, 187, 348
    Qwikster and, 210–13
HBO, 172–73, 306
Hewlett-Packard (HP),
    100–101
hierarchy of picking, 246–47
Hired, xx
hiring:
    hierarchy of picking and,
        246–47
    talent density and, **see**
        talent density

honesty, xviii, xxix, 265
    and spending company
        money, 88–89
    see also candor;
        transparency
hours worked, 59–60
House of Cards, xx, 98, 114,
    255, 348
HubSpot, xx, 76
Huffington Post, xxvii
Hulu, 306, 342
humility, 186
Hunger Games, The, 261
Hunt, Neil, 62, 68, 142–43,
    149, 232, 289
    downloads and, 219, 223
    and Netflix as team, not
        family, 257–58
    360s and, 291–92,
        293–94
    vacations of, 62

I

Icarus, 305–7, 342–44
India, 126, 221–22, 331–33
    Mighty Little Bheem in,
        337–42
industrial era, 396–97,
    399–400
industry shifts, xx–xxi, xxiii
Informed Captain model,
    210, 223–28, 319, 329,
    330, 341, 365
innovation, xv, xxiii, xxvi,
    127, 203–4, 234,
    399–401

innovation (cont.):
    decision-making and, 194,
        195, 202, 204
    and leading with context or
        control, 315–16, 319
Innovation Cycle, 210
    asking what learning came
        from the project, 230,
        233
    celebrating wins, 210, 228
    failures and, 210, 229–40
    farming for dissent,
        210–16, 237
    not making a big deal
        about failures, 231–33
    placing your bet as an
        informed captain, 210,
        223–28
    socializing the idea, 210,
        216–18, 237, 239
    spreadsheet system and,
        215–16
    sunshining failures, 230,
        234–40
    testing out big ideas, 210,
        218–23
International Olympic
    Committee, 343
internet, 219–23, 231
internet bubble, 5
iPhone, 194
Italy, 196–97

J

Jacobson, Daniel, 247–50
Jaffe, Chris, 231–36

Japan, 70–71, 271, 331, 332,
    379, 385
    in culture map, 359, 364,
        365, 366
    feedback and criticism in,
        370–78
    Japanese language, 372–73
    360 process and, 377
jerks, 51–55, 296
Jobs, Steve, xxix, 194
Jones, Rhett, 265

K

karoshi, 70
kayaking, 267
Keeper Test, xvi, 245–77,
    355, 357–58
Keeper Test Prompt, 267–71
Key Performance Indicators
    (KPIs), 123, 282, 308
Kilgore, Leslie, 22, 123, 143,
    255
    expense reports and, 93
    on hiring and recruiters,
        143–45
    "lead with context, not
        control" coined by, 72,
        307
    new customers and,
        123–24
    signing contracts and,
        224–25
    360s and, 284, 285–86,
        291–92, 293
King, Rochelle, 41–43
Kodak, xxi, 348

Korea, 331, 332
Kung Fu Panda, 327

L

Lanusse, Adrien, 223
Latin America, 205, 356, 366
 Brazil, 206, 225, 331–33, 359, 364, 366–68, 378, 389
Lawrence, Jennifer, 261
lawsuits, 260
layoffs at Netflix, 5–9, 14, 116, 250
leading with context, not control, 72, 305–49
 alignment in, 320–22, 341
 on a North Star, 321–26
 as tree, 327–41
 control versus context, 308–13
 decision-making in, 309, 318–19, 320
 Downton Abbey-type cook example, 311–13, 321
 error prevention and, 314–15, 324–25, 396–99
 ExxonMobil example, 314–15
 Icarus example, 305–7, 342–44
 innovation and, 316–17, 319
 Kilgore's coining of phrase, 72, 307

 and loose versus tight coupling, 317–20
 Mighty Little Bheem example, 337–42
 parenting example, 309–11
 spending and, 88–94
 talent density and, 313, 314
 Target example, 315–16
lean workforce, 120
letting people go, 257–61
 "adequate performance gets a generous severance," xv, xxvii, 254, 259–61, 357–58
 employee fears about, xv, 265–67, 271–72
 employee turnover, 274–75
 in Japan, 271
 Keeper Test, xvi, 245–77, 355, 357–58
 Keeper Test Prompt, 267–71
 lawsuits and, 260
 at Netflix, 274
 Netflix layoffs in 2001, 5–9, 14, 116, 250
 post-exit communications, 177–82, 271–73
 quotas for, 264
LinkedIn, 75, 77, 205
Little Prince, The (Saint-Exupéry), 317
loose versus tight coupling, 317–20
Lorenzoni, Paolo, 196–99, 202, 207

loss aversion, xvii–xviii
Low, Christopher, 380–83

M

Mammoth, 77–78
Management by Objectives, 308
Man of the House, 327
Massachusetts Institute of Technology, 126
McCarthy, Barry, 21–22, 84
McCord, Patty, 5–9, 13, 14–15, 22, 41–42, 62, 63, 80, 107, 257
  all-hands meetings and, 164
  departure from Netflix, 254–55
  expense policy and, 83, 91–92
  financial data and, 167
  salary policy and, 118, 122–23, 142, 145–46
  team metaphor and, 251
  360s and, 291–94
  vacation policy and, 60–61, 65, 68, 78–79
Memento project, 234–36
Mexico, 205–7
Meyer, Erin, xxvii–xxviii
  The Culture Map, xxvii, 28, 358–69
  Hastings' message to, xxvii–xxviii
  keynote address of, 28–29, 48

Netflix employees
  interviewed by, xxviii, 29–30
  in Peace Corps, xxvii
micromanaging, 194–95, 199, 200
Microsoft, 117, 186, 261–63
Mighty Little Bheem, 337–42
Mirer, Scott, 296–97
mistakes, 183–88, 400
  distancing yourself from, 236–37
  management style and, 314–15, 324–25, 397–98
  sunshining of, 235–36
  see also failures
Morgan Stanley, 187
Moss, Trenton, 77
Mr. Peabody and Sherman Show, The, 218
Munk de Alba, Marta, 265, 267
Musk, Elon, xx
Myers, Vernā, 357

N

Narcos, 197–98, 205
National Public Radio (NPR), 247–50
NBC, 124
Neal, Jessica, 8, 213, 322
Negotiating Your Salary: How to Make $1000 a Minute (Chapman), 130

Netherlands, 357, 359, 363, 365, 366, 370, 385–88

Netflix:

"adequate performance gets a generous severance" mantra at, xv, xxvii, 254, 259–61, 357–58

awards and nominations of, xix–xx, 115, 218, 245, 343–44

Blockbuster offered purchase of, xi–xii

children's programming on, 216–18, 334–41

content licensed from external studios by, xx, 114

content produced in-house by, xiii, xx–xxi, 113–15, 348

crisis in 2001, 5–9

culture of, xiv, xxvi–xxvii, xxviii, 68

Culture Deck of, xv–xviii, 256–57

diversity at, 356–57

downloading and, 219–23

employees as part of, versus working for, 164–65, 174

employees' love for, xx

Explorer project, 231–33, 236

financial information of, 398

founding of, xi–xii, 3–4

global expansion of, xix, xxi, 221–22, 331–41, 349, 353–41

American-centric culture and, 385

see also global expansion and cultural differences

"highly aligned, loosely coupled" mantra at, 320–21

internal competitiveness at, 263–64

IPO of, xii, xix, 166

layoffs at, 5–9, 14, 116, 250

leadership tree at, 327–41

meetings at
all-hands, 164
Estaff, 322, 360
length of, 365–66
Quarterly Business Review, 75, 96, 167, 173, 217–18, 322–26, 331–33, 360

Memento project, 234–35, 236

Qwikster, 211–13

and shift from DVDs to streaming, xiii, xx, 210–11, 348

stock price of, xix, 349

success of, xix–xxi, xxx, 6–7, 115, 116, 348–49

tagging and categorization of content on, 131

as team, not family, 250–53, 257–58, 367

Netflix (**cont.**):
  and transitions in
    entertainment and
    business environment,
    xx–xxi
  turnover at, 274
  viewer data of, 398
  Wii interface and, 231–32
Netflix Innovation Cycle, 210
  asking what learning came
    from the project, 230,
    233
  celebrating wins, 210, 228
  failures and, 210, 229–40
  farming for dissent,
    210–16, 237
  not making a big deal
    about failures, 231–33
  placing your bet as an
    informed captain, 210,
    223–28
  socializing the idea, 210,
    216–18, 237, 239
  spreadsheet system and,
    215–16
  sunshining failures, 230,
    234–40
  testing out big ideas, 210,
    218–23
New York Times, 245, 263
Nickelodeon, 38, 113, 217
Nieva, Jennifer, 100–102
Nishamura, Lisa, 344
Nokia, xxi
Northwestern University, 48
NPR (National Public
  Radio), 247–50

O

office politics, 279
OfficeTeam, 120
Olympic Games, 306, 343
"only say about someone
    what you will say to
    their face," 23, 279–80
opening the books, **see**
  transparency
Orange Is the New Black,
    xix, 114, 348
Oscars, xix, 245, 343
Outliers (Gladwell), 213
oxytocin, 32

P

Paris, 394–96
paying top of personal
    market, 113–51, 258
  creative positions and, 119,
    125–27
  form of payment and,
    120–22
  rare skill sets and, 128–29
  recruiters and, 141–49
  rock-star principle and,
    116–20, 122
  see also salaries
Peace Corps, xxvii, xxviii,
    20–21, 153, 353–54
Peña Nieto, Enrique, 207
penguins, elephants versus,
    257
Peppa Pig, 336
Perez, Kari, 205–10

performance:
  "adequate performance gets
    a generous severance,"
    xv, xxvii, 254, 259–61,
    357–58
  annual reviews, 282
  bonuses and, 121–27
  candor and, 26–30
  as contagious, 11–15
  differing levels in teams,
    9–11
  family business metaphor
    and, 247–50
  metrics and, 123–24
  hard work and, 59–60
  internal competitiveness and,
    263–64
  Key Performance Indicators,
    123, 282, 308
  performance improvement
    plan (PIP) process,
    260–61
  see also talent density
Peters, Greg, 68–69, 322,
    376–78
PlayStation, 231
pleasing the boss, 194–95,
    199–200, 229–30, 282,
    293
praise and compliments,
    32, 34
pratfall effect, 188
privacy, 183
Protector, The, xix
Procter & Gamble, 123
Pruckner, Gerald, 89
psychological safety, xv

Pure Software, xxi–xxiii, xxx,
    3, 4, 8, 9, 19–20, 83,
    96–97, 108, 153, 184–85,
    187, 348
pyramid structure, 194,
    327–29

Q

Quarterly Business Review
    (QBR) meetings, 75,
    96, 167, 173, 217–18,
    322–26, 331–33, 360,
    234–35, 236
quitting current job, reasons
    for, 120–21
Qwikster, 210–13

R

raises, 132–41
Ramachandran, Shalini, 265
Ramsey, Bella, 336
Randolph, Marc, 4
  Netflix cofounded by, xi,
    3–4
  in Netflix's offer to
    Blockbuster, xi–xii
rank-and-yank, 263–64
Reputation Institute, xx
Reguera, Ana de la, 205
responsibility, see freedom and
    responsibility
Rhimes, Shonda, xiii
Rites of Passage at $100,000
    to $1 Million+ (Lucht),
    145

rock-star principle, 116–20, 122

Roma, xiii, 245

Rosh, Lisa, 189

rules and process, xxii–xxiii, 348, 393–94

 when to choose, 396–99

 see also control, leadership by

Russia, 306, 343

S

Sacred Games, xix

safety issues, and management style, 314–15, 396–99

Saint-Exupéry, Antoine de, 317

salaries:

 adjusting down, 140–41

 bonuses and, 121–24

 changing companies and, 135–37

 form of payment and, 120–22

 negotiating, 129–30, 131

 for operational positions, 118

 paying top of personal market, 113–51, 258

  creative positions and, 119, 125–27

  form of payment and, 120–22

  rare skill sets and, 128–29

  recruiters and, 141–49

  rock-star principle and, 116–20, 122

 performance reviews and, 282

 and quitting current job, 120–21

 raises in, 132–41

 recruiters and, 141–49

 reviewing, 132–41

Sampaio, Leonardo, 366–68

Samsung, 98–99

Sandberg, Sheryl, xv, 195

San Jose **Mercury News,** 78

Sarandos, Ted, 37–40, 66, 143–49, 322, 339

 alien movie and, 193

 bungee jumping story of, 287–88

 on "hierarchy of picking," 245–46

 Icarus and, 306–7

 in leadership tree, 330–35, 339, 341–42

 360s and, 289–93, 298

Saturday Night Live, 211

Sausgruber, Rupert, 89

Schendel, Zach, 221, 223

Schlumberger, 355–56

Scorsese, Martin, xiii

secrets, 154–56, 166–67

 at HBO, 173

 reasons for keeping, 160–61

 SOS (stuff of secrets) information, 156–60, 236

 symbols of, 157–58

 trust and, 155–58

 see also transparency

Series of Unfortunate
Events, A, 218
severance pay:
"adequate performance gets
a generous severance,"
xv, xxvii, 254, 259–61,
357–58
in Europe, 357–58
sexual harassment, 397–98
signing contracts, 224–28
Silicon Valley, 116, 195, 203
Singapore, 359, 363, 365,
366, 370, 379–82, 385,
389
60 Minutes, 343
Sky Italy, 196–97
Slepian, Michael, 155
Smith, Frederick, 208–9
socializing the idea, 210,
216–18, 237, 239
Society for Human Resource
Management, 274
software, 116–18, 318
Songkick, 75
spending, see travel and
expenses; travel and
expense approvals,
removing
spin, 179, 183
Spotify, 203
spreadsheet system, 215–16
Stack, Jack, 162–65
stack ranking, 263–64
Stamberg, Susan, 248
Star Is Born, A, 44
status quo, xxx
stealing, 85

Stranger Things, xix, xx, 38,
113, 114–15, 119
streaming, 220, 231
downloading and, 219–22
shift from DVDs to, xiii, xx,
210–11, 348
Stuber, Scott, 246
subtitles, 336
Sundance Film Festival, 305,
344
Sun Microsystems, 8
sunshining, 159
of failures, 230, 234–40
systems, loosely versus tightly
coupled, 317–20

T

talent, 9–10
contagious behavior and,
11–15
and differing performance
levels in teams, 9–11
talent density, 9–11
building up and fortifying,
xxiv, xxv, 1, 2–16, 109,
112–51, 244–77
collaboration and, 252,
263–64
creating a great workplace
of stunning colleagues,
3–16
decision-making and, 196
family business metaphor
and, 247–50
hierarchy of picking and,
246–47

talent density (**cont.**):
hiring and, 246
internal competitiveness and,
263–64
Keeper Test and, xvi,
244–77
Keeper Test Prompt and,
267–71
and leading with context
versus control, 313, 314
and moving from family to
sports team metaphor,
250–52, 257–58
Netflix layoffs and, 5–9,
14–15, 116, 250
and readiness to release
decision-making controls,
200–202
stack ranking (rank-and-
yank) and, 263–64
360s and, 296
see also paying top of
personal market
talking behind people's backs,
23, 279–80
Tanz, Larry, 146–48, 288, 298
Target, 315–16
teams:
contagious behavior in,
11–15
differing performance levels
in, 9–11
dream, 115
feedback from teammates,
294–95
lean, 120
tensions in, 294

televisions, 4K ultra high
definition, 98–100
Tesla, Inc., xx
Thinkers50, xxvi
13 Reasons Why, 48–49
360-degree assessments (circle
of feedback), 40–41,
279–303
benefits of, 299–301
discussion facilitated by, 287
in Japan, 377
live, 291–301
stepping out of line during,
296–97
tips for, 295–96
written, names used in,
283–91
Thunell, Matt, 113–19
tight versus loose coupling,
317–20
transparency (opening the
books), 153–91
decision-making and, 196
difficult decisions in,
174–76
empowerment and, 165
and feeling it's better not
to know some things,
175–76
giving low-level employees
access to information,
165
and information that would
be illegal to leak, 161–69
knowing when to share,
160–61
about mistakes, 183–89

possible organizational restructuring and, 169–77

post-firing communication and, 177–83

quiz scenarios on, 161–89

privacy and, 182–83

risks of, 160, 166

sharing financial data, 163–68

sunshining, 159

360-degree assessments and, 287

see also secrets

travel and expenses:

flying business class, 96

honesty and, 88–89

rules for, 83–89, 96–97

spending company money as if it were your own, 86–87

travel and expense approvals, removing, 83–110

cheating and, 94–96

company's best interest and, 87, 90, 92, 100, 102–4

context and, 89–94

Freedom and Responsibility ethos and, 91–94

frugality and, 96–104

Trollhunters: Tales of Arcadia, 218

trust, 154–58, 164, 171, 181, 186–89, 236, 252

cultural differences and, 365, 366, 367

see also transparency

truth, 236

spinning, 179, 183

see also candor; transparency

Turkey, 237–40

turnover, 274–75

Twitter, 206

U

Uber, 203

University of Mannheim, 187–88

V

vacation policy, removing, xvii, 59–80, 84, 105–6

freedom and responsibility and, 79–80

Hastings' nightmares about, 61–62, 64, 67

Hastings' vacations, 66–67, 68, 71

Japanese workers and, 70–71

leaders' modeling and, 64–72

loss aversion and, xvii–xviii

and setting and reinforcing context to guide employee behavior, 72–75

value added by, 75–79

Vai Anitta, 147

values, xiv

Vanity Fair, 205, 262, 263

VH1, 327

Viacom, xiii, 103, 104

Virgin Management, 76
Visualsoft, 76
vitality curve, 263–64
vulnerability, 187–88

W

Wall Street Journal, 99, 265
Walmart, 247
Wang, Andrew, 113, 119
Wang, Karlyne, 379–83
Wang, Spencer, 168–69
WarnerMedia, 124
Washington Post, 98
Watchever, 221–22
Webcredible, 77
Week, The, 265
Welch, Jack, 263
Wells, David, 86, 90, 96, 289
West, Jerret, 198–99, 202

white-water kayaking, 267
Wickens, Brent, 94–95
Wii, 231–32
Worst Witch, 336
Wright, Brian, 38–40,
        113–14, 119

Y

Yacoubian, Aram, 330,
        337–42
Yahoo, 226, 227
Yellin, Todd, 221, 223,
        232
YouTube, 218, 219, 221–22
Yurechko, Mark, 174

Z

Zenger Folkman, 32